GROWING THROUGH TIME
An Introduction to Adult Development

GROWING THROUGH TIME

An Introduction to Adult Development

P. B. Walsh

Community College of Allegheny County

Brooks/Cole Publishing Company
Monterey, California

Brooks/Cole Publishing Company
A Division of Wadsworth, Inc.

Printed in the United States of America
10   9   8   7   6   5   4   3   2   1

Library of Congress Cataloging in Publication Data

Walsh, Patricia Buchanan, [date]
    Growing through time.

    Bibliography: p.
    Includes index.
    1. Adulthood   2. Personality.   3. Self-actualization
(Psychology)   4. Life cycle, Human.   I. Title.
HQ799.95.W34   1982   305.2'4   82–14590
ISBN 0–534–01214–0

Photo credits: Pages 15, 102 © Laimute E. Druskis/Jeroboam; page 37 © Dave
Bellak/Jeroboam; pages 54, 82, 179 © Rose Skytta/Jeroboam; page 121 © Budd Gray;
pages 141, 277, 294 © Frank Siteman/Jeroboam; page 160 © William Rosental/Jeroboam;
page 201 © Vince Compagnone/Jeroboam; page 224 © B. Kliewe/Jeroboam;
page 246 © Bill Owens/Jeroboam; page 266 © Randolph Falk/Jeroboam.

Subject Editor: *C. Deborah Laughton*
Production Editor: *Patricia E. Cain*
Interior Design: *Katherine Minerva*
Cover Design: *Jamie Sue Brooks*
Cover Photo: *The Image Bank West/© P. A. Simon*
Illustrations: *Ryan Cooper*
Typesetting: *TriStar Graphics, Minneapolis, Minnesota*

For Ron
and for Dan and Dave

Monterey

Preface

New models and new perceptions of the changes in adult life have emerged in the last decade. The years of research in human development have begun to pay off. The information now available is vital to students in many fields, not only for their understanding of the unfolding patterns in others' lives but for understanding the predictable dramas in their own lives. Sharing this information in appropriate textbook form involves a number of difficult choices.

With so much material to assimilate and so many perspectives on the issues of adult growth and change to acknowledge, how much can be covered in an introductory text without confusion? How strongly should research be emphasized? How can the greatest number of readers be reached? How can objective information be presented such that readers can experience it subjectively as well? My own answers to these questions have shaped this book.

The text is designed to introduce a broad range of readers to a developmental perspective of adult life and is appropriate as a resource for psychology, sociology, and human-development courses, for the helping professional, and for the nonprofessional, non-academic reader. The primary goal is to integrate clearly and concisely as much current material as possible. A second goal is to invite participation in the learning experience. Exercises in the text and in the Appendix allow readers to deal with the content on an experiential level. The text exercises tap into personal applications for the reader; the structured experiences in the Appendix may be used as either individual or group activities. Either way, participation can create a deeper level of involvement. A further goal is to give readers access to information about adult development from both a stage-theory perspective and a process orientation.

Growing through Time is divided into five parts. After a brief introduction, there is a background section on methods and models, a chronologically organized stage-theory section, a life-cycle process section, and a conclusion.

Part One, a single chapter, introduces the reader to "Adult Life Now." This chapter deals with our cultural myth of adulthood and the effects of that myth, with some current cultural realities of adult life, and with the issue of social change as it affects the potentials of adult living. Part Two, consisting of three chapters, presents the methods of developmental study and the models that have been developed to describe adult growth and change. Part Three discusses adult life from a chronological perspective and surveys the ages and stages approaches to adult development. Part Four focuses on the life-cycle process. Its three chapters examine biological, social, and psychological development, respectively. Part Five suggests some of the strengths and weaknesses of the stage and the process points of view and surveys current life-extension research, with its implications for future lives.

Each chapter concludes with three special features: "Terms and Concepts to Define" gives readers an opportunity to review the definitions of new terms they've encountered in the text, to enhance their understanding of the subject matter. The "Experiences" section lists those activities from the Appendix that are most applicable to the material covered in the chapter, giving readers a chance to become more involved with the concepts discussed. "Going beyond the Text" lists assignments to be carried out individually; the completed assignments can be the focus for group discussions. Again, the goal is to reinforce the reader's understanding by applying what has been learned to specific real-life situations. Suggested Readings are provided for those wishing to pursue specific topics.

The Appendix is an independent collection of experiences that may be used concurrently with the text or as a final recap. The three sections supply exercises in awareness, values clarification, and goal setting; each section is closely related to the sequential order of text materials.

I wish there were enough space to acknowledge each person who nurtured this book, but—lacking that—I want to deeply thank the teachers and students, friends and acquaintances who helped along the way. Individually, I must honor Dr. Clark Emery, Dr. Donald Clark, and Dr. William Bauer, who created the settings from which the book had its beginnings. I owe an eternal debt to Ram Dass, who places the human melodrama in its widest perspective. Thanks, too, to Dr. A. L. Dailey for her support and encouragement and to Betty Hershey and Bea Kearney for their dedicated typing of the manuscript. And to the editors, Todd Lueders, C. Deborah Laughton, and, most especially, Trisha Cain, my deepest gratitude for making this book a reality.

Finally, I thank the reviewers, who helped the rough draft become a finished product: Ellen Beck (Sinclair Community College), Jane M. Berger (Miami Dade Community College), James H. Booth, IV (Community College of Philadelphia), Louis H. Bronson (California State University, Sacramento), Jeffrey W. Elias (Texas Tech University), Janet J. Fritz (Colorado State University, Ft. Collins), Pauline Gillette (Northern Virginia Community College), Charles R. Kessler (Los Angeles Pierce College), Catherine M. Porter (Oregon Center for Gerontology), Phileon B. Robinson, Jr. (Brigham Young University), Fran Schmitt (North Seattle Community College), and Jean Pearson Scott (Texas Tech University).

P. B. Walsh

Contents

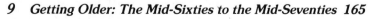

PART ONE

An Introduction

*Adult life can be understood differently now than it was in the past.
Part One is an introduction to the new information and new social conditions
that are changing our concepts of what happens in the adult years.*

1

Adult Life Now

When you have finished reading this chapter you should be able to:
Summarize the cultural myth of adult life.
List at least three aspects of reality that conflict with the myth.
Distinguish from each other the meanings of biocycle *and* life course *and*
    life structure.
Define the term cohort, *and describe your own cohort, in detail.*
Identify two social forces that are causing people to change their expecta-
    tions about adult life.

Only in the last half of this century have researchers in the behavioral sciences begun to study adulthood fully and systematically. As
information from the new field of adult development has become
available, the basic concept of adulthood has had to be redefined;
and our perception of how the central part of life is really experienced has begun to change. *Perception* is an essential concept in the
study of adult life: it means the way in which you understand and
interpret experience. A vital assumption of this book is that your
perception of adult life affects the way you live. This assumption is
based on the beliefs that your perception colors the way you see
other people in their lives, that it shapes the way you experience
your own life, and that it governs both the way you direct your life

and your expectations for the future. From this assumption, it follows logically that perceiving accurately is important to you. Are you aware of what concepts of adulthood you now hold?

As a first step in clarifying your perception of adult life, take a minute to define, for yourself, what being an adult means:

_____

_____

_____

_____

_____

After reading this chapter, you may find that your definition has expanded in some ways, because this chapter is an exploration of a powerful cultural myth about adulthood that blurs our perception. It is also an examination of some of the social changes that affect the realities of adult life.

A Myth: To Be Adult Is to Be Finished

Contemporary American culture supports a vague but widespread myth of adulthood. The myth has two parts, both involved with a definition of *adult* as "finished."

The first part of the myth is based on a three-stage concept of life: first you are a child, which means that you're immature physically and psychologically; then you're an **adolescent,** physically adult but psychologically still a child; finally, you become an adult. That's all there is. We have no other words to describe further phases of **development** (which basically means, after all, growth, or progression, and which will be further defined, as scientists have used it, in the next section). So adulthood seems to be the end of growth. The first part of the myth, then, is that to be an adult is to be a finished product.

Where did the myth come from? In the past, when life expectancies were shorter (we could expect to live for about 40 years at the turn of the century, for example), this myth was close to a reality for many people. Now we can reasonably expect that we will live for at least 50 years after the age of 18.

Can you live 50 years without developing in some way? Definitions of *adult* that are based in completion, maturity, and being finished unfortunately imply that you can.

For example, the legal definition of *adulthood* makes a one-time distinction (in most states in the United States, and in regard to most rights and responsibilities): before your 18th birthday you are not an adult; after it you are. There is no further change in status.

Most people would agree that age isn't the best indicator of maturity. Some other societal indicators, though, are considered by many people to be valid cut-off points for adulthood: marriage, for instance, or economic self-sufficiency (Neugarten, 1968a). "Today you're a man/woman!" sounds very close to "Today you're finished," meaning complete or grown-up.

Finished is a word that also suggests the second part of the cultural myth about being adult, which is that the only change to be expected in adult life is deterioration. From this point of view, after reaching whatever turning point is identified as "becoming adult," an individual begins "getting old"; adulthood is a time when the fading of youth and the coming of age slowly blur together until—suddenly—you're old. Fifty years of adult life are seen as one long, slow slide from adolescence to death. To become an adult is to be "finished," in the most negative sense.

Our culture's emphases on competitive sports and youthful sexuality are a part of this vision. Sex symbols who are "washed up" by their middle twenties and athletes who are "over the hill" at 30 are both the exploiters and the victims of our myth that biological peaking is the main event of living. The sources of this aspect of the myth lie in cultural traditions. American culture has inherited and exaggerated the traditional values of the Western world—physical power, productivity, and time, all of which may be at their peak in youth. Both modernization and industrialism, cornerstones of contemporary culture, foster negative attitudes toward aging (Cowgill & Holmes, 1972; Gruman, 1978). And, most importantly, America has been predominantly a youth culture for the last 30 years, bombarded with media and advertising aimed at the "baby-boom" generation, the largest generation alive, which was born in the years following the Korean War (Toffler, 1970).

Now we can sum up the reasons for the myth of a state of adulthood that can change only for the worse: the myth is sustained by a combination of the outdated expectations from the past and the media-created distortions of the present. Together these strong influences on our subjective perceptions of adulthood often have destructive effects.

One effect of the myth is to block realistic life planning. It can paralyze the decision-making processes of young adults, who may believe their decisions must last a lifetime and so feel that to make life decisions is a trap (Sarason, 1977). In older adults the myth may foster the unrealistic attitude that retirement is the end of productive living (Atchley, 1977). As a result, the alternatives and options of life may be prematurely closed down.

Another effect of the myth is that it lends negative imagery to maturing, which is perceived as nothing more than getting old. People in their twenties may feel that they're old already (Maynard, 1973). **Ageism,** negative stereotyping based on age, destroys self-esteem, social productivity, and physical and psychological health (Butler, 1975). Accepting the myth leads us to depression and despair. Rejecting the myth is not only much more productive, it's much more accurate.

A Reality: To Be Adult Is to Be Unfinished

All of the information on adult life gathered by contemporary behavioral scientists is in direct conflict with the myth that adulthood is a static state. Adulthood is actually an unfinished process. Development is indeed a reality in the adult years.

Developmental scientists—those who study how changes over time occur in people—vary in their orientations. Some emphasize how development is tied to age-related stages; some attribute changes to biological, social, or psychological processes; some view changes as the result of interactions among all of these factors. Which variables are most important in adult development becomes a matter of the kinds of changes that are being studied and of the biases of individual researchers. But from any point of view the evidence clearly indicates that we are not finished products until we are finished with the whole process of living.

A contemporary definition of **adult** is an unfinished person, growing through time. With that as a working definition, we can turn to the question of why this reality has been overshadowed by the myth.

One reason the reality wasn't apparent earlier is that information about adult development has been available only very recently. Early in the century developmentalists primarily studied infants, children, and adolescents. All three came under the heading of child psychology, which is still a growing field. But developmentalists have looked beyond adolescence now. By mid-century, sociologists, biologists, and specialists in the field of aging—gerontologists—were studying the issues of the last years of life. And gerontology, too, has expanded, extending back in time to include the causes of problems that emerge in later life. Most importantly, long-term studies of the middle years of life have reached their conclusions, and the gaps in life-span research have begun to close. The study of human **life-span development** has become a behavioral science in its own right, with the clear-cut goals of describing, explaining, and modifying the changes of life from conception to death (Baltes & Goulet, 1970).

A second reason why the reality of adult development hasn't been obvious is that the changes made in adulthood are much more subtle than the abrupt growth and maturation of early life (Troll, 1975). Biological change in adulthood tends to be gradual, almost imperceptible; changes in social behavior and psychological dynamics unfold slowly, over a much greater time span than youth's.

A third reason for the obscuring of the reality is that adult changes are extremely complex. Biological, social, and psychological events interact in ways that are not only complicated but highly individual. The outcomes of change in individuals are affected by many factors, external and internal, that are themselves changing (Levinson, Darrow, Klein, Levinson, & McKee, 1978; Z. Rubin, 1981).

Changing, subtle, and complex, adult development has one further aspect that deserves serious consideration: the changes of adulthood may be largely under individual control. Many behavioral scientists view the events of adult life as the results of unconscious or conscious choices—in any case, our own choices. From this point of view, the directions of our development are a function of individual awareness: the more life choices we are aware of and the more thoroughly we understand them, the more appropriately we can choose.

We live in a social setting that offers a wide range of alternatives in how to conduct our lives; and the options, too, are continuously changing. This hasn't always been the case. Before we deal specifically with the rate of change in contemporary life, we will digress a little, to put the social forces of the current era into perspective.

Life Processes: Biological, Social, and Personal

In some ways adult life is the same as it has been throughout human history. But, as much as we need to understand that, we need to see how our lives differ—from those of the past and from one another's.

Your life is like all lives,
> like many lives,
> different from many lives, and
> different from all lives.

Each of these summary statements reflects a point of view on the span of human life, and each point of view allows insights.

Your life is like all lives, on the biological level. All human beings experience the process of a shared **biocycle:** we are born; we grow from dependency to independence; we develop from immaturity to maturity; we may mate, may reproduce; we decline physically from maturity to senescence; we die—some early in the cycle, some late. The biocycle has remained unchanged since the beginning of recorded history. These shared experiences make human lives essentially the same in spite of cultural, racial, sexual, and personal differences, from the point of view of the biologist.

Your life is like many lives, on the social level. The culture that you live in, the geographical location, the historical time, the social setting, and the work that you do create a social framework for your life; they shape the way you live. The lives of others, those experiencing the same set of social factors, are shaped similarly. So much do the social and psychological factors complicate the human biocycle, in fact, that researchers call the biocycle by another name when it is combined with the social framework. They call it the **life course** (Levinson, 1980). For life courses to vary is normal, certainly—from culture to culture, from place to place, and from person to person. But, among people who are in the same place at the same time, one category of differences is particularly revealing—the historical one.

Your life is different from the lives of many who live at the same time and in the same place you do because you're a member of a specific cohort. A **cohort** is a group of individuals who share the same historical time period (Neugarten, 1968b). Members of your cohort will live lives different from those of most other people in your social setting. This is so because, as you and the members of your cohort develop, you experience the same social events: wars, economic changes, technological inventions, fads, and every other shared happening. Your level of education, your moral attitudes, the condition of your teeth—all may be a function of the cohort in which you were born (see Figure 1-1).

Members of differing cohorts tend to experience quite different life courses. A classic example of cohort differences is the "generation gap" between the cohort consisting of the parents of young adults and the cohort of the young adults themselves. The parental cohort may have a set of social attitudes, moral beliefs, values, interests, and personal styles that varies considerably from that of its offspring. Generation gaps of a sort may occur even between sisters and brothers of different ages.

A useful way to widen your understanding of cohort differences is to compare some of the elements characterizing your parents' cohort and your own. Make a quick list, considering lifestyles, experiences, and other factors.

Parental cohort	*Your own cohort*
1. _____	_____
2. _____	_____
3. _____	_____
4. _____	_____
5. _____	_____
6. _____	_____
7. _____	_____
8. _____	_____
9. _____	_____
10. _____	_____

Are there any differences reflected in this list that would make your life vary essentially from your parents'? Or are the differences just surface contrasts?

One difference that you may have noted is that of your own cohort's rate of social change. There have been stable periods in human history in which cohort could follow cohort in lives cut to the same pattern, whether comfortable or uncomfortable, with little variation. Had you lived two hundred years ago, for example, your

Cohort of people born in 1960;
most members will be dead by 2040

Cohort of people born in 1930;
most members will be dead by 2010

Cohort of people born in 1900;
most members had died by 1980

	1900	1910	1920	1930	1940	1950	1960	1970	1980	1990	2000
Economy	Industrialism			Great Depression	Boom years			Rising inflation			
Wars		World War I			World War II	Korean War	Vietnam War				
Technology	Electricity Telephone	Automobile	Radio	Air travel		Television Computer age Satellite communications	Space technology				

Figure 1-1 An age cohort is a group of people who are born in the same year or the same time period. Three cohorts are diagrammed here with some of their experiences, for comparison.

Use the space below to describe your own cohort in terms of the events and changing social attitudes that have shaped your lives.

grandparents' lives, your parents', and your own might have been notably similar. Today, however, we live in an unstable period of rapid social changes. Differences of ten years, even five years, between cohorts may result in very different lives (Toffler, 1980; Yankelovich, 1981).

All things considered, your life nevertheless is different from any other life ever lived. Personal uniqueness is more basic a sort of human variation than the differences caused by social environment or by living in a particular historical time. Each life is unique at the moment of conception, and, over time, the individuality is compounded; in a manner of speaking, we become more and more ourselves (Neugarten, 1968b). Unless you are an identical twin or a clone, you are biologically unique. And the experiences of your life and your responses to them—for twins and clones, too—make you psychologically and socially unique. Within your life course you are mapping a one-of-a-kind life structure, with your social choices, your thoughts and feelings, your hopes and dreams (Levinson et al., 1978); your **life structure** is the life course unique to you (see Figure 1-2).

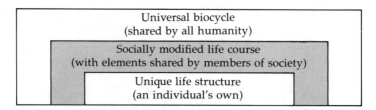

Figure 1-2 The universal biocycle encompasses all human experience, but for any individual its effect is strongly modified by a particular social setting—the culture, location, and cohort. Within the frameworks of the biocycle and the social life course, individuals consciously or unconsciously create their own unique life structures.

You may create your life structure consciously or unconsciously—either way, it will be built. And it will be built in a setting that you can't count on to remain familiar. People living their lives in contemporary, changing North American culture have the potential for individual choice in more aspects of their lives than any people ever living before.

Social Changes and Future Choices

In the previous section we considered, in a very general way, the relative influences on adult development of the social setting and biology. It is clear that the social forces are very powerful. Such biological realities as maturation and procreation are only a framework for adult life; cultural factors shape life courses that vary in complexity and form within that frame. For example, cohort differences can be powerful determinants of how people adjust their lives to their times.

To adapt to the times, people born into today's cohorts have to be more aware and creative than any people before them. A new social factor is operating on the adult life cycle—a dramatic acceleration of social change. In his best-selling analyses of contemporary cultures *Future Shock* (1970) and *The Third Wave* (1980), Alvin Toffler has described this acceleration, or speedup, in the rate of social change and also its numbing effect on people not ready to cope with "the premature arrival of the future."

Accelerated change makes difficult and risky the use of guidelines from the past, or even from the present, for direction in the future. In social terms, you can't assume that the ways older people are successfully handling their lives now will work for you when you reach their level of maturity. In biological terms, you can't be sure that your physical aging in decades to come will be anything like physical aging today. To plan for the future with guidelines so scarce isn't easy, but it does give you the opportunity to creatively shape your life in individual and new directions.

 Two directions of change that are already well under way are expanding the options for adult living. The first, which is general and social, is the emergence of an entire new culture of continuous accelerated change—and this in the midst of a social world that still looks to the past for stability. The new culture is a by-product of technology. Though begun by computerization and electronic miniaturization, no radical change in one part of the social environment can be isolated from the rest of it, so all of the interconnecting systems in society change with the technology—social institutions, organizations, information sources, and psychological and biological conditions (Toffler, 1980). Many of our attitudes toward work, sex, marriage, and child rearing have shifted in only one generation. Daniel Yankelovich—like Toffler an analyst of cultural changes—has found in widespread attitudinal surveys that there have been major turnarounds in the last 20 years. Of particular note are the turnarounds in acceptance of work outside the home as equally appropriate for men and women; of sexual relations outside of marriage as not necessarily wrong; of living together without being married as socially tolerated; of parenthood as an optional choice; and of child-care responsibilities being shared by men and women (1981). Our social expectations must be continually updated.

A second direction of change, more specific and biological, is the establishment of far more sophisticated life-extension technology. During your life span you may update several times the length of life you expect. Life extension isn't science fiction. It's a reality. Early in this century medical technology was focused on the control of infectious disease, for the most part. This focus allowed the average life span to increase 20 to 25 years (from 48.2 years to 68.9 for men and from 51.1 years to 77.4 for women). The increase of that era, however, was the effect of controlling disease and early death in the young. Current life-extension technology, centered to a large extent on chronic diseases instead, has extended life expectancy past the age of 65 by 200% since the beginning of the century. That is, for people who live to be 65, the average number of years remaining has increased from 5 to 15. Scientists now believe that the typical life span in our culture is rapidly increasing toward a life expectancy of 85 healthy years before an inevitable collapse and death (Fries & Crapo, 1981). Current research in the growing field of biochemical life extension is directed toward the goals of controlling and even reversing biological aging. We'll examine these aspects of life extension more closely in Chapter 15, but at this point it's useful to note that by fairly conservative estimates we can count on at least 20 years added to the average life span (Fries & Crapo, 1981; Rosenfeld, 1976).

One of the effects of social change and biological life extension in combination is to make our lives experimental models. Are you ready to perceive your adult life span in these new and different terms? Several questions may help you expand your perceptions: How long will you live? How much technological change are you apt to experience during the number of years you expect to live? How much change in social attitudes will you experience? Let's explore these questions concretely.

How many more years can you expect to live if the average life expectancy has increased to, say, 85 for both sexes by the year 2000?

60 or more   50 or more   40 or more   30 or more   20 or more

_____   _____   _____   _____   _____

Because of technological changes, how much different is life now from how it was 20 years ago?

not at all   slightly   moderately   noticeably   extremely

_____   _____   _____   _____   _____

If technological change continues at the current rate, how much different will life be 20 years from now? 40 years from now? 60 years from now?

not at all   slightly   moderately   noticeably   extremely

_____   _____   _____   _____   _____

How much have alterations in social attitudes (about sex, personal freedom, marriage, divorce, women's roles, men's roles, race, religion, work, credit buying, and other issues) changed life from the way it was 20 years ago?

not at all   slightly   moderately   noticeably   extremely

_____   _____   _____   _____   _____

If social attitudes change at the current rate, how much different will life be 20 years from now? in 40 years? in 60 years?

not at all   slightly   moderately   noticeably   extremely

_____   _____   _____   _____   _____

As you answered those questions, did you find any surprises? Had you previously over- or underestimated your life span? Had you been assuming that your life in the years ahead would be pretty much like life now? These responses are not uncommon.

If you use this text to become more aware of present realities and of some of the possible directions of change, you'll have used it well. You'll be more prepared to see your own life drama in the perspective of time and place, and you'll be more capable of deliberate and creative choices. Even though studies of lives in the present will be of only limited direct use to you in anticipating your future, you can use them to learn to identify the essential issues in adulthood. Then, as you meet these issues head on, you'll recognize them. You'll also learn to recognize some of the points that require choices, and you'll learn some ways you might handle them in your own one-day-at-a-time existence, within the unfolding drama of human life.

The Plan of the Book

This book is a limited survey of what is known, so far, about adulthood. It is broad rather than deep, an introduction rather than an in-depth study.

This first chapter has been written to help you sort out the myth of adulthood from the many realities of it, and to emphasize that the realities are changing. A central goal of the whole book is to encourage you to apply what you read personally, always understanding that, in your own cohort and in your own life, things will be a little different from the way they are in studies already published.

Part Two, which includes the next three chapters, will give you a background consisting of the methods and models that behavioral scientists have used to understand changes over the life span. We'll begin to survey the stage and process theories of Western culture in the 20th century.

The third part of the book is a long section of six chapters that describe developmental periods associated with specific years of adult life. The descriptions begin with the breakaway years of late adolescence and end with the breakdown years of senescence. Understanding the age and stage perspectives will familiarize you with some of the changing dramatic scripts of adulthood and their social framework.

Part Four gives you the contrasting perspective of continuity and process. Instead of emphasizing how changes are associated with specific ages, as in the preceding part, these three chapters describe life processes themselves—our lifelong biological, social, and psychological development.

Part Five has two goals: to encourage you to integrate all the preceding material into a holistic perception of lives growing through time, and to encourage you to look ahead, to anticipate the futures we may be approaching.

The Appendix is a collection of exercises of three kinds: for being aware of your beliefs and feelings about the issues of adulthood, for clarifying what you value in adult life, and for setting some tentative goals to fulfill over time. Some of the experiences can be done alone, others can be done with a group of people. Either way, they may be helpful explorations of what you can know about your life and the lives of other people.

Before we proceed, take a minute to define (perhaps in different

terms than you used at the beginning of this chapter) what being
adult means to you, now. To be adult means:

_____

_____

_____

_____

Summary

Contrary to the cultural myth, an adult is not a finished product: an
adult is physically full grown but psychologically and socially growing, developing over the span of life. Adulthood is a process of
changes that end only with death.

The myth that adulthood is essentially static—changed only by
biological decline—is created by outdated expectations from the past
and distorted images from contemporary media.

Data from recent developmental studies indicate that adulthood is
a time of subtle, complex changes that are under some degree of

personal control. Conscious choice may be a significant factor in how an individual develops.

Life processes in humans are based in much more than the bio-cycle of maturation, procreation, and death; the social life course is shaped by differences in culture, and by differences in historical time. The lives of members of a cohort tend to be shaped in similar ways, because the people in a cohort share a particular set of historical influences. Within any cohort, each individual creates a unique life course, which is called a life structure.

Our social setting is changing rapidly; even the biological aspects of adulthood may be changing. A fundamental effect of the accelerated rate of social change is to make the use of others' lives as guidelines a risky strategy for living. The speedup of change forces us to fit our lives to new living conditions rather than rely on familiar patterns. And the possibility of increased longevity requires us to understand the implications of living more years at an advanced age, and to attempt to plan for it.

In the process of recognizing the need for new life strategies we come face to face with the uniqueness of our own lives and our potential for living them responsibly. The life structure that each of us creates is made of our active choices, thoughts, and feelings and reflects our overall personalities. Awareness of the issues of adult life may be useful as we create our lives.

Terms and Concepts to Define

adolescence _____

_____

ageism _____

_____

biocycle _____

_____

cohort _____

_____

development _____

_____

life course _____

_____

life-span development _____

_____

life structure _____

_____

Experiences

To involve yourself with the concepts in this chapter, try these experiences described in the Appendix.

Alone
1. Experiencing your Life Course *at home*
26. Cohort Values

With Others
2. Uniqueness
3. Adults
23. Life Extension I
41. The Life Game

Going beyond the Text

1. Note advertisements and cartoons promoting the myth that adult is negative, young is positive.
2. Scan newspapers and magazines for articles about technological research and breakthroughs that may ultimately change how we live.
3. Interview at least one person from a cohort born ten or more years before or after your own. Try to get an in-depth understanding of living with another time reference.

Suggested Readings

Toffler, A. Future shock. New York: Random House, 1970.
Toffler, A. The third wave. New York: William Morrow, 1980.
Yankelovich, D. New rules. New York: Random House, 1981.

PART TWO

The Developing of a Developmental Approach

This part of the text surveys the ways that traditional and contemporary behavioral scientists have perceived adult development. After an introduction to the researchers' methods, we'll look at the two overall perspectives of the developmental approach. They are the chronological approach and the process approach.

2

Lifetimes: Methods and Models

When you have finished reading this chapter you should be able to:
Identify the disciplines that have been brought together to create the field of life-span development.
List and evaluate the methods used in the study of adult development.
Distinguish between cross-sectional studies *and* longitudinal studies.
Summarize the early theoretical models of psychological development: Bühler's, Freud's, Jung's, and Erikson's.

As you read Chapter 1 you may have begun to suspect that adult development is a difficult subject to study objectively. The events of every person's lifetime are so complex, so individual, so varied; how can adult development be treated in general—be described, analyzed, classified? If you had to systematically study your own development from birth to death, how would you do it?

Here's a line. Let's say that it represents your lifetime. Two parts of it are marked off: your childhood and your adolescence. What would you do with the rest of it? You know, now, that the adult years are too long and too varied to perceive as one time period. How would you divide them? Try it.

What were you thinking about as you considered how to deal with your life analytically? Were you thinking in terms of chronological ages or of biological aging? Were you considering social changes or psychological changes? How did you come to your decision—and why? Your "how" and "why" are your own. You'll find that its been done many ways. This chapter will sketch in the background of the study of life-span development and describe the early psychological models.

Taking It Apart/Putting It Together

The essential problem in understanding adult development in the modern world has been the problem of complexity. In each life so many kinds of development proceed at the same time, and so many factors have effect, that sorting them out was and still is a complicated task (Z. Rubin, 1981).

The more we know about the individual factors and the relationships among them, the better we eventually can understand the whole of development. The first step toward understanding is to separate out the factors. The second step is to pull the factors back together holistically. First analysis, then **synthesis.** That's the scientific route to understanding.

The behavioral science of adult development has emerged as the result of years of analysis—which was unplanned and unconnected and so difficult to synthesize. The problem was that biological, sociological, and psychological development were originally studied by people in separate disciplines, working at times on the same questions but sharing very little. Biological information belonged to research biologists and members of the medical professions; social data belonged to sociologists and anthropologists; psychological theory and techniques belonged to psychologists and psychiatrists. Each field had a specialized focus, a specialized terminology.

The first effect of such specialization was to isolate the disciplines from one another. But later, as specialization increased, it tended to bring the disciplines closer together; people who worked in the narrow areas ran across materials in other fields that were relevant to their own research. Cross-discipline sharing began. For example, sociologists specializing in cultural aspects of aging and psychologists specializing in the problems of mid-life crises could see that they needed each other. The realization spread that mind and body and social setting couldn't be understood separately. Then social psychology appeared, pulling together sociology, psychology, and anthropology. And the new field of **gerontology**—the study of maturity and aging—integrated the sociology, psychology, and biology of adult life. By the century's last quarter a comprehensive approach to the whole life span—a synthesis—was possible (Baltes & Schaie, 1973).

Now life-span development exists as a discipline in its own right, bringing together specialists in biology, sociology, and psychology in the study of adult life. Together they are tackling the next crucial problem in dealing with adult development: how to research it most effectively.

Questions, Methods, Samples, and Models

Three major issues that determine effectiveness of research in the human-behavior sciences are the issues of what information we need, how we're going to get it, and who has it. In fact, the usefulness of the experimental results depends on how these issues are resolved—with the hypotheses that we formulate, with our methods of getting information, and with our choice of the subjects to be studied. An additional factor in effectiveness is the overall model for the research.

The questions that are asked in a research study are composed to try out the researcher's **hypothesis,** which is the idea that the study is designed to test. The hypothesis is worded so as to prove either true or false. The questions the experimenter uses can also control the outcome because they always limit the answers. If you have a bias that to age is depressing, for example, you will probably choose a hypothesis that will reflect your bias: you might design a study that measures only the depressing aspects of aging and ignores other, positive factors. Also, the questions must be appropriate; they must be the central questions. And the questions must be comprehensive; they must leave out nothing important. Because each researcher has personal perceptions and expectations and belief systems, biases and blind spots will be built into every study. So to correctly interpret any study you will need to be sufficiently alert to identify the limitations of the questions being asked—and to consider what appropriate questions have been left out.

Research methods used in studies of adult development are the standard methods used in all behavioral sciences:

experimental research
analyses of statistical data (such as census figures)
surveys and questionnaires
standardized tests (such as those of performance and personality)
physiological measurements (for example of reaction time or endurance)
analyses of biographies and journals
interviews

This list begins with the most impersonal methods—those that interpret the subjects' responses strictly according to the experimenter's terms. In descending order, the methods move closer and closer to recording information in the subjects' own frames of reference, culminating in the face-to-face interview. With any of these methods, the information will be more or less accurate depending on the honesty and the self-awareness of the subject. Because some questions can't or won't be answered accurately, many research designs combine two or more of the techniques to gather information more reliably. Statistics may lie, individuals may lie, and test results may lie, but the more agreement we find among them the more assured we can be that the information is accurate.

The questions asked and the methods used to find answers are important, but the subjects that are chosen—the experiment's sample—are even more important. Who should answer the questions? In evaluating a sample, you must be aware of the influences of such variables as sex, race, and age, and of socioeconomic class and cohort. Should you expect data to be very similar for a group of urban, middle-class male executives and a same-aged group of female agricultural laborers? Probably not. As we review the research on development, you'll note the limitations of the samples chosen.

Here's an example of the problem of selecting a sample. Let's say you assume that a person's self-concept changes for the worse as he or she ages, and you decide to test that hypothesis. You design a study that includes several questions relating to self-concept, and you attempt to obtain data that's valid by using a combination of questionnaires and interviews. Which of the strategies below for using a sample in your study would be most appropriate?

_____ 1. I would question several groups of mixed sexes and ages—seniors in high school, people in their twenties and thirties, people in their fifties, and people in their sixties—about their current self-concepts. (To produce the results I would compare the answers.)

_____ 2. I would question a group of men and women who are seniors in high school about their current self-concepts. I would contact them again in 10 years, in 30 years, and in 40 years asking the same questions. (To produce the results I would compare the answers.)

_____ 3. I would question a group of men and women in their sixties about the self-concepts they had when they were seniors in high school, when they were in their twenties and thirties, when they were in their fifties, and their self-concepts now. (To produce the results I would compare the answers.)

Which sampling strategy did you choose? What makes that sample valid? In each sample, sex and age are taken into consideration. How about socioeconomic class distinctions? Did you consider the question of cohort differences?

If you chose the first group you chose a cross-sectional sample. It's the kind of sample that characterizes a **cross-sectional study,** which compares the answers (or scores) of people who are at different ages at one point in time (see Figure 2-1). Cross-sectional studies are practical because they are relatively quick and inexpensive. Their drawback is that, although a cross-sectional sample may seem to show change over time, it may in fact show only **age differences:** the way people differ who are in the various age groups at the time of the study. A cross-sectional study is also limited by **cohort differences—** the tendency of people of a certain age in one cohort to differ from people of that age in another cohort.

To filter out the effects of cohort differences as you identify the ways people change over time, you would have to choose the second or third sampling strategies.

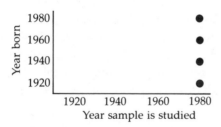

Figure 2-1 A cross-sectional study examines people from several different birth cohorts all at one time. The study illustrated was done entirely in 1980.

If you chose the second strategy, to contact the members of your sample several times during their adult lives and ask the same questions, you picked the strategy of a **longitudinal study** (see Figure 2-2). This strategy is to compare the answers (or scores) of people periodically over a long time span. Longitudinal studies eliminate age differences, because this type of study deals with only one group of people. And, because the cohorts represented in the group (which itself could be defined as a cohort) remain the same, longitudinal studies also eliminate cohort differences. (Correspondingly, the results may not hold true for people in cohorts that are extremely different.) The results of longitudinal studies are considered much more valid than cross-sectional data, because they are more apt to reflect real developmental changes. But full-scale longitudinal stud-

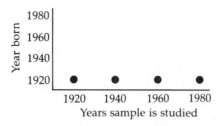

Figure 2-2 A longitudinal study examines people from a single birth cohort at several times in their lives. The study illustrated was conducted at 20-year intervals, concluding in 1980.

ies have some significant drawbacks: they're expensive, they involve years of research, and both researchers and subjects may drop out or die over the course of the years involved.

If you chose the third sampling strategy, to ask a group of mature people to reflect on their pasts and on their changes over time, you chose a **biographical study** (see Figure 2-3). This method may seem

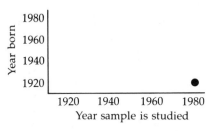

Figure 2-3 A biographical study examines people once in their lives, about the courses of their lives. The study illustrated, of people from one birth cohort, was done entirely in 1980.

questionable because it's based on material that's so subjective, but many researchers have used it productively. Although subjectivity is in fact a possible drawback, biographical interviews, old letters, and diaries may be used to piece together life histories successfully. The advantage of biographical studies is that the results are longitudinal, revealing developmental changes, but the research is not. So, compared to longitudinal research, biographical studies are neither long-term nor high cost.

The three kinds of studies are not equally effective. Longitudinal studies isolate similarities in people's life structures at specified ages and so may pick up developmental sequences of interest to researchers; for example, emotional changes typical of mid-life may come to light. Cross-sectional studies, however, although they may point up trends, most often reflect the differences between cohorts. For instance, although in a cross-sectional study of recreation playing bingo might appear age related, it's probably just some cohorts' idea of fun. As for biographical studies, because they reveal individual life histories from the perspective of hindsight, they often reflect genuine similarities in development, as well as cohort differences.

Now let's go back to the hypothesis of the example study: that self-concept deteriorates with age. As it happens, a cross-sectional study that included the question of change in self-concept, among many other questions, suggests that the hypothesis isn't necessarily true. The research was done in the late 1970s and published in 1977 by Marjorie Lowenthal, Majda Thurnher, and David Chiriboga. Their sample consisted of four groups of men and women from the same socioeconomic background: groups of high school graduates (ages 16–18), young newlyweds (ages 20–38), middle-aged parents (in their fifties), and preretirement couples (in their sixties). For eight hours each subject responded to checklists and to standardized tests and underwent interviews. An analysis of the self-concept differences indicates that the high school men were insecure and discontent; men in their twenties and thirties were energetic but lacked control; men in their fifties were more cautious and controlled; and men at 60 were easygoing. All of the male groups were low in self-criticism. In contrast, the female groups were highly self-critical. High school women were very insecure; women in their twenties and thirties also were insecure; the women at 50 were most negative and unhappy; but at 60 the women were assertive and competent.

Does this study indicate that men get progressively more self-governed and easygoing over the years, while women struggle painfully to a late self-acceptance? No. Because it's a cross-sectional study, it gives us only the age differences in self-concept of a particular sample, from a particular socioeconomic group, in a particular city in the early 1970s. Nevertheless, the study does illustrate well-designed contemporary research in adult development. Although Lowenthal, Thurnher, and Chiriboga included in their study the question of deterioration in self-concept according to age, the question was not intended to be verified by their cross-sectional research. Rather, the researchers intended the cross-sectional study only to provide a sound base of information about a specific sample of people. They've planned to retest their sample in 5 years; when the results of retesting are available, their cross-sectional study will have become longitudinal, possibly showing developmental changes in individuals. So not only the sampling strategy and the hypothesis but also how the sample and strategy are used to formulate results are critical to a study's validity.

The questions a study asks, the methods used to find answers, and the subjects who participate, it is well to remember, all are chosen by the researchers; and the way these elements are used is a function of the researchers' specific **theoretical model.** A theoretical model is a temporary system of ideas used to organize information in such a way that researchers can explain what is happening in an experimental situation, can predict what will happen, or both. Although theoretical models are temporary, they are useful, especially because they suggest hypotheses that can be tested for validity by research.

The first research in this century on developmental changes in adult life structures was based on a series of theoretical models that were created by psychologists. In this chapter we will review the models of four of these pioneers: Bühler, Freud, Jung, and Erikson.

Bühler and Biography

The earliest 20th-century psychological model of lifelong adult development was the work of a woman, Charlotte Bühler. Bühler's theoretical model was based on the ideas that human beings strive for fulfillment in life and that they achieve fulfillment through satisfying their needs, adapting to their environments, achieving creativity, and ordering their inner lives (Bühler, 1977).

Bühler's method was to collect and study and analyze (with the help of her students) biographies and autobiographies, looking for sequences of development. She and her students did find similar patterns in their life-structure histories; the patterns seemed to follow a curve of biological growth and decline. The patterns involved more than simple biology, however. To Bühler, individuals seemed to grow in another way—in relation to their goals in life. Based on the information from hundreds of biographies, Bühler expanded her model to connect chronological age, biological changes, and life goals. The life model has been divided into five phases, four of which are adult phases (see Figure 2-4).

Bühler describes the first 15 years of life as a time of progressive biological growth, during which a person's goals are dictated by parents and the social world. After 15 and until about 25, a person tries out one or more goals that they have tentatively chosen for themselves; these goals may include finding a mate and beginning a family. Between the ages of 25 and 45, Bühler found evidence that people commit themselves to their own goals and work to accomplish them. The period of the years between 45 and 65 includes an assessment of how well or badly those goals have been fulfilled; this

Age	Biological phase	Goal phase
0–15	Progressive growth	No self-determined goals
15–25	Continued growth/sexual reproduction	Self-determination of goals
25–45	Stability of growth	Culmination of defined goals
45–65	Loss of sexual reproduction	Self-assessment of goal success
65+	Biological decline	Fulfillment or failure of goals

Figure 2-4 Bühler's model of goal fulfillment integrates chronological age with phases of biological development and goal development.

What's useful about Bühler's model? _____

_____

Was the research method appropriate? _____

_____

What are the model's weaknesses? _____

_____

Does this model fit your life? How? _____

_____

_____

is a period that can give rise to new striving toward fulfillment or can produce negative self-perceptions. In Bühler's model, life satisfaction in the years of biological decline, from 65 on, is strongly colored by the fulfillment or failure of goals.

Life, for Charlotte Bühler, is a continuous process through interlocking biological and psychological phases, with the continuity of the process emphasized more than the separateness of the phases. The forces that propel the individual's development are the natural organic drives to meet physical needs and the natural human drive toward goal fulfillment. Bühler spent most of her own life testing and extending her model. She summed up the results in *The Course of Human Life*, published in 1968 and co-edited by Fred Massarik.

Although you will see direct similarities between Bühler's work and some current models, her work wasn't well known or widely accepted during her life. She was a humanistic psychologist in a time when the two major schools in psychology were the behavioral and the psychoanalytic. As contemporary humanists attempt to blend the focus on external action of the behaviorist and the focus on internal conflict of the psychoanalyst in a more holistic understanding of the person, the value of Bühler's work has finally been acknowledged (Bischof, 1976).

The psychoanalytic school controlled the American mental-health establishment from the 1920s until the late 1950s. Even now it dominates the field of psychotherapy in modified forms—although it has been seriously questioned in recent years (Gross, 1978).

Freud and Fixations

The psychoanalytic school of psychology originated in the work of Sigmund Freud, who lived and worked in Vienna 30 years before Charlotte Bühler began her research. Freud created a deep and complex theoretical model of personality development, and it made profound contributions to the understanding of human behavior: his concepts of the unconscious mind, of defense mechanisms, of internal conflicts, and of essential sexuality are invaluable for therapists. But Freud's attention was not on the developmental changes of adulthood. In fact, the Freudian model of human development obscured the profession's vision of adult life as a time of growth (Yankelovich, 1981).

One of the basic ideas in the Freudian model of personality is that personality is formed in the first 5 years of life. He believed that need satisfaction is the deepest human drive. In the psychoanalytic model, childhood experiences that involve oral and anal satisfactions and the establishment of sexual identity are the inevitable shapers of adult personality. Freud's theory was the product of his observations in clinical practice. His technique was to encourage his clients to talk about everything that occurred in their inner worlds: memories, dreams, events that caught their attention in daily life. By tracing back emotional, social, and even biological problems to early childhood experience, he created his model of personality development in the early years (see Figure 2-5).

Freud describes personality as the product of the child's inner, psychosexual conflict between the desire for pleasure and the necessity to deal with reality. He presents five stages of development. The first, beginning at birth, is a stage governed by the need for oral

Age	Psychosexual stage
0–8 months	Oral: Personality growth characteristics centered on experiments with the mouth (sucking, biting)
8–18 months	Anal: Personality growth characteristics centered on experiences with the anus (holding in, expelling)
18 months–6 years	Phallic: Personality growth characteristics centered on experiences of the body generally (particularly the penis, in the male)
6–11 years	Latency: (No personality growth)
11+ years	Genital: Personality growth characteristics centered on genital experience

Figure 2-5 Freud's model of need satisfaction associates personality development according to psychosexual stages with biological periods in childhood.

What's useful about Freud's model? _____

_____

Was the research method appropriate? _____

_____

What are the model's weaknesses? _____

_____

Does this model fit your life? How? _____

_____

_____

satisfactions, such as sucking and biting. The second stage, taking place sometime between 8 and 18 months, is controlled by the need for the anal satisfactions of holding back and expelling feces. A third stage that covers the period from 18 months to 6 years involves the struggle of the child to balance its sexual relationships with its same-sex and opposite-sex parents (the "Oedipal crisis"). This is called the "phallic" stage, in reference to the child's generalized sexuality. After the phallic stage, Freud considered that no personality growth occurs until about the age of 11, which begins a genital stage—the final formation of personality. In Freudian theory, any serious trauma (painful or frustrating experience) at any stage may cause a "fixation" of the person in that stage. The person who becomes fixated, or stuck, at one of the childhood stages then continues to exhibit behaviors that are typical of the stage and so are immature.

In Freud's model, then, development depends on the experiences of infancy and early childhood, when conflict between satisfaction and frustration forms the personality. Fixations in the child determine the behaviors characteristic of the adult. This is only the barest outline of a complex and important theoretical model, but it does lead you to some understanding of the limits the psychoanalytic model imposes on adult development. Not only does it make the genital stage the only adult stage, it makes "full genitality" almost impossible to reach. The stages are reversible. You may pass through them successfully, but you can always slip back, or "regress," at any time in adulthood. From Freud's point of view, your adult life is controlled by your childhood (Freud, 1953).

Jung and Individuation

Although Freud was the founder of the psychoanalytic school he was not its only major figure. Two of his students—Carl Jung and Erik Erikson—went beyond the Freudian conception of development to make important contributions to the psychology of adult life.

Carl Jung studied with Freud. Jung learned Freud's methods of therapeutic analysis, and Jung's own method became similar, but his model was very different. To Freud's analytic study of the contents of a client's conscious and unconscious mind, Jung added another sort of analytical study—of the images of myth, religion, and culture that are expressed in dreams and symbols. From Freud's idea of an unconscious that is driven to satisfy basic biological needs, Jung moved to a concept of an unconscious that struggles in the development of its spiritual needs—struggles, in fact, in the development of the human soul (Jung, 1964). Jung's theoretical model rests on the idea that adults develop through their own internal psychological unfolding and through the external and internalized forces of the environment. In the adult years, development involves the struggle of **individuation** (a process that begins at 12 and intensifies at age 40). Jung's term *individuation* means the process of becoming a person who can balance the conflicting inner forces that he felt we all carry in our personalities.

Jung divides life into four stages, with three of them taking place in the adult years (Figure 2-6). "Youth"—from 12 to 40—is a time of moving away from the issues of childhood and into involvement with the community, work, and family. Jung's second stage, the "adult years"—between 40 and 65—is a period in which attitudes become more stable and solid. In youth, horizons widen; in adulthood, they harden. "Old age," from 65 on, is the period in which Jung conceives the most meaningful psychological and spiritual growth to occur; it is then that the mature self works to reconcile its inner opposing forces.

*Age
(approximate)   Stage of individuation*
0–12   Childhood: Infantile dependency
12–40   Youth: Widening horizons
40–65   Adult years: Gradual hardening of attitudes "Stability"
65+   Old age: Reconciling opposites within

Figure 2-6 Jung's model associates four approximate biological periods with psychological stages through which a person develops or, in Jung's term, individuates.

What's useful about Jung's model? _____

_____

Was the research method appropriate? _____

_____

What are the model's weaknesses? _____

_____

Does this model fit your life? How? _____

_____

_____

Jung's model, described in *The Stages of Life* in 1933 (see Jung, 1971), was the first widely accepted model to encompass all of life and to present it as a natural progression—that of individuation until death. In Jung's model, as in Bühler's lesser known one, growth is essentially the unfolding of a more conscious humanness.

Erikson and Epigenesis

A more recent and more influential model that emphasizes both the psychological and the social evolution of human life appeared in the 1950s, in the work of Erik Erikson. Erikson, like Jung, was trained in the psychoanalytic tradition; like Jung he modified it in his own theoretical model of development. While Freud emphasized the sexual nature of human beings and Jung leaned toward the spiritual, Erikson was more interested in our social nature. In fact, he perceives development as being a psychosocial process.

The Erikson model of human development is more traditionally Freudian than is Jung's. Erikson's first stages of life are based on the Freudian stages of childhood. Like Freud, he bases his theory on clinical experience with clients. Like Freud, he perceives psychological energy as based on inner conflict, but Erikson conceives only part of a person's psychological energy to have an internal source. The rest of the psychological energy comes from conflicts caused by the natural unfolding of a person within a social setting. This social focus and this emphasis on development beyond childhood take Erikson far beyond Freud.

Erikson's term for the unfolding of an individual in a social setting is **epigenesis.** Epigenetic development is growth toward final maturity, with roots at the beginning that extend through each stage of development, so that it is like the growth of a plant from a seed. Epigenesis occurs on an individual basis and for the members of each generation. Erikson believes that personality develops as a person becomes aware of and interacts with his or her social world, and that society is structured in such a way that development can occur in an orderly sequence (Erikson, 1963).

Although Erikson's definition of "epigenesis" suggests a continuous process, his model is based on a series of separate stages of human development. He divides life into eight "ages," only three of them adult (see Figure 2-7).

Each of Erikson's stages involves an age-appropriate conflict that, if resolved, leads to growth. In the stages of childhood and adolescence, growth comes through attempts to resolve the basic issues of trust in the world, autonomy, initiative, and industry, and to establish an identity as a separate and unique self-in-the-world. The major issue of adolescence, identity, calls on the earlier resolutions and

Time period (approximate)	Psychosocial stage
Birth–first year	Trust versus mistrust ("hope")
2	Autonomy versus shame and doubt ("willpower")
3–5	Initiative versus guilt ("purpose")
6–11	Industry versus inferiority ("competence")
12–20	Ego identity versus role confusion ("commitment")
20–40	Intimacy versus isolation ("love")
40–65	Generativity versus stagnation ("care")
65+	Integrity versus despair ("wisdom")

Figure 2-7 In Erikson's model, the life course is divided into eight psychosocial stages that roughly correspond to chronological periods. *(Based on* Childhood and Society *(2nd ed.), by E. Erikson. Copyright © 1963 by W. W. Norton & Company, Inc. Reprinted by permission.)*

What's useful about Erikson's model? _____

_____

Was the research method appropriate? _____

_____

What are the weaknesses of the model? _____

_____

Does this model fit your life? How? _____

_____

_____

is itself reworked again and again in life's later changes. The adult stages in Erikson's model begin with a struggle in the twenties and thirties to establish intimate relationships with others. (To the degree that intimacy isn't achieved, a person experiences isolation.) In the forties and until age 65, the issue is becoming "generative," which means *productive*. (Lacking generativity, a person stagnates.) The next struggle is to reach self-acceptance, which he calls integrity. (Without integrity, a person views life with despair.) In addition to this progressive development, each person continues to reiterate the issues of earlier stages. The age-related conflicts are never completely resolved, although we struggle onward, away from our childhood fears and anxieties (Erikson, 1963, 1968).

Erikson's is a model that describes both social and psychological growth across time, through personal choice. In Erikson's view, we have responsibility for our own growth. Our lives are what we make them.

The psychological models that are reviewed in the next chapter have been strongly influenced by Erikson's work, which has dominated the field of adult psychology for the past 30 years (and which is compared to other early models in Figure 2-8). One related result of Erikson's influence is that in many of the contemporary models specific tasks are connected to stages of development that are considered relatively discrete. Another, quite different result is that continuity and process also are emphasized by contemporary theorists; development is perceived as unfolding naturally, ultimately all of a piece. To hold at the same time the perspectives of individual stages and of an overall course of development is quite possible, and eclectic theorists do just that.

			Experimental self-determination
	Youth	Intimacy versus isolation	
			Self-determination
Genital stage	Adult years	Generativity versus stagnation	
			Self-assessment
	Old age	Integrity versus despair	Fulfillment or failure
Freud's model (one stage)	Jung's model (process: individuation)	Erikson's model (process: epigenesis)	Bühler's model (process: fulfillment)

Figure 2-8 In early models, development in adulthood (the only portion of the life span illustrated here) is presented as a time of few changes, and they occur at wide intervals. All the models except Freud's distinguish separate stages, although the stages are viewed as segments of a continuous, long-term process.

Summary

Creating a discipline to study adult development took many years because of the subject's complexity. First, the many kinds of development going on at once had to be sorted out. Second, each kind of development—biological, social, and psychological—was the specialty of a separate scientific discipline, and these disciplines had to join as a single field of specialization: life-span development.

Even since the field of adult development has been successfully established, gathering data effectively has been problematic. Gathering data involves stating a hypothesis, selecting methods, and choosing samples. The usefulness of a study of adults may be limited by biases built into the hypothesis or by a choice of inappropriate methods; an even more frequent difficulty is selection of an inappropriate sample.

The most common kind of sample is cross-sectional. That is, it compares responses from people who vary in age at the time of the study. However, cross-sectional study results show age differences and cohort differences rather than developmental changes. Longitudinal studies, which compare responses from the same set of people given at several different times, indicate developmental changes more validly. Biographical studies, too, are helpful in showing genuine developmental changes.

Data is gathered to create and test theoretical models of adult development—temporary systems of ideas that organize information. The theoretical models of several psychologists—Bühler, Freud, Jung, and Erikson—were among the first attempts to understand and predict the course of adult life.

Bühler's model was based on biographical studies, and it emphasizes biological growth and goal-directed psychological development. Freud's model was based on clinical observation, and it emphasizes childhood experience as the dominant shaper of adult personality. Jung's model, also based in clinical observation, integrates social, psychological, and spiritual changes across the entire life span. Erikson's model, too, was based on clinical observation. It emphasizes the psychological and social development of the person across time, which occurs partly through a natural unfolding and partly through social pressure. Of these models, the most influential in the field of adult development has been Erikson's.

Terms and Concepts to Define

age differences _____

_____

biographical study _____

_____

cohort differences _____

_____

cross-sectional study _____

_____

epigenesis _____

_____

gerontology _____

_____

hypothesis _____

_____

individuation _____

_____

longitudinal study _____

_____

sample _____

_____

synthesis _____

_____

theoretical model _____

_____

Experiences

To involve yourself with the concepts in this chapter, try these experiences described in the Appendix.

Alone
5. Individuation
42. Goal Setting I
11. Intimacy/Isolation
27. Values over Time

With Others
31. Intimacy
4. Autobiography

Going beyond the Text

1. *Try doing a brief cross-sectional study to test a hypothesis of your own about time-related changes in adults (for example, "as a person grows older he or she becomes more politically informed"). Choose your sample carefully. Will your results actually tell you anything about development? That is, based on the sample you chose, will the results be valid?*
2. *Scan the* Reader's Guide to Periodical Literature, Psychological Abstracts, *and the* Social Science Index *for reports of current, ongoing*

longitudinal studies (such as the work being done at the University of California's San Francisco and Berkeley campuses, at the University of Massachusetts, and at the University of Chicago).

Suggested Readings

Erikson, E. Identity, youth and crisis. *New York: Norton, 1968.*

Jung, C. Man and his symbols. *New York: Doubleday, 1964.*

Lowenthal, M., Thurnher, M., & Chiriboga, D. Four stages of life. *San Francisco: Jossey-Bass, 1977.*

3

Life Stages:
Chronological Perspectives

When you have finished reading this chapter you should be able to:

Identify several of the complex influences on your life structure.

Describe Erikson's major contributions to current research in adult life change.

Distinguish between the stage *perspective on development and the* process perspective.

Summarize Gould's model and Levinson's model. Explain how Gould's and Levinson's models are alike and how they differ.

You can get some sense of the complexity of the problem of creating a theoretical model of development for the course of life by tapping into your own perceptions. By looking back and evaluating the experiences that you have had, and by looking ahead and anticipating the experiences that you will have, you can generate at least the beginnings of your own theoretical model. One way to do this is with a simple time line—in this case a life line—that represents your life course as you now perceive it. In tracing the development of your life, year by year, from birth onward, you will be establishing a chronological perspective.

In the figure that follows, the horizontal life line marks off years of life; the vertical axis measures quality of life (in terms of self-satisfaction) that you identify with those years, from a low of 1 to a high of 10.

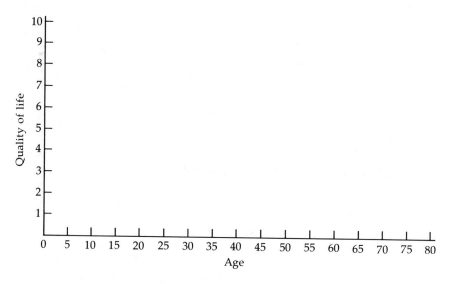

The first step is to divide your past experience from your future expectations by drawing a vertical line from the bottom of the chart to the top, at the point representing the year that you are now living. Next, decide which year has been the worst, the time of your least satisfaction with life; put a dot over the year at that low point. Then in the same way dot the high point of your life so far (considering carefully how high you want this maximum to be on the scale of possible highs and lows). Next fill in all the years of your past, dotting the ups and downs. When you have finished with your past, do the same with your future, predicting the highs and lows that you expect. (In the process you can choose how long you want to live.) Connect the dots.

Creating your life line may have put you in touch with feelings about the course of your life. Probably the life line hasn't given you much objective information; it's too simple. Still, it's a first step toward clearly experiencing the complexity of life seen whole.

A second step in sketching out your own theoretical model of development could be to analyze the causes of your life line's ups and downs. What makes life change radically? A change in direction may have many sources. Which of these sources do you see as the causes of your previous and future highs and lows? Check one or more of the blanks:

	My body*	My inner self	My parents	My society	Other
Most of the high points were caused by	_____	_____	_____	_____	_____
Most of the low points were caused by	_____	_____	_____	_____	_____
The level periods were caused by	_____	_____	_____	_____	_____

*Including age and health

Where are most of your checks? If you found that your parents, your inner self, or the two combined seem to control the course of your life, your perception would support the model of development put forth by Freud. If you checked more in the body and inner-self columns, your understanding of causes is closer to Bühler's. If your checks are scattered through the biological and psychological and social columns, you are perceiving complexity of development, such as Jung and Erikson—especially Erikson—perceived.

Erikson's Influence

Erikson's model of human development has been the most influential because it allows for the complexity of the subject. That is, Erikson's model involves both the inner, psychological struggles and the outer, social conflicts, in the unity of a growing personality. He recognized that people grow through similar sequences of changes that can be described as stages, yet that each individual goes through those changes differently, so that the process is both continual and ever new (Erikson, 1968).

The wide scope of Erikson's model makes it acceptable in widely different schools of thought in the fields of human behavior. His work is acceptable to traditional Freudians because his stages of development build on Freud's basic psychosexual theory, especially in the stages of childhood and adolescence. Erikson is equally acceptable to the school of the less traditional (but still psychoanalytic) ego psychologists, because of his double focus—on ego development as well as social development. Behavioral psychologists and sociologists find the social aspects of the model appealing, because both their fields emphasize the influence of the environment. Last, the humanists' and growth psychologists' schools of thought are founded in the same notion of unfolding and individuation expressed in Erikson's epigenesis concept. Although Freud and Jung and Bühler all made important contributions to the models of adult development now current, Erikson's work is the cornerstone of both of today's two perspectives on adult life, which seem to oppose each other: stage theories and process theories.

Recent work on adult development can be roughly divided into two points of view. One, called **stage theory,** presents adult changes as age-linked biological, social, and psychological stages. The other, called **process theory** or continuity theory, presents adult changes as individually differing processes that are either basically biological, social, psychological, or a combination of these and that proceed at varying rates over the life span. This is a rough division; some important concepts overlap in the two perspectives, so stage and process theories can't be considered to be in actual opposition to one another. Stage theories, for example, also include concepts about process—actually it is the processes that are seen as causing the stages. And process theories, on the other hand, do include some guidelines about the ages when people are most open to change, although the emphasis in process theories is on continuity, and age links are not considered essential or even meaningful.

Stage theories are based on the fact that our social setting encourages us to move through our lives doing more or less the same things others do and at the same ages; things such as marrying, having children, and retiring. Process theories examine the fact that individuals may move through their lives in time frames of their own: marrying or not marrying, having children or not, retiring or not retiring on their own schedules. Both theoretical positions are useful, each in its own way. In this chapter we look at the stage theory.

Ages and Stages

In terms of our cultural heritage, age-linked stage theories are not at all new; descriptions of ages and stages actually have existed for centuries. Ancient Greek, Hebrew, and Chinese descriptions of the stages of human life clearly outline developmental time periods, and their frameworks are much alike, as you can see in Figure 3-1 (Levinson et al., 1978).

Two additional descriptions of age-linked stages, much more modern although quite similar to the ancients', appeared in the 1970s at almost the same time. They have made an important impact on contemporary perceptions of the changes in adult life. These two descriptive models are the work of two young psychologists who found complex sequences of development in adulthood, almost by chance, in the courses of their very different research. The names of the psychologists are Roger Gould and Daniel Levinson.

Decade	Solon: A classical model	The Talmud: A Biblical model	Confucius: A non-Western model
Twenties	ripening powers (21–28)	seeking occupation	learning
Thirties	procreation (28–35)	reaching full strength	planting feet firmly
Forties	breadth of mind (35–42)	understanding	end of perplexity
Fifties	peaking of mental powers (42–56)	giving counsel	knowing heaven's will
Sixties	able, but less able (56–63)	wisdom	listening to heaven's will
Seventies	time to die (63–70)	white hair	a right heart
Eighties		renewal	

Figure 3-1 Daniel Levinson has pointed out that even in ancient times people were perceived as moving through a sequence of age-linked life changes. In Western culture, which is based on both classical and Judeo-Christian Biblical attitudes, we have been more apt to accept Solon's assessment of later life—as decline—than to accept the Biblical vision of the last years—as a time of wisdom and renewal. *(Adapted from* The Seasons of a Man's Life, *by D. Levinson, C. Darrow, E. Klein, M. Levinson, & B. McKee. Copyright © 1978 by Alfred A. Knopf, Inc. Reprinted by permission.)*

By the time Gould and Levinson began their work, a wide range of material on the subject of adult life was available to them. There were several existing theoretical models—Freud's, Jung's, Bühler's, and Erikson's—and there was a growing body of research that applied, tested, proved, disproved, explained, and illustrated the work of these major theorists. Biologists, sociologists, psychologists, anthropologists, and gerontologists were focusing more clearly on adulthood as a whole. And several longitudinal studies begun earlier in the century had begun producing data that sheds new light on the adult years. Life-span-development studies had become a new and very exciting frontier.

In addition to the rich sources of information now available, another new environmental factor was reflected in both Gould's and Levinson's models: social change. The social changes of the middle of the century were becoming obvious; people were struggling to cope with an extended and more complicated life course. Gould encountered people involved in this struggle in his work as director of the psychiatric outpatient department of the University of California at Los Angeles. Levinson encountered people in the same struggle during the course of his research at Yale on men in their middle years.

The Gould and the Levinson research projects varied in many ways: in setting, in sample, in methods, and in theoretical point of view. Gould was on the West Coast; Levinson was on the East Coast. Gould's first subjects were random groups of outpatients in a psychiatric clinic; Levinson's subjects were a systematically selected sample of "normal," well-adjusted men. Gould's research was cross-sectional; Levinson's work was biographical. Gould is an ego psychologist in the Freudian tradition. Levinson has an eclectic point of view, with Jungian leanings and a theoretical connection with Bühler (through her co-worker and his mentor, Else Frenkel-Brunswik). In spite of all these differences, the research done by Gould and Levinson and their associates produced results that are very similar.

Gould and Levinson share three essential tenets. First, they each have identified a sequence of age-related stages in the course of development and have found the sequences to have almost identical timing. Second, both Gould and Levinson believe that the stages are, most importantly, indicators of inner developmental work—although they both recognize that outer events contribute to the process. And third, both researchers perceive the individual as able to consciously create developmental changes, as an alternative to confusion and struggle.

Roger Gould

As assistant director of a psychiatric outpatient clinic in the late 1960s, Roger Gould listened to his resident psychiatrists discuss their clients' case histories, and he discerned a pattern. Gould heard what sounded to him like a connection between the ages of the clients and their specific life problems. In the teen years the issue was parents; in the twenties it was work, personal relationships, or both; in the thirties the issue became stagnation and frustration; and in the forties it was discontent with age and time. Sensing that the pattern in these problems was developmental, Gould designed an initial study to check whether his perception could be confirmed. He set up a team of investigators to monitor the issues that came up in age-graded therapy groups. The monitors found that group issues could be divided into two general categories: problems that are common to people of all ages and problems that are clearly age linked.

Working from the hypothesis that a sequence of age-linked developmental stages could be identified, Gould and his assistants used the data they had gathered from the therapy groups to design a questionnaire for nonpatients. When the questionnaire was given to a white, middle-class sample of educated men and women the results correlated with the earlier observations. Clearly, the evidence showed adulthood to be a time of "active and systematic changes," showing evidence of "a series of distinct stages" (Gould, 1972). When the *American Journal of Psychiatry* published this research, mail from Gould's colleagues poured in supporting his belief that "adulthood is not a plateau." His book *Transformations: Growth and Change in Adult Life* was published in 1978.

The theoretical model that Gould presents in *Transformations* is essentially psychoanalytic: he sees our childhood experiences as powerful influences on our adult lives. The **transformations**—the changes in form that occur—Gould presents as the long-term undoing of the beliefs of childhood, which continue throughout adult life. He describes two forms of consciousness in the adult. The first is a **childhood consciousness** of self-centered rage, separation anxiety, and false illusions of security; the second is an **adult consciousness** of fairness, reasonableness and realistic recognition of limitations. At sensitive times in our lives, Gould believes, these two types of consciousness come into conflict. The conflict allows an awareness of the childhood consciousness and so permits us to discard its false illusions. The conflict also provides an opportunity for a fuller adult consciousness to evolve.

The process that carries the individual from stage to stage in Gould's model is each individual's inner developmental struggle to transform childish dependencies into self-responsibility. Gould has called the energy that drives us toward adult consciousness "maturational push" (Gould, 1980). The framework that supports the stages is a person's responses to external occurrences. It is the sequence of adjustments to events that are part of life in our cultural setting.

In Gould's model, adult life is divided into five time periods (Figure 3-2). During each time period we are called on to make new adjustments, to face the loss of another of the childhood assumptions that have given us an "illusion of safety." "Leaving our parents' world" is the stage of progressive movement away from the family of origin that a person experiences between the ages of 16 and 22. In this stage we must lose the assumption that we'll always live with our parents and be their children. After we have resolved our initial separation we recognize that we are on our own: "nobody's baby." And with this the second childish assumption is lost: that parents will always help out. A new awareness of self-responsibility then creates a new stage, "opening up," between the ages of 25 and 35. Our parents' "version of reality" is exchanged for our own—eliminating the assumption that parents are always right. From 35 to 45 is the "mid-life decade," the time of developmentally processing one's own sense of reality and of ultimately understanding that the belief security is possible, too, is only an illusion. By 45, in Gould's model, a person has the potential to emerge into full adult consciousness. It takes a long time to grow up (Gould, 1978)!

Gould's model in *Transformations* doesn't deal with developmental changes beyond the forties, but his later work suggests that the "maturational push" of transformation may continue throughout adulthood (Gould, 1980).

Daniel Levinson

While Gould was doing the first studies on age stages on the West Coast, Levinson was designing and redesigning his research project in the East.

Age	Time period	*False childhood assumptions that we must lose*
16–22	Leaving parents' world	We'll always live with our parents and be their children.
22–25	Nobody's baby	Our parents will always be there to help us out.
25–35	Opening up	Our parents' version of our reality is correct.
35–45	Mid-life decade	There is no real death or evil.
45+	Adult consciousness	

Figure 3-2 Roger Gould's model of inner transformations includes five stages of adult development. As we leave home and take responsibility for our own lives, as we come to know ourselves, and as we struggle to accept our own reality, Gould considers that we are evolving toward adult consciousness. When we lose our childhood illusions of safety and face reality, we are fully adult. *(Adapted from* Transformations: Growth and Change in Adult Life, *by R. Gould. Copyright © 1978 by Simon & Schuster. Reprinted by permission.)*

What's useful about Gould's model? _____

_____

Was the research method appropriate? _____

_____

What are the model's weaknesses? _____

_____

Does this model fit your life? How? _____

_____

_____

Daniel Levinson and a team of researchers at Yale University originally set out to do a study on men in their "mid-life decade"—from 35 to 45. To do this they picked a sample of 40 men who had been born between 1923 and 1934, men who were at various points in the mid-life decade in 1969, the year that the study began. The sample was fairly balanced for occupations: it had 10 hourly workers, 10 executives, 10 scientists, and 10 writers. And the subjects came from social backgrounds that varied too: working class, middle class and upper class.

Levinson calls the method that he and his research team used "biographical interviewing." It involved structured interviews on specific topics, clinical interviews about feelings, and informal interviews—informal conversations. In addition to the interviews, each subject was given a Thematic Apperception Test, a "projective" test of personality in which the subject projects, or invents, stories to explain a series of pictures. The goal was to learn the subjects' life stories and to determine general truths about middle life based on these biographies.

As the team members began to collect interview material, they found that they needed more background information. (How can you understand the middle of a life if you haven't understood its beginning?) Before long, Levinson and his team realized that creation of a theory of adult development had to start from adulthood's beginning. That was something they hadn't planned on.

As the research continued, the team was surprised again; age-linked eras began to show up. The eras of adult life that the Levinson research "discovered" were not correlated with age exactly—there was some individual variation. But the sequence was sufficiently obvious to constitute a concrete model of the male life cycle that is closely age linked.

The book that describes the Yale research was published in 1978: *The Seasons of a Man's Life,* by Levinson and his associates. The model described in the book is based on a broad and eclectic theoretical background, integrating the work of Freud, Jung, Erikson, and Bühler, as well as concepts drawn from existential and phenomenological psychology, sociology, and the humanities. In a sense, Levinson's work has done for the 1980s what Erikson's did for the 1960s: the Levinson model brings together many disciplines to foster a more complete understanding.

In Levinson's model, a person is described as a biological, social, psychological being who lives as what Levinson calls a "self-in-relationship-to-a-world." (Self and world are so interrelated they can't be separated.) An individual life is an **evolution**—the gradual process of a unique life structure that changes.

Each of us, in Levinson's theory, has the ongoing, lifetime work of building life structures, then questioning them, then modifying them and building new ones. Life proceeds from stability to unstable transition periods, and on again to new stability. Each stabilized structure leaves out some part of the personality, which struggles to be expressed in the transitions and becomes a part of a new stable structure. The process is a struggle for inner and outer balance; and it is the struggle that generates the energy for change (Levinson et al., 1978).

In Levinson's account of the life structures that make our individual lives our own, he includes our universal biocycle. The eras of the biocycle are seen as "seasons," each different, but all of equal value. Like the seasons of the year, the seasons of life are broken by periods of change and instability as one season gives way to the next one. Also, underlying the changing of the age-linked stages of life, and so also underlying the lengthier changing of the seasons, a life structure is evolving over the entire course of adult life. The life structure unites the inner development of the person and the outer social environment, in Levinson's model. These three layers of growth combine biological and psychological maturation and social adaptation (Levinson, 1980).

You can look at the stages in Levinson's model in two ways (see Figure 3-3). If you look at it one way, he has divided adult life into the traditional three overlapping eras: early, middle, and late adulthood. But if you look at it in terms of the specific time periods that Levinson describes, adult life is broken into at least 11 periods between adolescence and old age. At the same time, these two ways of perceiving work together; the three long eras create a large framework, within which the shorter developmental time periods are defined.

As you read about Levinson's model, keep in mind that his subjects were all male, and that they were males of one time-period cohort. People who are female or who are born in an earlier or a later cohort may find that their timing is slightly different. Specifically, women may tend to experience the developmental changes earlier (Sheehy, 1976), and people from more recent cohorts may go through the transitions slightly later.

Levinson identifies 11 developmental periods that are each 5 to 7 years long. These periods alternate between stages of transition and stability. The **transition periods** are those stages in which the life structure is reevaluated and is modified or changed. The **stable periods** are the more settled stages, when the new forms of the life

Age	Time period	Era
17–22	Early adult transition	
22–28	Entering the adult world	
28–33	Age 30 transition	Early adulthood
33–40	Settling down	
40–45	Mid-life transition	
45–50	Entering middle adulthood	
50–55	Age 50 transition	Middle adulthood
55–60	Culmination of middle adulthood	
60–65	Late adult transition	
65–80	Late adulthood	Late adulthood
80+	Late late adulthood	

Figure 3-3 Levinson's model of evolving life structures of men suggests that a man's life work—building and changing his life structure—never quite gets completed. The self changes in relation to the world, and the world changes in relation to the self; evolution is a constant state.

What's useful about Levinson's model? _____

_____

Was the research method appropriate? _____

_____

What are the model's weaknesses? _____

_____

Does this model fit your life? How? _____

_____

structure are consolidated. Levinson sees this continuous alternation of transition—"structure changing"—and of stability—"structure building"—as an ongoing, developmental reworking of our self-and-world relationships. Rather than focusing on the achievements and products of development, Levinson has focused on the personal growth tasks and the processes of development (Levinson, 1980).

Each period in Levinson's model carries developmental tasks that are essential to that stage of the life structure. As we review adult life from a **chronological** perspective—a perspective that follows the sequence of time—we'll make use of these descriptions. At this point, however, be aware mainly of the chronology itself.

Levinson describes an "early adult transition" between the ages of 17 and 22, in which preadulthood must be left behind and early adulthood begun. When you reach this age, new relationships with the world at large, the people in your life, and even yourself must be formed. From 22 to 28 the life structure formed in the transition is tested and solidified, in a stage called "entering the adult world." Between 28 and 33 a new transition is necessary: the first adult structure needs to be revised and reshaped in a more satisfying way. This stage is called the "age 30 transition." After the transition into the thirties, a long "settling down" stage occurs, as you establish a firm place in the social world; from 33 to 40 your life structure is fairly stable. But between 40 and 45 a new transition is necessary—the "mid-life transition"—because it's time to rebuild your life structure for middle adulthood. From 45 to 50 another stable period follows, called "entering middle adulthood," and in turn it is followed by another transition period between 50 and 55: the "age 50 transition." "The culmination of middle adulthood," between 55 and 60, is stable. Then once more a new transition to a new era is necessary: this time it's a "late adult transition." Late adulthood begins at 60 in this model, and the tasks and possibilities after 60 are in Levinson's view what they were for Jung and Erikson—the final integration of the inner world (Levinson et al., 1978).

The stages in Levinson's research were clearly age linked, with a two-year range above and below the average ages of the subjects in each stage. The subjects were all male; however, some initial research suggests that the model fits women as well, although with differences in the stages' issues and in the strategies used to resolve them (Levinson, 1980). Levinson's model, although it is based on the lives of people who lived in the first half of the century, is being used in the present—in therapy to help people to adjust to life transitions (Brill & Hayes, 1981). Will future lives develop differently from those of Levinson's subjects?

Passages

In the period since Gould's and Levinson's subjects lived the major events of their lives, cohort factors may already have altered the boundaries of the ages and stages those researchers identified. More options about the timing of the major events of life—about the ages to marry, have children, or both; the years to enter or reenter the work place; the ages of retirement—may also allow us more options in the scheduling of our inner developmental work. Nevertheless, Gould's and Levinson's models have already taken effect, changing the average person's perception of adulthood, because Gould's and Levinson's ideas not only were available two years before their books were published, they were available as the basis of a best-seller. (See Figure 3-4 for a comparison of Gould's and Levinson's models.)

In 1976 a book called *Passages: Predictable Crises of Adult Life*, by a journalist named Gail Sheehy, was topping the lists of best-selling nonfiction. Sheehy had researched, interviewed, and pulled together everything she could find about adult life. She read everything she could find in print. She collected biographical interviews of men and women at varying points in life. She rounded up the work of Daniel Levinson at Yale, Roger Gould at UCLA, George Vaillant at Harvard, and Bernice Neugarten at the University of Chicago. Sheehy absorbed all the information she could collect, and then she synthesized it.

Passages describes the ages-and-stages perspective on adult growth in an exciting, readable format. With the new perspectives she de-

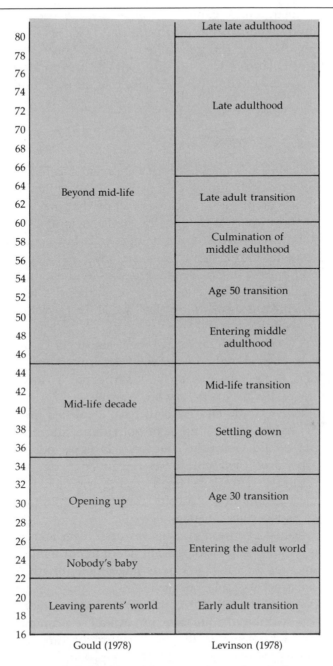

Figure 3-4 Gould and Levinson have identified very similar sequences of developmental time periods in the early and middle adult years.

scribed, adults gained a framework for transcending the cultural myth of adulthood. Adult life could be seen as a time of growth. By popularizing the age-linked, chronological perspectives of Gould and Levinson, Gail Sheehy helped incorporate them in our everyday view of adult life. We have that, now, to build on.

Summary

Erikson's model of adult development has had an influence on current research stronger than that of any other early models because in its complexity it includes factors that make it acceptable to most of the schools of thought in the behavioral sciences. His work contributed to two seemingly opposed (but actually complementary) contemporary perspectives on adult development: stage theories and process theories. Stage theories tend to emphasize the order and sequence of adult changes; process theories tend to emphasize the specific processes—biological, social, and psychological—that unfold in adult life.

Two contemporary stage theorists, Roger Gould and Daniel Levinson, have identified a series of age-linked developmental time periods. Each man has created a theoretical model of chronological stages, basing his theory on research.

Roger Gould and his staff have identified time periods in a series of cross-sectional studies of outpatients and nonpatients in California. Gould views the time periods as periods when people discard aspects of their childhood dependency on their parents. He describes this work as finally being completed in the forties, when most people have evolved from their "childhood consciousness" to an "adult consciousness."

Daniel Levinson and his research team identified time periods in the course of their biographical studies of men in middle life. Levinson sees the time periods as stages in a growth process; in it, people construct a stable life structure, outgrow its limitations and, in a period of transition, reconstruct it in a new, more stable form. Levinson describes the life structure overall as a complex creation of self-to-world relationships that evolves through time. In his view, the work of this evolution is never fully completed.

A journalist, Gail Sheehy, has combined and popularized Gould's and Levinson's ideas—in addition to other research—in a best-selling book called *Passages: Predictable Crises of Adult Life*.

Terms and Concepts to Define

adult consciousness _____

_____

childhood consciousness _____

_____

chronological _____

_____

evolution _____

_____

process theory _____

_____

stable periods _____

_____

stage theory _____

_____

transition periods _____

_____

transformation _____

_____

Experiences

To involve yourself with the concepts in this chapter, try these experiences described in the Appendix.

Alone
22. *Stable You/Changing You*
8. *Lifestyles*
43. *Goal Setting II: Short-Term Goals*

With Others
6. *Childhood Consciousness*
7. *Transitions*
28. *Seasons*

Going beyond the Text

1. *Interview a person who is at least 50 years old about his or her life course up to this time. Plan the interview ahead, so that you can draw out information about periods of change and stability and about central issues of life during these periods. Take notes. Analyze your notes for similarities to Gould's or Levinson's model.*
2. *Scan newspapers and magazines for materials that reflect chronological stage theories and the breakdown of the myth of static adulthood.*

Suggested Readings

Brill, P., & Hayes, J. B. Taming your turmoil: Managing the transitions of adult life. *Englewood Cliffs, N. J.: Prentice-Hall, 1981.*

Gould, R. Transformations: Growth and change in adult life. *New York: Simon & Schuster, 1978.*

Levinson, D., Darrow, C., Klein, E., Levinson, M., & McKee, B. The seasons of a man's life. *New York: Knopf, 1978.*

Sheehy, G. Passages: Predictable crises of adult life. *New York: Dutton, 1976.*

4

Lifetime Changes: Process Perspectives

When you have finished reading this chapter you should be able to:

Identify the major process perspectives on adult life.

Define multidisciplinary and contrast the multidisciplinary aspects of the stage and the process perspectives.

Describe your own social and biological "clocks."

Discuss variability in maturation, socialization, and adaptation.

Summarize the process models of development designed by Neugarten, Havighurst, Vaillant, and Loevinger.

The recent stage theories that we have reviewed are focused on changes that are periodic. That is, the changes appear at specified times in the course of a typical adult life. In these models, the emphasis is on age-related changes that elicit seemingly new versions of a person. Gould calls them "transformations"; Levinson calls the changes "evolutions." The processes that underlie these changes—biological maturation, socialization to new roles, and psychological adaptations to change—are left combined in these stage models; the processes of inner growth that together foster the delineation of stages simply are not considered. The stage theorist's main concern, after all, is with what constitutes the whole picture and its structural divisions, rather than with its underlying elements. The stage theorists pay more attention to what happens than to the details of why and how it happens.

The stage theorists don't ignore process, of course, although they may use the word in varying ways. (Our few words for different kinds of process force the word to carry many different levels of meaning, but the reader can understand the intended meaning through the context.) Erikson, Gould, and Levinson all base their theories of development on their own perceptions of the complex interaction of biological, social, and psychological processes. Erikson describes development as a psychosocial process, and as a part of the process of "epigenesis." Gould describes development as a psychological process that involves both the social experiences of leaving home, working, and marrying and the biological experience of "maturational push." Levinson describes the evolution of the life structure as combined inner psychological processes and outer social processes, in the framework of life's seasons, which are biological.

Each of these stage models deals with the underlying life processes as interrelated, which clearly they are. But life processes may also be dealt with in another way: individually. They must, in fact, be studied individually, if we are going to find out why and how they work. And they must be studied in the lives of individual people, if we are going to understand individuals' differing ways of development. Process perspectives consider the tremendous variability in individual lives. So, in addition to the stage theories, research biologists, sociologists, and psychologists are producing other theories of adult development—from the perspectives of their individual disciplines.

In this chapter we'll review some approaches to the study of adult life with the perspective of continuous individual processes rather than generalized stages. This point of view emphasizes change as continuous rather than periodic. Whether this continuous change is age related is of less concern to the process theorists than the regulation of change, the effects of varying environments on change, and individuals' differences in development. Compared to the stage theorists' approach, the focus of process researchers is quite specialized. Researchers in medicine and physiology, in sociology and social psychology, and in adaptation and personality theory investigate specific aspects of the major processes of adult life: biological, social, and psychological change (see Figure 4-1).

	Process perspectives		
	Biological	*Social*	*Psychological*
Chronological age factors	Maturation, aging	Age grading, social events	Biological and social factors plus self-perception
Regulating factors	Biological clock	Social clock	Biological and social factors plus self-perception
Environmental factors	Stress, nutrition, activity	Social norms, social roles	Biological and social factors plus self-perception
Individual factors	Functional age	Personal lifestyle	Adaptive style— personality plus self-perception

Figure 4-1 Biological, social, and psychological influences combine to shape our adult lives complexly, so that within any age cohort people exhibit variation as well as similarity. From the perspectives of these three processes, change occurs continuously, rather than in age stages.

Multidisciplines

Although we need the broad overview that the stage theories contribute, we also need the intensive research that the process perspective generates. We need all of the information that we can get. People from both perspectives agree that understanding adult development requires an integration of effort from every discipline—a **multidisciplinary** approach (Figure 4-2). Stage models have given us a broad view on the theoretical level. Process models will show us the products of a group of individual disciplines that integrate their concrete findings using the multidisciplinary team approach. Each separate process has important things to tell us about development, but for a more complete understanding the pieces have to be put together.

Biological Processes

When you developed your own life line (in Chapter 3) and analyzed the causes of your life changes from birth to death, what percentage of these changes were connected to your body? In the circle graph

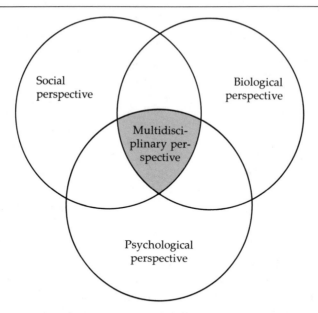

Figure 4-2 A multidisciplinary perspective integrates information from the major process perspectives on adult life.

below, which represents all changes in adult life, how much of the whole would you designate as caused by biological change? Draw a wedge in the circle that stands for your perception of biological influence.

Biological changes are important in childhood and early adolescence, but in adulthood biological change becomes less significant for many people. Body changes are a focus again in the lives of women during their childbearing years and, perhaps, around menopause. And of course physical impairments may complicate the lives of both men and women. But, between adolescence and the last years of adult life, biological changes usually aren't dramatic. Nevertheless they take place. Because biological changes in adults are continuous, subtle, and individually very different, they do often go unnoticed, and the medical profession has never established a chronological timetable for physical changes in adulthood. Medical care for children is labeled "pediatrics," medical care for the aged is "geriatrics," and all the rest—except for the minor field of adolescent medicine—is adult care. Puberty is the beginning of adulthood, medically speaking, and senescence the beginning of the end (Katchadourian, 1976).

It might be helpful here to distinguish among three different nontechnical terms that we will be using in particular ways in this text to describe the broad physical changes in adult life: *maturation, aging,* and *senescence.* **Maturation** is the final stage of development of any bodily systems, organs, tissues, and cells; **aging** is the gradual decline of efficiency in any systems, organs, tissues, or cells over time; **senescence** is the rapid aging that occurs in the last years of life. It's possible, during the early adult years, for some parts of the body still to be maturing while others have been aging for some time.

The rates of maturation, aging, and senescence and even the time of death seem to be controlled to some extent by the body's **biological clock.** Each of us experiences periodic changes in biological function. Those that take place in the course of a day are *circadian,* and the day-long period itself is a *circadian rhythm.* We also go through monthly cycles and perhaps yearly and semiannual cycles under our biological clock's control. The biological-clock concept is a way of describing the physiologically controlled regularities and predictable changes in bodily functions. Its location—in the endocrine system, or the brain, or in the cellular DNA—is still in question, but its effects are not. It may even control the decline in cell efficiency over time. The biological clock is apparently genetic, yet it may be slowed down or sped up by environmental influences (Wantz & Gay, 1981).

You can monitor the clockworks of your own biology by completing the following checklist of factors in aging:

Did your grandparents "age" early or late?

grandparent 1	early _____	late _____
grandparent 2	early _____	late _____
grandparent 3	early _____	late _____
grandparent 4	early _____	late _____

Did your parents "age" early or late?

parent 1	early _____	late _____
parent 2	early _____	late _____

To what ages have your grandparents lived?

grandparent 1 _____	grandparent 3 _____
grandparent 2 _____	grandparent 4 _____

To what ages have your parents lived?

parent 1 _____   parent 2 _____

Is your environment stressful?

physical stress	high _____	moderate _____	low _____
psychological stress	high _____	moderate _____	low _____
environmental pollution	high _____	moderate _____	low _____
environmental complexity*	high _____	moderate _____	low _____

What biologically risky factors does your lifestyle include?

high risk: overeating _____

       abuse of alcohol, nicotine, or other

          harmful chemicals _____

       little physical activity _____

       no self-regulation of stress responses _____

moderate risk: fairly good nutrition _____

       little use of harmful chemicals _____

       moderate physical activity _____

       some self-regulation of stress responses _____

low risk: optimal nutrition _____

       no use of harmful chemicals _____

       high level of physical activity _____

       high self-regulation of stress responses _____

*Complexity refers to the amount of stimulation present in the environment; too much stimulation causes stress. For example, living near an airport may be stressful if the noise level is high.

Do you have any of these individual risk factors?
   a self-stressing personality pattern _____
   a chronic disease _____
   a risky physical condition _____

All of these factors may have some effect on the biological clock that will control the physical changes of your adult life: you can see what your genetic potential may be, and what other factors may affect your timing. What is your probable rate of aging, considering these factors?

Studies of the biological processes of adult life were originally limited to the biological changes of aging and senescence; they were the work of gerontologists. Gerontology and geriatric medicine were initially focused on the changes of old age. More recently, however, both fields have expanded to include middle age. An example of this trend is the Duke Longitudinal Study of Aging, a classic multidisciplinary, longitudinal study. In 1955 the Duke study was designed to trace the medical, social, and psychological case histories of a randomly selected sample of men and women who were then 60 years old or older. By 1968 a second phase of this study had begun, this time with the starting age of the sample lowered to 46, to investigate the adaptations to aging of a group of middle-aged subjects (Palmore & Jeffers, 1971). In addition, exercise physiologists, tracking the changes in efficiency of body function across adulthood, have been able to close the gap in biological information by working from the other direction—studying development from the early years toward the later (deVries, 1975). Slowly a whole picture has emerged of development at every level of biological function—entire bodily systems, individual organs, and single cells.

One of the most important results of the study of adult physiology is the finding that people change at varying rates. Chronological age has little correlation with the biological age of the systems or the organs of the body in adults, a fact that has given rise to the concept of **"functional age."** Functional age is a measurement of age according to efficiency of bodily function, rather than an accounting of the number of years lived. You and a friend may be the same chronological age yet may vary significantly in functional age. A second important finding is that the parts of every person's body mature and age at different rates. You might, for example, have a very functional skeletal-muscular system but a very worn and inefficient heart. A third factor in the condition of the biological clock is that the amount of exercise you get has a direct relationship to your functional age. The damages of a sedentary lifestyle may be more destructive biologically than the changes of aging. That is, your life-style could wear you out more than time weathers you (deVries, 1975; Fries & Crapo, 1981; Weg, 1976).

The concept of *functional age* underscores the fact that individual biological clocks vary widely in their timing. In childhood, individuals' timetables of maturation are fairly similar. By puberty maturation may vary by six years and still be considered normal; in adulthood aging and senescence are even more variable. People may differ considerably in genetic inheritance, and all people differ at least slightly in lifestyle, in terms of stress, nutrition, activity, and personal habits. Actually, with so many ways adults vary in their biological processes, it's amazing that people in the same year of life age as similarly as they do.

In spite of variability among individuals, the similarities in the patterns of aging in any age cohort are far more evident than the patterns of individual variations. All of us are aware of stereotypes of skin condition, facial expression, body posture, speed of movement, and other physical characteristics that we use—consciously or unconsciously—to estimate a person's age. If these samenesses in aging patterns are not biological, where do the stereotypes come from?

The source of the sameness is social. In addition to the biological processes of adult life, there are a series of social processes that may synchronize adult changes far more strongly than biology.

Social Processes

Looking at the changes of adult life from the perspective of social processes gives us an immediate insight into the sources of another sort of age-change stereotypes. These stereotypes are social expectations about age-appropriate ways of thinking, feeling, and behaving, and they have a direct effect on how we conduct our lives as we grow older.

From the social-processes point of view, many changes in adult life are the result of social learning, which is also called socialization. Messages from a number of sources in our social environment communicate—both indirectly and directly—how we should feel, think, look, and act at various times in our lives. And we all absorb these messages, even when we're not aware of it. This information about social expectations and social processes shapes us all, to some degree, to fit the social stereotypes (Levinson, 1980).

How are you being socialized to adulthood? Rank the items in this list of social networks, of social institutions and media, and of pursuits and artifacts of our society from 1 (highest) to 15 (lowest) in their power to shape your perceptions and expectations about adult life:

_____ parents
_____ family
_____ friends
_____ acquaintances
_____ church
_____ school
_____ law
_____ government
_____ visual media (such as tv, movies)
_____ print media (such as books, magazines)
_____ work
_____ recreation
_____ consumer products
_____ technology
_____ art, including music

Messages from all of these sources socialize us, with the intent of making us smoothly functioning members of our social world. Most of the time their messages are more or less in agreement; but sometimes their messages are contradictory and confusing—especially in times of rapid social change.

Socialization begins at birth, and it never really ends. We are even socialized in our attitudes about our death. Our social world instructs us continually in the status, the normal behavior, and the appropriate social roles of different age groups (Kimmel, 1974).

Every society has some system for designating the levels of status of its members, and one of the criteria that determine status is age. This system of assigning status according to age, called **age grading,** includes information about the positive or negative status that is connected with a particular age group; it also dictates the rights and responsibilities, the privileges and constraints that go with certain ages. In our social setting, for example, old age is given a very low status, and it carries no responsibilities, few privileges, and many constraints.

In addition to a system of age grading, every society also maintains a set of expectations that pressure all the members of the social group to behave in similar ways. These expectations (and the similar behaviors) are called **norms.** Social norms are learned early, and often they become so much a part of our perception of the world that we are liable to think of them as the natural way of things; we find questioning them confusing and painful. Social norms are helpful when they make society run smoothly, giving us reasonable expectations about the behavior of others. Norms are not helpful when they lock us into automatic ways of behaving that are mindless or unhealthy or destructive. Norms concerning age most often are not helpful. Yet they exist, powerful enough to pressure us unknowingly into expected ways of leading our lives. They may control our behavior and how we perceive ourselves. They may push us into choices we're not ready to make, or may hold us back from change that we need. One of the most negative aspects of age norms is that by their nature they change much more slowly than does the social environment. Invisible and unquestioned, age norms from the last century still affect our social worlds and our inner thoughts, thereby distorting our perception of current reality. Can you think of some?

Age grades, age norms, and age constraints are the stuff of which social roles are made. A social **role** is a sort of social script that we learn to act out and to expect from others. All of us play sex, work, and age roles quite unconsciously, having learned them early and, for the most part, indirectly (Romer, 1981). Like norms, roles are useful when they facilitate social interactions: for people to behave in the ways that we expect allows us to be comfortable. Doctors are supposed to act like doctors; children are supposed to act like children. When a doctor acts like a child, we're startled and uncertain (and children can get into trouble for "playing doctor"). But though roles make knowing how to act easier, they are not useful when they become rigid stereotypes and so inhibit creativity and flexibility. And, most importantly, they are not useful when they prevent us from being ourselves. Age roles can do just that.

All of us do anticipate age roles, learn them, master them, and outgrow and replace them. They are learned so well that, hypothetically, you could base your performance as "young adult" or "middle-aged person" or "older person" entirely on role prescriptions. However, although following the directions from your social world may be a strategy that's easy to adopt, it also may be stressful and destructive to actually carry out. For example, if you feel social pressure to accept the role of "middle-aged person" at the age of 45 when your functional age is 10 years younger, you may be painfully frustrated. In fact, reducing your physical activity level to conform to that role might destroy the level of functioning you had formerly maintained. Playing "old," it turns out, is one of the most physically debilitating factors in later life. Awareness of age roles and of their degree of influence over you is essential to your understanding of social development.

In essence, the constraints society imposes are the clockworks of adult life—they constitute the **social clock.** Unlike your biological clock, your social clock comes from outside you; eventually, however, it is directly or indirectly learned and becomes the source of your perceptions of social timing.

First identified by Bernice Neugarten and her associates (1968), the social-clock concept is a way of describing the timing of predictable social changes in adult life. The social clock tells us what we "should" be doing in each age and time period of our lives. It regulates the age-status periods of life, telling us when men and women are "young," "middle-aged," and "old." (The clock, incidentally, is sexist: its timing of these age grades is different for men and women.) It also regulates the ideal timing of important life events and activities. We know, in social-clock time, at what ages men and women "should" marry, "should" have children, and "should" enter and leave the work force. (The clock is also slow: its "shoulds" are based on norms from the past.)

Though sexist, slow, and often inappropriate, still the external social clock imposes age grades, norms, and roles. From a sense that we're behind clock time, we may push toward a goal we're not ready to reach; getting ahead of our inner sense of timing may cause us to slow down our efforts. There is a strong possibility that we're operating on the basis of a clock that's plain inaccurate.

The survey on which the clock concept is based questioned people who were middle-aged in 1965, and they were in strong agreement—within social classes—on the timing of social changes (Neugarten, 1968a). In the last 20 years, however, the external clock they recognized has been subject to new influences. In mid-century, for example, the American family cycle went into a remarkable speed-up. People married and had children at earlier ages; their children left home earlier and in turn had their children at earlier ages, so that the people who became grandparents were in their mid-forties (Neugarten, 1977). But the clock's norms have not adjusted for the change: grandparents are still, in common fantasy, nice old folks with white hair. By the 1980s the social clock as an external regulator of social processes in adult life was noticeably weakening (Neugarten, 1980) as a result of new social attitudes of age irrelevance, most probably related to changing lifestyles.

As an internal regulator, however, your social clock is still ticking. Examine your concepts of your actions corresponding to a timetable by completing these statements:

I finished/will finish my degree	early ____	on time ____	late ____ .
I began/will begin working	early ____	on time ____	late ____ .
I married/will marry	early ____	on time ____	late ____ .
I had/will have children	early ____	on time ____	late ____ .
I've "settled down"/will "settle down"	early ____	on time ____	late ____ .
I retired/will retire	early ____	on time ____	late ____ .
I've gotten/will get "old"	early ____	on time ____	late ____ .
I will die	early ____	on time ____	late ____ .

Your social clock can control your lifestyle not only at these major junctures but in detail: women in their thirties cut off their long hair, because it's "too young" for them; men in their forties sell their motorcycles, being "too old" to ride them now. Your choice of clothes, home, car, recreation—all can be determined by rigid age expectations. Or you can choose to time your own social processes, styling them to be appropriate for your own life.

The strengths and weaknesses of living on social-clock time has been one of the many concerns of a pioneer in the field of social and psychological processes in adult life—Bernice Neugarten. Neugarten has been a long-time associate of the University of Chicago's multidisciplinary, longitudinal, and cross-sectional Kansas City Studies, which began in 1952. The Kansas City Studies series has examined men and women in their middle and later years of adult life who represent all social levels. With more than a thousand subjects studied, these investigations have been influential in current thought on adult life.

Neugarten's early work, including the research that established the social-clock concept, was focused on the social factors affecting age norms and age constraints. At first, adult development seemed a process of socialization; the older the subject, the more completely he or she internalized social norms and roles (1968b). But hindsight reveals that finding to be an apparent cohort effect, rather than a developmental reality. Our society, Neugarten now feels, is fast becoming "age irrelevant" (1980).

The longer that Neugarten has worked in the field of adult development, the more strongly she has become convinced that chronological age is a poor predictor of adult life stage. Better predictors, she believes, are found in lifestyles and body condition and in the family and economic status of the individual (1977, 1980). Neugarten's model of development consists of a loosely age-related sequence of the major life events that each person experiences on his or her own biological, social, and psychological terms. These terms vary with sex, race, social class, and the individual (see Figure 4-3). External social controls keep life patterns fairly even, and so do inner personality factors. Rather than moving from crisis to crisis, Neugarten sees social development as moving from event to event: events become crises only when they are timed badly (1977). Personality is described as developing through increases in the "executive processes of personality"—self-awareness, selectivity, control, mastery, and competence—as impulsiveness is brought under control (1977). Also, personality develops through accumulation of experience and perspective, as life events are experienced (1977). The bottom line in personality development, for Neugarten, is that we become "more and more ourselves" (1968b).

Neugarten's beliefs themselves have evolved over time, and they have been based on empirical research, especially on studies of people in their middle years and later. Stemming from her training as a gerontologist, Neugarten's approach has been multidisciplinary, with perhaps more emphasis on the social processes of change than on individuals' psychological processes of change. The combined social clock and biological clock are, for her, the framework of personality changes in adulthood.

Age (varies with sex/ race/class/individual)	Group	Tasks
20+	Young adults	Entering work force Marriage Parenting
40–50	Middle-aged	Empty nest Grandparenting Body monitoring Leaving work force
55–75	Young-olds	Losing loved one Sex-role reversals
75+	Old-olds	Senescence

Figure 4-3 Neugarten's model of life-cycle development

What's useful about Neugarten's model? _____

_____

Was the research method appropriate? _____

_____

What are the model's weaknesses? _____

_____

Does this model fit your life? How? _____

_____

_____

Another influential developmentalist who shares this point of view is Robert Havighurst. Like Neugarten, Havighurst was involved in the Kansas City Studies—he was, in fact, an initiator of the research. He bases his model of development on Erikson's, but he uses the Erikson model simply as a framework for a list of developmental tasks that he has identified as essential achievements in adult life (Figure 4-4).

The sources of Havighurst's tasks change over time. Before adult development begins, he delineates tasks that are psychological—like Erikson's, they are the essentials for creating a personal identity. With early adulthood the tasks become socially oriented, involved

Early adulthood (ages 18–30)

_____ Selecting a mate
_____ Learning to live with a marriage partner
_____ Starting a family
_____ Rearing children
_____ Managing a home
_____ Getting started in an occupation
_____ Taking on civic responsibility
_____ Finding a congenial social group

Middle age (ages 30–60)

_____ Assisting teenagers to become responsible, happy adults
_____ Achieving adult civic and social responsibility
_____ Reaching and maintaining satisfactory occupational performance
_____ Developing adult leisure-time activities
_____ Relating to spouse as a person
_____ Accepting and adjusting to physical changes of middle age
_____ Adjusting to aging parents

Later maturity (ages 60+)

_____ Adjusting to decreasing physical strength and health
_____ Adjusting to retirement and reduced income
_____ Adjusting to death of spouse
_____ Establishing affiliation with one's age group
_____ Meeting social/civic obligations
_____ Establishing satisfactory living arrangements

Figure 4-4 Take a minute or two to check off the tasks on Havighurst's developmental task model that you feel you will accept in the coming years. You don't have to accept all of the tasks on the list. Conversely, tasks may not be listed that you will want to create for yourself. *(From DEVELOPMENTAL TASKS AND EDUCATION, by Robert J. Havighurst. Copyright © 1972 by Longman Inc. Reprinted by permission of Longman Inc., New York.)*

with establishing social roles. In middle age and later maturity Havighurst shifts to tasks of adjustment and adaptation to social and biological losses, which again draw on psychological resources. The time periods in this model are extremely wide, and the tasks have no specific chronological age links. For Havighurst, adult life is an ongoing checklist of accomplishments that initially are social and later are personal (1972).

Havighurst sees all tasks, whether they are biological or social or psychological, as adaptive: successful accomplishment of the tasks yields social acceptance, personal happiness, and the likelihood of success with future tasks. Adaptation is, to Havighurst, the key to development.

In a sense, **adaptation**—introduction of stress-reducing changes—has been an essential element in all of the models we've reviewed. Bühler presents growth toward adult "self-fulfillment" as the interaction of an innate, inner striving to achieve goals, of an environment that may or may not support our striving, and of an "integrative system" that adapts both the environment and the self, each to the other. Erikson connects personality development directly to the ways an individual adapts to the social world—ways that either stunt and block personal growth or that allow personal unfolding. Gould explains developmental changes as the product of interaction—that of the "childhood consciousness" and the social changes experienced, from which emerges an adaptive "adult consciousness." Levinson describes development as evolution of our continuous-but-changing life structure as we adapt and readapt our inner selves and outer worlds each to the other. Neugarten recognizes development as an interplay between the cumulative personality and the timing of life events, resulting in more functional—more adaptive—self-perceptions. But social and biological adaptation are not the whole picture. Developmental changes have also been explored from a third perspective—the essentially psychological perspective.

Psychological Processes

Biological and social development are both central to psychological development. Both biological and social clocks may regulate our **interpersonal** relationships with others, but they also shape our **intrapersonal** changes—the changes within each person individually, in thoughts and feelings. Biological and social changes require us to make new adaptations to new conditions; they also provide situations that may (or may not) prod us to grow. Two essentially intrapersonal and psychological processes that have been the subjects of extensive long-term study are our adaptive style and our personality (including ego development).

Adaptation may be defined as the way that we fit our inner selves to our outer environments. Adaptive styles are a matter of personal perceptions of life events and of coping skills used to interact with events, things, and people. Our styles may allow us to adapt comfortably, or they may be maladaptive to the point of mental and physical illness. We may adapt passively, conforming to the situation, or we may adapt actively, changing the situation to fit our own needs. We may adapt consciously, making an effort to deal effectively with change, or we may adapt unconsciously, trying to defend the inner self from conflict. Certainly, over the life span, events challenge our adaptations (Lazarus, 1976; Newman & Newman, 1981).

An unconscious aspect of our adaptive style that Freud first labeled the *defense mechanism* has been the subject of an extensive longitudinal study by George Vaillant, at Harvard. Vaillant inherited his sample from the long-term Grant Study of Adult Development, which has been carried on at Harvard since 1939. In 1967 Dr. Vaillant joined the staff, and in 1969—30 years after the study began—he selected a follow-up sample from the original group.

The original subjects in the Grant Study were 268 of the most well-adapted and productive students at Harvard, between 1939 and 1942. In 1968, Vaillant interviewed the members of his sample to find out "what had gone right in their lives." He wanted to explore his theory of mental health. For Vaillant, being mentally healthy means having the ability to adapt to problems in a way that doesn't distort the person or the environment and that allows the person to function well. He was particularly interested in the relationship between ego mechanisms of defense and adaptation to life changes. What Vaillant was looking for was a deeper understanding of satisfactory adaptations in men's lives. What he found (among other points) was that psychological development continues through life, that adaptive styles determine health or pathology, and that adaptive styles can mature (Vaillant, 1977).

The unconscious adaptations of defense mechanisms have traditionally been considered by the psychiatric community to be unhealthy, but Vaillant has pointed out that individual defense mechanisms can be classified into categories of age appropriateness (see Figure 4-5). A defense that, like "denial," is perhaps psychotic in an adult may be more appropriate in another stage: in this case, childhood. The defense of deep "fantasy" is fairly appropriate and healthy for an adolescent; "displacement" or "intellectualization"

Typical age for defenses	Level	Defenses
Childhood	I/Psychotic (infantile)	Denial Distortion Delusional projection
Adolescence	II/Immature	Fantasy Projection Hypochondriasis Passive-aggressive behavior Acting out
All ages	III/Neurotic	Intellectualization Repression Reaction formation Displacement Dissociation
"Healthy" adults	IV/Mature	Sublimation Altruism Suppression Anticipatory planning Humor

Figure 4-5 In Vaillant's model of adaptive defense mechanisms, a hierarchy identifies defenses that are appropriate to some ages and inappropriate to others. *(Condensed from* Adaptation to Life, *by G. E. Vaillant.* © *1977 by George E. Vaillant. By permission of Little, Brown and Company.)*

What's useful about Vaillant's model? _____

_____

Was the research method appropriate? _____

_____

What are the model's weaknesses? _____

_____

Does this model fit your life? How? _____

_____

_____

may be an appropriate, if slightly neurotic, way in which an adult can handle serious stress. Vaillant identifies a number of defenses as being not only mature but integrating and adaptive. "Altruism," "humor," "suppression," "sublimation," and "anticipatory planning" are all adaptive behaviors that may be inappropriate at some times in life; but in adulthood they may also be extremely productive. Vaillant feels, in fact, that they are the hallmarks of the further reaches of psychological development. He sees the ability to adapt as evolving through a hierarchy—a scale of changing values—from a psychotic and infantile level toward a healthy and mature level.

Vaillant's perception of the maturation of ego defenses is supported by the work of Norma Haan and Jack Block at the Institute of Human Development at Berkeley. In a longitudinal study of the influences of adolescence on later personality development, Block and Haan found that, in a sample of both men and women, such defenses as reaction formation and fantasy diminished, whereas defenses such as altruism and suppression increased. Over time, mature defenses became more common. This maturity occurs in a framework of personalities that are consistent in their various types and that mellow slightly with time (Block & Haan, 1971).

This distinction between adaptive styles and personality is an important one. Remember that Neugarten also perceived developing "executive processes" of the personality, including self-awareness, and that she believed we become more and more ourselves over the years; our personality is more than just our adaptive style.

A **personality** is a pattern of consistent behavior, a tendency to react in the same ways to similar situations. The concept of personality enables us to understand and predict the behavior of others with some degree of accuracy. Some psychologists, especially behaviorists and social psychologists, believe that personality is primarily shaped by interpersonal interactions, beginning at birth. Other psychologists, including psychoanalysts, cognitive psychologists, existentialists, and physiological psychologists (and even ethologists and sociobiologists) describe personality as an expression of inner drives, or needs, or goals, or memories, or ways of thinking. Developmental psychologists—since Erikson—have usually taken the position that personality has both interpersonal and intrapersonal sources.

Psychologists working on the infant years of development recently have made some contributions to our understanding of adult personality. One contribution is demonstration of the relationship between the infant's genetic "temperament" and its later personality; another contribution is an illustration of the correlations between an infant's "attachment" pattern and its later patterns of behavior.

Some of the first work on temperament—the individual's usual reactions to stimuli—was done by Stella Chess. She observed a sample of 136 infants and identified four consistent patterns of behavior; difficult (excitable or irritable), easy (relaxed and undemanding), slow to warm up (unresponsive), and mixed (not very consistent). Chess classified the infants into these four categories by recording their intensity of responses, their activity levels, their regularity of sleeping and eating, and other criteria. A longitudinal study has indicated very strongly that the individuals had the same temperament ten years later (Chess, Thomas, & Birch, 1968). Temperament at birth, as created by the sensitivity and efficiency of our nervous system, endocrine system, and digestive system, seems to be the core of personality (an idea that is supported, incidentally, by current studies of twins reared apart).

Do you have any idea what your temperament was like at birth? Do you still react and behave in similar ways?

As an infant my temperament was _____

_____

As an adult my temperament is _____

_____

The way you react as an adult may reflect your genetic temperament, or it may not. Early emotional and cognitive learning also apparently shape the later personality.

Developmentalists such as Jerome Bruner (1968) at the Center for Cognitive Studies have shown not only that infants learn in the first weeks of life, but that what they learn then significantly affects their lives. Infants make associations between events and behaviors, remember these associations, and change their behavior as the result. An infant's cognitive style and its emotional needs and goals are shaped by its earliest stimulations from the environment. And the patterns of behavior begun early in life form a foundation for the patterns consistent in later life.

Because early learning is so fundamental, one of the most crucial kinds of experience that an infant has is in its first human relationship. A baby's first intense relationship, called "attachment," is with its mother or the person who gives it the most care in its first year of life. A pattern of interacting developed in response to the first caretaker may have an important influence on the baby's later interactions with other people, on reactions to such emotional events as separation and loss, and on the cognitive styles used in solving problems. Building on the work of Mary Ainsworth and John Bowlby, child psychologists have been able to show clear connections between the interactions of a child and its caretaker and the child's later patterns of behavior (Sroufe, 1978).

Genetically inherited temperament and environmentally learned early emotional behavior, then, make up the core of the predictable patterns that we call *personality*. Our core is the basis on which we strive to make sense of our experience and to master our environment.

Striving toward integration has been identified as the dynamic behind another model for the development of the inner self—the work of Jane Loevinger. Loevinger is an ego psychologist who has described psychological process as movement through hierarchical levels of ego development that proceeds from the spontaneous and impulsive level of immaturity through "self-protective," "opportunistic," and "conformist" levels, toward the "conscientious," "autonomous," and "integrated" levels of maturity. Loevinger, like Bühler, Jung, Erikson, Gould, and Levinson, expresses the belief that there is a natural unfolding of the self (or ego) in interaction with the social environment. She describes the ego as a complex structure of a variety of factors, including character, control of impulses, characteristic concerns, and ways of thinking, morals, and styles of interacting and relating. This inner self develops through transformations or evolutions of its structures (or both) in a developmental sequence (see Figure 4-6). So temperament (genetically inherited) may remain stable, but personality changes (Loevinger, 1976).

Although Loevinger is often called a stage theorist, what she is actually describing is a continuous process of development, one that is not age linked, although the three least-evolved states are clearly not functional for normal adults. In this model, the process of development begins with the "presocial" and "symbiotic" conditions of the infant, which are characterized by nonexistent self-identity and extreme dependence. The next stage in the process is called the "impulsive"; it's associated with lack of impulse control and with simplistic, black/white, good/bad thinking. Beyond the impulsive lies the "self-protective" stage, in which fragile controls are developed. At this point in the development process, the individual focuses on getting away with as much as possible, manipulating other

General age	Continuous states of development process
Infancy/childhood	Presocial
	Symbiotic
	Impulsive
	Self-protective
Adolescence/adulthood	Conformist
	(Conscientious-Conformist Transition)
	Conscientious
	(Individualistic Transition)
	Autonomous
	Integrated

Figure 4-6 Loevinger's model of ego development depicts evolution and transformation of personality development that, although they are not linked to age, do reflect the trends toward autonomy and integration described by stage theorists Bühler, Jung, Erikson, Gould, and Levinson. *(Adapted from* Ego Development: Conceptions and Theories, *by J. Loevinger. Copyright © 1976 by Jossey-Bass Inc., Publishers. Reprinted by permission.)*

What's useful about Loevinger's model? _____

_____

Was the research method appropriate? _____

_____

What are the model's weaknesses? _____

_____

Does this model fit your life? How? _____

_____

_____

people, and refusing self-responsibility. A person functioning self-protectively, in Loevinger's terminology, would tend to be rigid, defensive, and blaming. The next stage—the "conformist"—involves gaining identity from the social group, conforming to rules, and stereotyped, simplistic thinking. Further development of the ego leads to a transitional level, the "conscientious-conformist" level, in which the individual gradually becomes aware of his or her inner life and begins to perceive alternatives and exceptions to rules. At this level there begins a self-consciousness and flexibility of thought.

From Loevinger's point of view, most late adolescents and adults develop to the two last-mentioned phases, with the average adult at the conscientious-conformist level. Four further reaches of development are possible, however, in this model: the "conscientious" stage, the "individualistic" transition, the "autonomous" stage, and the "integrated" stage. Conscientious persons become self-responsible, in terms of goal setting, self-evaluation, and self-criticism. The self-recognition characteristic at this stage allows recognition of others, so that mutuality in relationships becomes possible. At the individualistic-transition level yet more tolerance of self and others develops, as does more recognition of inner and outer complexities. The autonomous stage involves, like Jung's individuation, a reconciliation of polarities, a deep recognition of the meaning of autonomy, identity, self-expression, self-fulfillment, and existential humor. Beyond autonomy lies the integrated stage of full personal growth. These last developmental stages are rare, but potentially possible.

Loevinger's model, unlike the others we have seen, is not based on clinical research, although she has made many research-based contributions to the science of personality measurement. It is based, rather, on a painstaking review of all the conceptions and theories of ego development and on a synthesis of cognitive, humanistic, psychoanalytic, and stage theories of personality. Although Loevinger's model shows the possibility of psychological development over time, it is free of chronological ties.

To understand the patterns of adult development we must clearly understand that there is a chronological factor in adult life and that there is also a process factor. The two—time and process—may or may not be correlated. We will examine them separately, first life's chronological framework and then life's processes apart from chronology. Separating them allows us the security of becoming familiar with each one in detail while we maintain the freedom to recognize that, although age doesn't necessarily cause a process to develop, age often is correlated with specific developments. Shared timing in social development may create some chronological similarities; shared tendencies in biological development may create chronological similarities; shared psychological experience may create some chronological similarities. They are the framework, these similarities, in

which the individual differences in the patterns of our lives unfold. For this reason, in the next section we'll survey development first from the chronological perspective.

Summary

Stage theories and process theories both recognize a framework of chronological age and a content of biological, social, and psychological development in adult life. The difference between the two perspectives is in their emphasis. Stage theories emphasize age-related changes in the general population; process theories emphasize continuity of change, specific processes of change, and individual differences. Although both stage and process theorists agree that understanding adulthood must be a multidisciplinary effort, process theorists are more apt to be expert in one discipline yet involved in a team approach. The major perspectives taken by these teams are biological, social, and psychological.

Biological process in adult life has no real theoretical model: the findings in this area are simply sets of empirical findings by gerontologists and physiologists. An important contribution from these specialists is the recognition that biological changes in adulthood are only loosely correlated with age—instead they are a function of the individual's "biological clock," which in turn is regulated by genetics but also lifestyle and environment.

Social processes in adult life also are regulated—by a theoretical "social clock," which is a term for the system of age grading, age norms, and age roles that determines the timing of social events. The society's social clock and its reflection on individual timing is sexist, slow, and inaccurate; however, in recent years it seems to be growing less influential.

Bernice Neugarten, whose early research dealt with the social clocks of middle-aged persons in the 1960s, has developed a model of adult development based on four loose age categories during which a sequence of life events occur. In her model, social controls and personality factors keep the timing of most individuals' life events fairly similar, but each person times his/her own development. Neugarten considers personality development a function of social development; over time, experience accumulates, impulse control increases, and one's personality reveals itself more clearly.

Robert Havighurst has created another model of socially based development, which is based on Erikson's model but identifies a series of primarily social tasks that adults must accomplish to achieve a satisfactory adaptation to life.

Adaptation and personality growth are psychological processes of development in adult life that have also been a major focus of research. George Vaillant, for example, has presented a model of the psychological processes of adaptation to life change based on a hierarchy of defense mechanisms. Unlike Freud in his classic model, Vaillant defines several defenses not as immature but as mature and integrating. Temperament and attachment may be the early bases of personality growth, but our ego development seems to move toward responsibility, autonomy, and integration; the model of Jane Loevinger supports this possibility.

Each of the processes underlying lifelong development—biological, social, and psychological processes—exhibits its own continuity, its own variability, and its own (to use Gould's term) "maturational push." Therefore change over time is apparently inevitable.

Terms and Concepts to Define

adaptation _____

_____

age grading _____

_____

aging _____

_____

biological clock _____

_____

functional age _____

_____

interpersonal _____

_____

intrapersonal _____

_____

maturation _____

_____

multidisciplinary _____

_____

norms _____

_____

personality _____

_____

roles _____

_____

senescence _____

_____

social clock _____

_____

socialization _____

_____

Experiences

To involve yourself with the concepts in this chapter, try these experiences described in the Appendix.

Alone
1. *Experiencing Your Life Course*
29. *Mature Defenses*
44. *Goal Setting III: Lifetime Goals*

With Others
9. *Social Norms*
21. *Social Roles*

Going beyond the Text

1. *Find a number of people (either in person or in biographical sketches) who don't fit the typical development chronology—either biologically, socially, or psychologically—but who have developed in a positive way in their own time frames.*
2. *Update the social clock; survey a large number of people about their timing concepts for major life events (such as marrying, having children, and retiring) or for age categories (such as "young," "middle-aged," or "old").*

Suggested Readings

Loevinger, J. Ego development: Conceptions and theories. *San Francisco: Jossey Bass, 1976.*

Neugarten, B. Ed. Middle age and aging. *Chicago: University of Chicago Press, 1968.*

Vaillant, G. Adaptation to life. *Boston: Little, Brown, 1977.*

PART THREE

A Perspective: Ages and Stages

Part Three is a first overview of the course of adult life from the chronological perspective. Contemporary stage theorists provide the core of information in this section, which is expanded with relevant information from many other sources. It's important to remember as we make our first survey of adulthood in this section that stage theories are formulations of the timing of developmental changes that may hold true on an average, but they are not guidelines for individual lives. *They offer a way of perceiving adult changes—not a new set of "shoulds."*

5

Getting Ready:
The Late Teens to the Late Twenties

When you have finished reading this chapter you should be able to:
Define what Keniston means by "youth."
Discuss the central conflicts of the twenties decade.
Identify White's "growth trends" in the twenties.
Summarize the tasks that Erikson, Gould, Levinson, and Havighurst identify
with the twenties.

We are biologically (and legally) adult by the age of 21, but, socially and psychologically, at that age our adult lives are just starting.
During a time period that lasts from 10 to 15 years, depending on
the person, we're all beginners, working on the first developmental
tasks of adulthood. This period starts in the late teens and may end
as late as the middle thirties (Gould, 1980; Levinson et al., 1978).

In this chapter we will focus on the twenties decade itself and on
the insights about this time period that have been contributed by
developmentalists. In this period most of the work of becoming a
young adult gets done. The work load of social and psychological
tasks is heavy in these years, particularly with externally and internally generated "shoulds," or imperatives, that "ought" to be accomplished before the decade is over.

The Twenties Decade: An Overview

Without expert assistance you're probably already fairly familiar with the social and psychological demands of your environment as well as with your own personal requirements for the twenties decade. As an introduction to the subject, identify some of them:

The social clock requires that people should have accomplished the following tasks by the end of their twenties:

_____

_____

To be psychologically normal, people should behave/think/feel in the following ways by the end of their twenties:

_____

_____

My own expectations are/were that by the end of my twenties decade the following tasks will/would be accomplished:

_____

_____

As you examined your own perceptions of the twenties imperatives and those of society did you find any differences? Did your own expectations match those of others? A decade is a time span sufficiently broad to allow general agreement. However, if there were discrepancies between the social and personal shoulds, there are good reasons why they exist.

One reason that **conflicts**—struggles between opposing forces—may exist between individual imperatives and those of society lies in the mixed messages given about which experiences are most appropriate for this time of life. The cultural myth of youth carries one set of messages about your twenties; the social structures of work and family carry a second set.

You're only young once, and these are the years for adventure and romance, strength and beauty, risk and challenge; this is the message of the cultural myth. Conversely, the myth hints, once you're no longer young you're finished. At the same time you're urged to get on with it; these are the years for responsibility and commitment, plans and decisions, stability and serious considerations. This is the message of social survival. With "you're only young once" coming in one ear and "get on with it" coming in the other, a person who is 20 and confused experiences a classic **double-bind:** a trap between conflicting demands. Double binds breed confusion, indecision, impulsive choices, and irrational behavior. The twenties can be a painful period of internal psychological conflict and uncertainty.

Another source of conflict is the result of social changes that only now are becoming clearly visible. Kenneth Keniston has described this period of life as a new developmental stage that has emerged in the latter part of the 20th century—in much the same ways that adolescence as a separate developmental stage emerged in the last part of the 19th century. A pause for a more extensive education—a time of economic dependency before entering the work force—became necessary in the urban-industrial society at the turn of the century. This period became known as **adolescence,** which hadn't existed as a concept before that time. In the rapidly changing, highly technological society of this century, a longer pause for an even more extensive education and so even more extended economic dependency before beginning a career has become more and more common. This has given rise to a new phase of development that Keniston calls **youth.**

"Youth," in Keniston's concept, is a stage of psychological transition between adolescence and young adulthood. A youth is neither an adolescent nor a young adult; a youth is a person who is trying to find himself or herself, a person who is struggling with individuation. In the struggle, the person separates self and environment in order to evaluate each of them, often painfully and critically, in their strengths and weaknesses (Keniston, 1977b).

Not every young person experiences the stage of youth as Keniston describes it, but mass education on the college level has introduced masses of people to the kinds of thinking that are typical of the new developmental period: objectivity, responsibility, and relativity. Young people who are educated to think about themselves and their society with some objectivity are apt to perceive their lives in a different way. Learning that we can shape and reshape our own lives may give rise to an uncomfortable sense of responsibility; but it also suggests that all things are possible. Learning that many of the norms and roles of our society are simply stereotyped behaviors, and that they may be very different in other cultures, can stir up feelings of emptiness and phoniness. However, this information also brings an awareness that we can create our own roles and standards. And that choice is paralleled by another. The new freedoms of thought may generate frustration and rebellion or they may lead to an earlier psychological maturity (Lidz, 1976).

Yankelovich has identified a radical shift in American values. It began with the youth on college campuses in the 1960s and has spread to encompass an estimated 80% of the population in the 1980s. For many people now in their twenties, the shift reflects a change of the issues to be resolved. The major change—a demand for self-fulfillment rather than self-sacrifice in sexuality, in work, in family life, and in environmental safety—appears most strongly in samples of single people under 35 who have had some college education. On one hand, this new ethic of fulfilling our human potential often conflicts with the hard economic realities of contemporary life. On the other hand, new social norms in which marriage is viewed as not mandatory and parenthood is seen as not essential relieve some of the pressures on decision making in the twenties decade. New freedoms of choice, and the accompanying new ethics of **commitment,** may ultimately create a cultural requirement for a self-fulfilling lifestyle for everyone, rather than only for those who purposefully struggle to achieve it (Yankelovich, 1981).

Those people who do experience youth's extended time-out from "getting on with it" have opportunities for working through many personal issues that—otherwise—crop up throughout adult life, often disastrously. Youth presents a chance to work through sexual identity more completely before marrying or parenting. It provides the possibility of shifting from dependency relationships with peers and elders to mutuality in equal relationships. It offers the potential of developing to a level of commitment to life, sophistication of thinking, and awareness of spirit that—without the time-out of youth—might never be reached (Keniston, 1977b).

So far we have identified two of the central conflicts of the twenties decade: mixed messages from the social environment and the changing conditions of the social environment that have created the somewhat optional developmental stage of youth. A third conflict lies much closer to home. The collision of parental expectations and youthful perceptions are an almost universal source of trouble.

When social change speeds up, the realities of early adulthood become very different for each generation. Parents are often quite unaware of this. Their expectations—their requirements, which they communicate indirectly and directly to their sons and daughters—may have been appropriate for their own cohort, but they might be totally unrealistic for the next generation. Messages such as "When are you going to settle down in a serious job?" or "Don't you think it's time you thought about marriage?"—followed by "Why, when I was your age . . ."—are infuriating to a young person who desperately feels the need for the time-out of youth. Parental expectations and youthful realities in many cases don't match (Schenk & Schenk, 1978).

Social expectations about psychological and social autonomy in young adults are now in their third shift in the 20th century, and social norms haven't yet completely caught up with the second shift. Early in the century young people stayed with their parents, only gradually becoming psychologically independent and economically self-supporting. The next generation's members may have maintained an extended psychological dependence on family in many cases, but because of the economic boom at mid-century they could start work and could marry early in their twenties. Their children have tended to become psychologically independent earlier but have found that to become economically self-supporting takes a long time.

Parents who were in the twenties cohort of the 1950s, when jobs and money were plentiful, were more apt to encourage early independence in their own children. Some of them now have trouble understanding why their expectations don't fit the lives of their daughters and sons who are trying to find their places in the tight job market and inflated economy of the 1970s and 1980s. The parent generation hasn't anticipated the need now for extended education, the opening up of sex-related work roles, and the emphasis on the individual's life satisfaction that have become key factors for contemporary cohorts (Yankelovich, 1981). And so a third source of conflict—family struggle—contributes to an extended transitional stage in the twenties, as young adults work at breaking away, getting free, cutting loose. Economically discriminated against by employers and insurance companies, requiring expensive education for the complex skills needed to find work, young people living out this transition are torn between the need for autonomy and the necessity of dependency. Conflicts between young adults and parents over control, life styles, attitudes, and issues make this launching period one of the most difficult times of life for both groups (Freedman, 1978; Lowenthal et al., 1977; Schenk & Schenk, 1978).

The Late Teens and Early Twenties

The two developmental tasks that are most basic to your autonomy in young adulthood are those of beginning individuation—becoming an individual person, separate from your family of origin—and of creating a social network outside your family structure. The first task confirms your identity and permits you to live on your own; the second allows you to form close and supportive relationships, with friends, a mate, a new family.

Erikson's labels for these tasks are "ego identity" and "intimacy." Erikson describes the establishment of **ego identity** as a lifelong process with its roots in childhood development and with a first flowering essential in adolescence. By the late teens, from Erikson's point of view, ego identity should be fairly clear; you should be aware of appropriate social and sexual roles, your social status, and your personal abilities and beliefs. Once this ego identity is established, you have the capacity to commit yourself to others in friendship and intimacy. In Erikson's model, the task of the twenties is intimacy—including the capacities to love deeply and to work effectively. With these abilities you can begin to leave your family of origin.

Leaving your family of origin is the first phase of adult life that Gould has identified. He calls it "leaving our parents' world." Gould sees the process as beginning fairly early in adolescence, around 15, and ending at about 22.

During this developmental phase, Gould feels, we are dropping our childhood illusion that we'll "always belong to our parents and believe in their world." The process of dropping this belief may be easy or difficult; to be free of parental controls we must believe that we are strong enough. Gould's criteria for leaving our parents' world are the knowledge that independence won't hurt us or our parents, that believing different things than our parents believe is all right, that we can create our own security, that we can establish our own new network of friends and loves, and that our bodies are our own. The events of our early twenties that separate us either physically or intellectually from our parents—college, travel, military service, moving out—help us to reach these understandings on an emotional level. The assumptions that have kept us in our parents' world drop away. We move a step toward autonomy (Gould, 1978).

Breaking free from the parents' world is also essential from Levinson's point of view. Levinson describes the "early adult transition" as a time of breaking down the adolescent life structure and beginning an early-adult life structure, as **novice** (beginning) adults.

In Levinson's view, terminating adolescence involves **separating** from your parents: moving out, supporting yourself, and accepting new roles are external signs of separation. The internal signs are gaining psychological distance, recognizing differences between yourself and your parents, and reducing emotional dependency. It's the beginning of what Levinson feels is a lifelong process of separation.

The second task, to create an early-adult life structure, is being accomplished as you work on the first one. It may mean going to college and finding new attitudes and new skills. It may mean getting a job and experiencing new responsibility and importance. It may mean exploring a world of people and places that your parents never knew (Levinson et al., 1978).

A first step into adult life may include all three aspects of creating an early-adult life structure: new training, a new position, and a new social world. It most certainly includes taking on some new, more adult roles, paying more of your own way and buying more possessions yourself, finding your own personal space outside of "home," and building your own social status outside of your family's. All this doesn't happen overnight, or all at once. But it has to happen if a person is going to make an adult separation from his or her family of origin (Schenk & Schenk, 1978).

Early marriage can look like a shortcut to accomplishing all these tasks of the early-adult transition. Everything seems to get done at once: new role, new economic unit, new home, new status. But the key word here is *seems*. Levinson points out that while early marriages may be a conscious attempt to seem more adult, they may be an unconscious attempt to replace a parent. An insecure young man gets a mother substitute to manage his living arrangements. An immature young woman gets a father replacement to support her economically and to protect her emotionally (Levinson et al., 1978).

Gould (1978) makes this point, too. He adds that another motive in early marriage is to get a partner who will help us escape our parents' control. Sheehy labels these marriages "piggyback" and "jailbreak" marriages. She points out that they are the classic way in a sexist society for women to get out of their parents' worlds (Sheehy, 1976). Vaillant (1977) found that early marriages, made before the partners had developed the capacity for real intimacy, were those most often in serious trouble. Divorce statistics are the dramatic bottom line: marriages made before the mid-twenties are statistically the most risky.

By the age of 22, most people have begun to establish a base of intimacy and autonomy. Vaillant, however, identified a small group of "perpetual boys" in his sample, men who never really left their mothers for intimacies and responsibilities in the outside world (Vaillant, 1977). There is no research that identifies the women who stay "perpetual girls." We could predict that the female group would be larger than the male group, in a society that has traditionally socialized women to be dependent rather than autonomous. As a study of mental-health professionals has shown, the female stereotype and our cultural definition of *adult person* don't always match (Broverman, Broverman, Clarkson, Rosenkrantz, & Vogel, 1972). In spite of the difficulties in pulling up roots, however, most people seem to be approaching autonomy by their middle twenties.

The Middle Twenties

The mid-twenties is a time of life that is particularly sensitive to the shifts of social change. Extended education spreads into these years; deferred marriage and parenting hit hardest here. Although most members of the parental generation of today's youth and young adults were married by the time they reached 25, the contemporary pattern is quite different. The current census shows that in 1979 more than a third of all 24-year-olds and more than 27% of all 29-year-olds were still single. From the baby-boom cohort onward, the single lifestyle has increased in popularity among young adults. The changing work expectations among young women, the increased competition for jobs in a tight job market, and the inflated economy all contribute to the new mid-twenties—and the youthful time-out described by Keniston is also an important factor. A prevailing social attitude among young people is that it's important to "find themselves," to "get their acts together" before they build structure into their adult lives.

Robert White, an ego psychologist who has investigated personality change in the case histories of adults, has identified a series of psychological "growth trends" that echo the major themes of youth. The first trend, "stabilizing ego identity," is the tendency to move toward a more solid sense of who we are as we struggle to fit ourselves into the social roles of early adulthood. A second growth trend is the "freeing of personal relationships." There seems to be a movement away from perceiving other people in terms of our needs, fantasies, and stereotypes and toward seeing them as real people who do not exist simply to fulfill our expectations. As our own identities become more stabilized, in other words, we become more aware of the identities of others. "Deepening of interests" is a third growth trend. White finds an apparent movement from passing interests and tentative commitments toward more serious involvement. As competence and mastery grow, perceptions become more sophisticated. Values become **humanized**. The "humanizing of values" is another trend; from being reactive, shallow, and oversimplified, values become deeper, and they reflect a more complex understanding. The final trend that White describes, "expansion of caring," is a movement toward empathy and concern for others. As such it is a natural outcome of the other trends (White, 1975). White's sample was a group of college students, so his findings can't be validly projected on the broader population. But both White and Keniston agree that there is important psychological work that may occur in these years, given the time and space, creating the possibility that contemporary young people may develop very different perceptions than the generations of the past.

As Yankelovich has indicated, there is some reason to believe that the expectations of people in their twenties are changing. And in a survey based on a life-history questionnaire and a sample of interviews, Sheehy, too, has identified a number of basic attitudes that seem to prevail mainly in some young men in the twenties cohort that is current. The respondents were predominantly middle class and college educated, young professionals or managers—clearly people who could be considered to have experienced Keniston's "youth" and as having had time to work through White's "growth trends" (Sheehy, 1979).

Sheehy calls these young men "the postponing generation"; she finds that their expectations are quite different from the traditional values of the American middle class. They reject hard work and the belief that work is what gives life meaning; they emphasize their need for personal growth; their goal is a balanced life of love, leisure, and freedom to express themselves. Ambition and responsibility have little appeal for them; yet money and the good life are very important (Sheehy, 1979).

What are they **postponing**—putting off? Apparently they aren't postponing the psychological tasks of these years that involve self-identity and individuation.

Gould has found that there may be several years—from around the age of 22 until about 28—during which this sense of self-identity comes and goes. There is a seesaw for many people between independence, with responsibility for their own personal space, and dependency, with the security of leaning on parents. The essence of this struggle is getting free of the assumption that if we do things our parents' way we'll get results but that if we get tired or can't cope, they will take over. Once we find that our parents' way isn't necessarily right for us and that our parents aren't always there to bail us out, Gould believes that we can deal with our lives more rationally and can focus less self-centeredly on the world around us. Unloading this assumption may be difficult, however. To do so we must get rid of the related childhood illusions that rewards will be automatic if we obey the "shoulds," that there is only one right way, that if we falter our families will take over, and that reason, commitment, and hard work will always pay off. Once we know that all of these "truths" aren't necessarily true for us, we're a step closer to Gould's "adult consciousness" (Gould, 1978). Clearly the young adults in the Sheehy survey have not postponed this step. They seem to be quite aware that their parents' solutions won't work for them.

The men in Sheehy's sample don't seem to be postponing the integrating work that Levinson identifies with this time period either; that is, they are not putting off the creation of the first life structure. Levinson's label for these years is "entering the adult world," a time of beginning to be adult, of entering adult life gradually. It may seem to be a time of establishment, because people appear to be making total commitments in career education or work, or in marriage and family. But Levinson feels that this illusion of solid commitment covers the reality that people in their mid-twenties are dealing with two conflicting tasks. The first is to remain "loose," and to explore life's options; the second is to create a stable structure. But to be both loose and stable at the same time is impossible. So most people seem to deal with this contradiction by creating a life structure that looks stable from the outside but which they know can never last (Levinson et al., 1978). Levinson's conflicting-tasks concept may explain why many young adults are ambivalent about their careers and why early divorces are a common outcome of early marriages (Schenk & Schenk, 1978).

What the "postponing generation" is postponing is dealing with the expectations of their social world, their social clock. The outmoded timing of the social clock may be suggesting that by the mid-twenties a man and a woman should have finished school, married, and started a family. Men should have started a career. Yet the changing social environment of the end of the century requires new timing, new time-outs, postponement of the standard life events.

It's important to be aware that the young people who are postponing social responsibility and are allowing themselves personal space are not necessarily immature at all. Youth allows room for the emergence of new kinds of psychological maturity (Keniston, 1977a); the tasks of individuation of self and mutuality of relationships are in reality vital tasks of personal growth. A quick review will make this apparent.

Keniston describes "youth" as an incomplete stage of transition, in which the relationships between the self and society may be worked out, relationships between the self and others can become more equal, and strategies for personal development may be tested. Moral and cognitive growth are possible on a wider scope when a youthful time-out is possible.

What's positive about that from your point of view? _____

_____

_____

What's negative about that from your point of view? _____

_____

_____

White identifies a series of interdependent "growth trends" in these years (and earlier) as "stabilizing of ego identity," "freeing of personal relationships," "deepening of interests," "humanizing of values," and "expansion of caring."

What's positive about that from your point of view? _____

_____

_____

What's negative about that from your point of view? _____

_____

_____

Gould maintains that the middle twenties are the years in which personal decisions triumph over parental rules. Physical and emotional separation from parents needs to be accomplished in these years.

What's positive about that from your point of view? _____

_____

_____

What's negative about that from your point of view? _____

_____

_____

Levinson supports the position that separation is the core work of these years. He adds that the relationships and perceptions of adolescence must be left behind and a new life structure must be created—a temporary structure for the beginning of adult life.

What's positive about that from your point of view? _____

_____

_____

What's negative about that from your point of view? _____

_____

_____

Havighurst's list of tasks of early adulthood (in Chapter 4) isn't quite so time bound; he uses the age of 35 as a cutoff point for establishing a sound marriage, a family, a home, an occupation, a social network, and a sense of civic responsibility. The same tasks are required of everyone.

What's positive about that from your point of view? _____

_____

_____

What's negative about that from your point of view? _____

_____

_____

All four of these models emphasize the struggles of the twenties decade (see Figure 5-1). Personal growth is apparently possible in the middle twenties if separation from parents and preparation for self-sufficiency can be accomplished. The social tasks can wait—but not too long.

The Twenties Decade

	Erickson	Gould	Levinson	Keniston
20	"Intimacy versus isolation"	Ending of "Leaving parents' world"	Ending of "Early adult transition"	"Youth" (Optional)
22		"Nobody's baby"	"Entering adult world"	
24				
26		Beginning of "Opening up"		
28				
30			"Age 30 transition"	

Figure 5-1 Several stage theorists describe the twenties as a time of conflicts, transitions, and struggles with life decisions. Erikson, Gould, and Levinson describe the difficulties of these years in past cohorts; Keniston reflects on the time-out that has been necessary for many young adults of current cohorts.

The Late Twenties

For most people, the late twenties seems to be a time of transition. It is a time of looking backward to see how life has progressed so far and of looking ahead to see where it may be going. The outward attention to the social formulas for successfully becoming an adult, for getting through the first phases of adult life, seems to shift; attention turns inward as the twenties decade draws to a close.

Gould describes the years that begin at about 28 and may last until 34 as the time of "opening up to what's inside." The false and childish assumptions that start to conflict with real experience in the real world are the assumptions that life is simple and controllable and that we have no inner contradictions.

Life on the outside is beginning to seem manageable for most of us by the late twenties: we've had a chance to live and work in the world outside of our parents' homes; we've had a taste of life on our own. With any success at all in our ventures, we start to build the confidence necessary to take responsibility for our own lives. Gould feels that now we must "break the contract of our twenties"—the contract of obedience to the social imperatives—the shoulds. This is a time for making a new, reasonable, and realistic deal with life. To do this we must drop some deeply held illusions. The illusion that we're not at all like our parents has to be rejected; in some ways we probably are quite like them. The illusion that our minds and our emotions are synchronized has to go. So does our illusion that we are capable of perceiving our own reality accurately, without important blind spots. And the illusion that nothing can harm us—the classic illusion of youth—also has to be dropped. As these illusions are left behind each of us becomes more able to look at our personal reality directly. We can face our own contradictions and ambiguities. We can recognize our weaknesses; we can admit to our fears; we can accept our strengths (Gould, 1978).

The transition of the late twenties may not be comfortable, but it is important to experience. Levinson, like Gould, feels that most people in every cohort, every generation, go through a difficult transition period from the end of the twenties into the early thirties. He calls this the "age 30 transition." People who go through the changes smoothly are those who either have modified their first life structure to fit their developing lives appropriately or have shut down their awareness of the need to change—a strategy that may cause serious problems later in life. The developmental tasks that

Levinson associates with this period are revision of the first life structure and creation of a more satisfactory structure. In Levinson's model of adulthood as an ongoing process of building, tearing down, and rebuilding the structures of our lives, the late twenties bring the second rebuilding. This new structure must be ready to support the anticipated serious, restricted, and real life of the thirties (Levinson et al., 1978).

The novice phase of adulthood is almost over. By the end of the twenties we have learned a lot about what being adult means. We may have taken on the tasks of early adulthood and completed many of them, or we may have postponed the outer-world tasks and responsibilities and taken time to deal with inner development. Class differences and sex differences and lifestyle differences cause variations in how young lives unfold, but by the age of 30 there is an almost universal awareness that the time has come to get on with it.

Summary

The twenties decade is a time period when all of the initial shoulds of adult life must be dealt with. But contemporary social changes have confused these social imperatives, creating a number of conflicts in early adult life.

One source of conflict is the clash of the cultural myth of youth as all there is and the cultural reality that this is the time when serious commitments must be made. A second source of conflict lies in the social changes that have made an extended time-out from adult responsibility during these years a necessity while further education is completed. This time-out has become a recognized stage, which Keniston has named "youth." A third and related conflict area is that parental expectations seldom match the demands of the cultural setting or the needs of young adults.

In the late teens and early twenties a number of difficult social and psychological issues must be faced. Erikson has identified the need of the young to achieve intimacy with others. Gould has found the issues of separation and autonomy crucial in this first step toward adult consciousness. Levinson's tasks for this period include establishing social independence and emotional independence, as well as creating a tentative early adult life structure.

By the mid-twenties the conflicts mentioned above are often intensified. More parental and economic pressures make extended youth difficult. Yet the young person may be doing psychologically productive inner work at this time. White has identified a number of "growth trends" in college students that may be reaching their conclusions by the mid-twenties. These trends are growth toward intrapersonal identity, interpersonal mutuality, commitment, values, and caring. Gould notices that, as internalized autonomy deepens, people become freer of the external pressures of the perceived imperatives. Levinson sees the mid-twenties as the time when a person reconciles the contradictions of youthful freedom and adult-like stability by building a seemingly stable life structure. It's important to recognize that the inner struggles of this period don't reflect immaturity; what they reflect is a new way of adapting positively to a changing social environment. Time enough remains for the stabilizing tasks of early adulthood that Havighurst has listed.

The late twenties give rise to transitions. In the process of evaluating the recent past and anticipating the near future, inner developments may accelerate. Gould describes this inner work as the acceptance of our own responsibility for our lives and the recognition of our internal contradictions. Levinson describes it as an integrating and reintegrating evaluation of our whole life structure, a transition to the more stable period of the thirties.

Class, sex, and lifestyles may cause variations in timing and resolution of this transition, but by the age of 30 most people are beginning a new phase of adult life.

Terms and Concepts to Define

commitment _____

_____

conflict _____

_____

double bind _____

_____

ego identity _____

_____

humanized _____

_____

novice _____

_____

postponing _____

_____

separating _____

_____

youth (in Keniston's view) _____

_____

Experiences

To involve yourself with the concepts in this chapter, try these experiences described in the Appendix.

Alone

5. *Individuation*
27. *Values over Time*
45. *Planning Strategies I: Taking Steps*

With Others

10. *Being 22*
31. *Intimacy*
30. *Adult Family*

Going beyond the Text

1. *Analyze your own early twenties as either traditionally "adult oriented" or "youth oriented," in Keniston's terms. What qualities of what he calls "youth" have you experienced?*
2. *Scan newspapers and periodicals for articles that illustrate changing educational patterns, economic conditions, and sex-role expectations that may add pieces to the puzzle facing those now in their twenties.*

Suggested Readings

Keniston, K. Youth: A new stage of life. In L. Allman & D. Jaffe (Eds.), *Readings in adult psychology.* New York: Harper & Row, 1977.

Schenk, Q., & Schenk, E. Pulling up roots. *Englewood Cliffs, N. J.: Prentice-Hall, 1978.*

Yankelovich, D. New rules: Searching for self-fulfillment in a world turned upside down. *New York: Random House, 1981.*

6

Getting Set:
The Early Thirties to the Late Thirties

When you have finished reading this chapter you should be able to:
Explain why the thirties decade is difficult to deal with chronologically.
Define maturity.
Discuss Gould's and Levinson's descriptions of the early, middle, and late thirties.
List the mid-thirties changes that have been identified in the lives of women.
Describe your own life goals for the thirties.

As the twenties come to a close and the thirties decade begins, the developmental tasks of establishing ourselves socially and economically become even more important. The twenties are for getting ready; the thirties are for getting set.

This chapter deals with the 10-year time span of the thirties. It's not an easy time of life to pin down chronologically; as a life stage, the thirties don't present a clear set of characteristics. One reason for this lack of clarity is that social attitudes about the thirties are vague: when the subjects of the original "social clock" studies were asked to identify the time periods of adult life, they described "young adulthood" as lasting from 18 to the middle twenties and "middle age" as beginning at 40—the thirties had no name (Cameron, 1969; Neugarten, 1968a). There is reason to believe the attitude still exists, that people in their thirties are no longer young but not yet middle aged (Sheehy, 1979).

A second reason why age links are unclear in the thirties is that there are so many variations in lifestyle at this time. Men and women are often in different points in their family careers, work careers, or both. That is, there exists a variation according to sex. In addition to variability related to sex roles, there are other differences in lifestyle due to individual timing of life events: some people are well on their way in the social tasks of autonomy, marriage, work, and parenting; some people are just beginning; and some people remain single and child free. These differences in life structures make up the core of variability within this decade.

Social class, ethnic or racial background, and cohort factors—singly and together—also cause chronological variations, adding to the problem of chronological clarity. Perhaps because of this variability, research on this decade is limited. Most of the studies that are relevant to development in the thirties are done from the process perspectives, from the point of view of work and family roles and of other developments that are not necessarily identified with specific ages. Neugarten and Havighurst, for example, emphasize the sequence of life events rather than the ages at which they most often occur. Gould and Levinson, however, do maintain a chronological framework, and Vaillant and Sheehy contribute some age-linked insights into the lives of men and women in their thirties. They give us a chronological framework that can be filled in later, in the process-oriented section of the text.

The Thirties Decade: An Overview

Begin with an overview: What is your perception of this decade? What are your expectations for this time of life? Fill in the blanks in the following sentences:

People are _____ when they're 30.

In their thirties people have _____ responsibilities.

Marriage is _____ for people in their thirties.

Sex in the thirties is _____ .

Family involvement is _____ in the thirties.

In their thirties people are more _____ psychologically.

Religion is _____ when you are in your thirties.

Politically, the thirties are _____ .

Social life in the thirties is _____ .

Financially, people in their thirties _____ .

Friends are _____ when you are in your thirties.

Education in the thirties _____ .

Work becomes _____ in the thirties.

Physically, the thirties are a time of _____ .

What's left out? You may want to originate some statements of your own:

In the thirties _____ .

In the thirties _____ .

In the thirties _____ .

You may see this decade as a positive and challenging time of life; you may also look at it as a dull or difficult time, depending on your personal perspectives. Contemporary social attitudes tend to be less than positive about turning 30. The 30th birthday, the "Big 3–0," is often seen as a traumatic experience.

One explanation for the trauma of entering the thirties is social. The slogan of the 1960s "never trust anybody over 30" established the age as the cutoff for understanding the social changes that involved so many members of this cohort. It may have been a paranoid perception, but it expressed a basic social attitude. The generalized social expectation is still that by the time most people are in their thirties they have established some deep commitments to careers, marriages, families, or material things. They have something to lose. This prevailing social attitude runs deep and sends strong messages: the years of the thirties decade are the years of getting set, of establishing a solid style of life, of becoming more fully adult. A 30th birthday may be a social warning signal that it's time to get very serious about "making it."

Another explanation of the emotional difficulty of this particular birthday is psychological. Our psychological sense of aging is probably more deeply tied to cultural reminders that time is passing than it is to biological changes (Sarason et al., 1975). A birthday, especially one that begins a decade, is a cultural reminder of our growing older that carries considerable power. The outside pressures to make commitments that seem permanent—such as career choices, marital choices, and lifestyle choices—may become internalized. "I'm 30 already, and my life is drifting away. I'm not getting any younger. There's still so much I have to do." Being past 30 may bring an uneasy **psychological aging.**

Like psychological aging, the experience of biological aging is often uncomfortable in a society that is unrealistically youth oriented, a setting in which any kind of aging is automatically thought of as negative. A third explanation, then, of the problem with becoming 30 is biological. We have a strong social stereotype in America that a person is biologically "over the hill" at 30. Behind that stereotype is a very small truth. That truth, however, is only really important in the lives of highly trained athletes, whose peaks of physical condition may decline significantly after their thirties, or in the lives of women who have postponed childbearing, which may become slightly more risky after 35. The larger truth is that **biological aging,** which consists of noticeable changes in appearance and conditioning, is only loosely related to chronology, and this truth is lost in our social setting.

Behind the unease about social, psychological, and biological changes that so many experience with their 30th birthday lies a reality—the reality of **maturity.** Maturity is readiness; maturity is fullness. It is not an end in itself, but a potential to be used. In the thirties biological maturity is complete, social maturity is growing, and psychological maturity is within reach. The pressure of time is a reality; the potential for readiness to become a full adult is a strong possibility. A 30th birthday may be the beginning of 10 years of life that are demanding and challenging, and by 30 many people are aware that they have the competence of maturity to deal with these challenges.

The first years of the decade seem to be involved with finishing up the unfinished business from the late-twenties transition period. When that's accomplished, there may be a few steady years of work toward functioning in the young-adult community. At the end of the decade that steadiness may falter: new uncertainties may emerge, and new transitions may be called for.

The Early Thirties

It's hard to get everything right the first time. That's true of any new and complex skill that you learn, and it's especially true of styles of life.

By the end of your twenties, you've developed a lifestyle that is the outcome of your choices. You have made choices about intimate relationships, marriage, friendships, family ties, work, recreation, religion, politics, and community. You may enter the thirties with a lifestyle that works for you in some ways but, in others, does not work. An inner awareness that life doesn't quite fit, that it needs alterations or major changes, remains from the difficult twenties. That awareness is probably growing stronger. The transition that began internally in the late twenties may be beginning to affect your external world by now. Age 30 is, for example, a peak year for divorce; marriages made at 21 have had both the American average of 7 years to come apart and sufficient extra time for the legal action necessary to undo them (Sheehy, 1976). Marriages initiated later may have suffered from the partners' transitional·struggles in the late twenties. A career begun in the early twenties may have become old and dull or proved to have been a mistake.

Gould describes the struggles of the early thirties as a continuation of the process of "opening up to what's inside" that began in the late twenties. That deep psychological self-exploration may be unsettling, but Gould sees it as part of our need to give ourselves permission to keep developing. If we're going to go on growing we will have to face the flaws in our inner and outer worlds and repair them. That's why this questioning stage is so important (Gould, 1975).

Dissatisfaction, Gould has found, is common in these years, both with our careers and our relationships. Dissatisfied with work, people are apt to change jobs if they can't renew a sense of commitment to the jobs they have been doing. Men and women both may go back to school at this point, to get more training or to learn new skills that will help them to change their lives.

Dissatisfied with their relationships, both married and single people may be looking for new ways of relating. Couples renew their commitments or drift into infidelity or divorce; they begin families or decide to increase the number of children they have, shifting patterns of relationships; they move into new environments. It's time for a change. Single people feel it, too, and may feel the need to settle down, to stop moving, to establish a deep commitment to relationship. These changes often are linked to unresolved adolescent conflicts that have been left on hold during the twenties. The conflicts may be sources of transitional depressions and confusion (Gould, 1978).

Levinson, who also found reactivation of adolescent conflicts in people in their early thirties, sees it as positive: a chance for us to work out our doubts and conflicts now that we have the resources to deal with them. Levinson calls it the "age 30 transition." It begins in the late twenties with uneasiness and a sense that something is missing from life and ends in the early thirties with new energy and direction for the future.

Whether we have made life commitments early in the twenties or have postponed making them until the late twenties, Levinson feels that at this point we're under both inner and outer pressure to get more purpose and order into our lives, to find deeper attachments and fulfillments. The "novice phase," in which we learn how to navigate adult life, is almost over (Levinson et al., 1978).

According to Levinson, four tasks are essential functions of the novice phase, if we are going to create a satisfying life structure. These are to form a "dream," a mentor relationship, an occupation, and a love relationship. We must form these goals and relationships actively; they don't just happen to us as side effects of development.

According to Levinson, perhaps the most essential of the four is what he calls the **dream.** This is not an impossible fantasy: it's the ideal image of ourselves as part of the adult world. We create such a dream from the possibilities we imagine for ourselves. Our dreams are vague at first, but over time they become better defined. They take on reality, if we let them. But, if we never give them a chance to become real, if we betray them and sell out to our parents' or our mate's dreams, our dreams will always stay with us as regrets. Can you describe your ideal image of yourself—your dream? Try it.

_____

_____

To make real the sort of dream Levinson describes, we need help. To get this help, Levinson suggests that we each must form a relationship with a mentor—a combination teacher, guide, model, and sponsor. A mentor isn't a peer and isn't a parent, but he or she is often older and more experienced than we are. The mentor relationship that we form is a transition between dependency and autonomy as we create the outer-world part of our dreams. Have you had or do you need a mentor? Have you been a mentor? Describe the relationships you've had and would like to have.

_____

_____

_____

The settings for the dream images we hold are most often work situations, but usually these involve more than just jobs. Forming an occupation means learning the skills, earning the credentials, getting to know the people who share the occupation, and becoming known by them. It's a social and psychological process that's demanding and draining. Accomplishing it requires support from the inner-world part of the dream. What occupation would help you fulfill the outer-world parts of your dream? Are you forming this occupation? How?

_____

_____

_____

The inner aspects of the dream involve forming love relationships. To be able to do that you have to be able to form an intimate peer relationship with another person. You have to accept yourself and your "significant other"—your lover—and you have to accept the children that may be born to the relationship. Intimacy and responsibility and loving acceptance are hard to maintain in a long-term relationship. Levinson points out that the difficulty is eased if the mate you find is one whose dream fits your dream, so that you can share them and live them out together. How do your love relationships fit into your own version of what Levinson calls the "dream"?

_____

_____

_____

Levinson believes if you end your novice phase with a dream that can be translated into real-life goals, with a mentor who can guide you, with an occupation that you can grow in, and with a loving partner to support you, you're all set for fully adult living (Levinson et al., 1978).

Sheehy has pointed out that if married men lack a love relationship at home at this time, their outer world may provide one. She describes the **"testimonial woman"**—a female acquaintance who gives an unfulfilled husband the admiration that he's not getting at home. (It's also quite possible that an unfulfilled wife might seek out a male acquaintance to meet the same needs.) If a man is bored by the "substitute mother" that he married or if a woman is disappointed in her "substitute father," the perceptions of marriage of the twenties may need reworking. The relationship also may be in need of work if the partners have fallen into a closed-couple pattern that has limited their support from outside friendships and activities and has weakened their involvement in the social environment. To get through the dissatisfactions of the transition into the thirties, both partners have to be aware of what's missing and to be willing to make changes. The time has come for "rooting and extending," for making emotional and financial investments in the adult world (Sheehy, 1976). In the early thirties the career ladder becomes more important and life goals become more concrete. After the shakedown of transition, and after we've brought to bear our own solutions, we're ready to get into our middle thirties.

The Middle Thirties

Toward the middle thirties most lives tend to level out. Sheehy calls this phase "rooting and extending," Levinson calls it "settling down," and Vaillant calls it "career consolidation." All these labels clarify what's happening. People who have been married since the early twenties may be deeply involved with child rearing and the PTA; people whose marriages have broken up are busy restructuring new life patterns. People who are settled into careers are beginning to push for advancement; people who are entering new careers are working to get settled. In these years, there are new involvements in community, in politics, in churches, and in social organizations.

Gould recognizes a deep desire for stability and continuity among people in their thirties. He describes a feeling of timelessness that people have at this age as people involve themselves in work and marriage. But Gould doesn't see these years as a separate time period; he includes them in the "mid-life decade," which starts at age 35 and ends at 45. This is a decade of finally facing the realities of adult consciousness.

Overinvolvement in work in the middle thirties is identified by Gould as a protective device we use to keep from facing adult realities: work makes us feel important, like full-grown adults; it lets us identify with a larger group, and makes us feel significant. However, the busywork of involvement in life outside the home during these years also may be only a cover for a slowdown, which is to follow. Marriage, too, can be used as a protective device, according to Gould. Women, especially, may use it as a way to avoid the acceptance of personal power and of responsibility for their own lives. Within marriages, **marital conspiracies,** in which couples act out stereotyped roles that keep their relationships in balance artificially, may also act as protective devices to avoid recognizing a partner as a fully adult person (Gould, 1978).

Levinson, unlike Gould, has identified the middle and late thirties—from 33 to 40—as a clearly defined time period, which he calls "settling down." By the mid-thirties, he believes, most people have a sense of themselves as full-fledged adults. We reach our middle thirties with a new or at least newly altered life structure, one that will carry us farther into adulthood. The dual developmental tasks of "settling down" are to establish our places in society and to advance in our work (Levinson et al., 1978).

Each of us has a place in society, a "niche," that Levinson believes is dictated partly by what he calls our "dreams" and partly by the social world in which we live. These are the years of fitting the dream to the reality. Each of us also imagines some level of advancement that will meet our expectations or ambitions. We may picture our career ladders as having only two rungs and make rung two our goal; or we may see our ladders as having endless rungs and aim for the top—in any case, the mid-thirties is the time to start climbing.

There are several possible outcomes of the career climbing that goes on in the early years of the "settling down" phase. Levinson describes five of them. The first, which is the smoothest course of advancement, takes place within a stable life structure: a person who has built a structure that is adequate for the work-advancement possibilities of the thirties is in good shape. A second outcome of career climbing is also advancement, but it is advancement for which a new life structure is often required, often calling for a new lifestyle: a new home, a new social network, a new set of attitudes and values. Promotions that carry demands for a new lifestyle may be accompanied by an adaptation period that is shaky, but they also carry new opportunities for growth.

Advancement isn't the only possible outcome, unfortunately. A third possibility in the struggle toward career goals is that, even within a stable life structure, a person can try to get ahead, and still fail. It's possible to adapt to failure, but that's never pleasant. A dead end at this time of life, as at any other time, may bring with it any number of problems: alcohol abuse, emotional troubles, psychosomatic illness. Another possibility is that a dead end may bring the individual to a fourth outcome: breaking out.

Breaking out of a career in the middle thirties requires that a brand new life structure be created—a process that Levinson found was difficult for the people in his study. Their lives stayed in a state of confusion for an 8- to 10-year period while they regrouped. The only outcome that brought more problems was the fifth possibility: struggling with an unstable life structure (Levinson et al., 1978).

Instability isn't a comfortable condition for most people in these years of "making it." In general, adult human beings have a strong need for stability, and if changes must be made we're apt to make small ones. This is no time to rock the boat.

The middle thirties are not the most colorful time of life in most cases. Vaillant describes this period in the lives of the men in the Grant Study as dull and narrow and materialistic. It is a time of "career consolidation," and Vaillant defines **consolidation** as a forced stability. Conformity is at its peak, which is understandable in a period of assimilation into the work world and community. Men and women both seem to use these years to get established. Both seem to be willing to settle for self-deception rather than to be forced to change anything in their life patterns. Vaillant points out that, in spite of the calm on the surface, the thirties are a time of establishing the difficult balance between putting down roots and striving to get ahead. After all, getting ahead often involves moving—pulling roots out of a community instead of strengthening them. However, striving to advance is sometimes in conflict with the responsible parenting that becomes so crucial at this stage of family development. Parents are faced with hard choices: Should the husband accept a new and better job if that requires moving the children in the middle of a school year? Should he accept it if that requires the wife to sacrifice a career she's just begun? What if it means leaving the network of friends and relatives that has supported the family for years? Choices between career and family welfare, between financial gains and personal losses, are common causes of stress in the thirties (Vaillant, 1977).

In some ways the middle thirties may seem to be peaceable years, years of self-satisfaction. After all, the struggles of the twenties may be resolved, and adult competencies and capabilities may be serving well. However, pressures are forming under the surface that will emerge in the years ahead. The internal, psychological work of self-questioning and of developing self-awareness that are characteristic of adolescence and the late twenties and early thirties are on hold in the mid-thirties.

For the time being, people let their social roles take over. They are work roles—college-professor or iron-worker roles, labor or management roles. They are parent roles—somebody's mother or somebody's father. They are assorted social roles—voters, consumers, member of groups. People in their mid-thirties are busy achieving, while they can. Their lifetimes are halfway over on the social clock: 35 is half of the currently expected life span of 70 years. Men are beginning their prime of life; women may have reached their limits as sex objects but they're still in their years of most responsibility (Neugarten, 1968a).

Sheehy has identified an extremely difficult developmental moment at age 35 that is special to women and her observations are supported by current studies. Many women are triggered to survey their progress toward their life goals by one or more of the following: a last child beginning school, a return to work outside the home, an awareness that they are getting close to the end of childbearing, or a remarriage after divorce. The age-35 survey is for some women a "last-chance" overview of where their lives have been and where they are headed in the middle years. Discrepancies in their goals and actual lives may be resolved by becoming a "runaway wife" or by having another child, by infidelity or changed marriage; by new life goals or reeducation (Pellegrino, 1981; Sheehy, 1976).

Havighurst considers people in their thirties to be middle-aged. Remember that, in Havighurst's model, middle age begins at 30 and lasts until 60 (see Figure 6-1). We looked at the developmental tasks that he has identified as the tasks of middle age in Chapter 4. Most of them are beginning to make themselves felt by our middle thirties. Civic and social responsibilities are a part of many of our lives by now. A two-way responsibility to family may be developing, too—as our children grow older, so do our parents, and relationships with them may be shifting from dependence to support. Also, an awareness of the physical changes that come with the middle years begins to sneak up on us in the thirties. Havighurst has used *acceptance* rather than *awareness* to describe our attitude toward health. However, more and more of us, instead of becoming acceptant of decline in functioning, are becoming aware that exercise and improvements in diet further a healthy physical condition. In comparison, few of us are sufficiently sensitive to the need for developing varied leisure-time activities that will carry over into the years

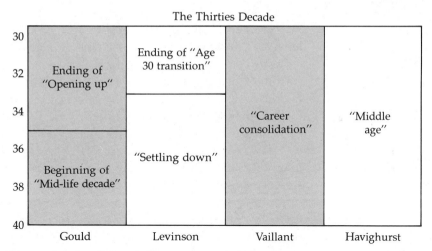

Figure 6-1 By the mid-thirties, several stage theorists describe a temporary stability in the lives of many people in their samples: Gould found that his subjects were finishing the psychological work of establishing autonomy at this time; Levinson perceived a balancing of the self in the social world by the mid-thirties; Vaillant found it to be a serious time of consolidating developmental gains; Havighurst felt that most of the social developmental tasks are accomplished by 35.

of retirement. (As Vaillant says, in the middle thirties we tend to be "narrow.") All of these tasks are ongoing in the middle years. They become more important as time goes by (Havighurst, 1972).

And time is going by. We no sooner level off in our middle thirties when new transitions begin appearing in our lives. As we enter our late thirties, the changing once more intensifies.

The Late Thirties

The last years of the thirties decade bring us into a developmental phase that Bühler has called "culmination." Our life goals—those in our dreams, to use Levinson's word, should be clearly defined by now. We know where we're going and what we want in life. We also have a good idea of how much we're going to get. These are the years when we begin to see life clearly and see it whole.

Gould's "mid-life-decade" is well under way in the last years of the thirties. The final realities that have to be faced if we are going to develop what he calls "adult consciousness" now press to be acknowledged. The last major assumption of childhood has to be challenged: "There isn't any reality to evil or death." In giving up this childish belief we are giving up all our illusions of security. We can't continue to deny our inner rages and pains left over from childhood; we can't go on pretending that the terrible things that happen in the outside world can't happen to us. To break through to adult consciousness, Gould feels, it's necessary to drop our belief that we're safe from evil, to recognize that we and the people that we love will die, to admit that we can survive alone, to abandon the stereotyped family roles that we play, and to admit that nobody is innocent—not others, not ourselves. These beliefs are not abandoned all at once. In fact, if we stop growing and dig in to defend our illusions, somewhere along the way, they may not be dropped at all. The naked vision of authenticity that Gould has described as adult consciousness is a painful acceptance of existence. It is realistic acceptance of the worst that can happen, and knowing all of the worst can make us stronger and wiser and better prepared for whatever our future brings. To achieve an authentic adult consciousness, to be a person who can relate to other people in an open and compassionate way, we have to dump denials and play acting.

Gould has pointed out that the mid-life decade presents opportunities to be more real. We may have faced a serious sickness by this period of life, or a personal disaster, or an accident. We may have had to face a parent's death, or the loss of a child, or the loss of a friend. As we learn to cope with these events, we learn to accept our limitations and our strengths (Gould, 1978).

Levinson's description of the late thirties includes some of these inner-world struggles, but it focuses more specifically on outer-world adaptations. He gives these years a kind of sub-period status within the general developmental stage of "settling down." This stage applies to men, and it applies to career-oriented women, who go through similar changes during these years (Hennig & Jardim, 1977). These last years of the thirties are a time when many of us become confident adults, finally. We're affirmed by others as being competent. We feel a stronger sense of independence and authority. It feels good. And the new confidence seems to bring back a more youthful sense of ourselves, so that we're full of energy and imagination. And yet this new sense of power may bring with it a feeling that we're being restricted and held back. Surprisingly, childish rebellions and insecurities are common reactions to constricted competence. Struggles between dependency and independence, authority and conformity are typical of this period. Even though one may have become one's own person, life can still be full of frustrations. These late, "settling down" years may find us still fairly unsettled (Levinson et al., 1978).

Looking back over the thirties, we can see that in spite of the rough places here and there, the thirties can be our years of integration. In the transition into the thirties we try to integrate our inner sense of self with the new life situation of being taken seriously. In the middle years of the decade we try to integrate our outer, social self with the environment. As we get closer to 40 we're ready to pull together our inner and social selves, for a new level of integration in our lives.

Gould has given us a picture of this decade as opening with a reexamination of the inner world and closing with a movement toward giving up our last childhood illusions and accepting the realities of adult living and dying. What's positive about Gould's picture, from your point of view? What's negative about it from your point of view?

Levinson has described the thirties decade as beginning with an uneasiness and introspection that then works into an all-out attempt to get settled in the adult world; the decade ends with both a sense of competence and mild frustration. What's positive about Levinson's conception of the decade, from your point of view? What's negative about it from your point of view?

_____

_____

George Vaillant has presented these years as the years of "career consolidation," conformity, and commitment, as we try to balance stability and the changes involved in getting ahead. What's positive about Vaillant's picture, from your point of view? What's negative about it from your point of view?

_____

_____

What is your own perception of the thirties? Ideally, what should they be or have been in your life? Taking into individual consideration Havighurst's framework of social tasks, Gould's framework of psychological development, and Levinson's framework of integration (and keeping in mind Vaillant's concept of career consolidation and Sheehy's observation about womens' life surveys), construct or reconstruct the broad life goals of your own thirties decade in the paragraphs that follow.

Considering the social tasks Havighurst believes integral to the thirties (mate selection, marriage partnership, parenting, home management, occupation, civic responsibility, and becoming part of social groups), my own goals are or were:

_____

_____

_____

Considering Gould's model emphasizing psychological development that includes self-exploration, dealing with work and relationship dissatisfactions, breaking down marital conspiracies, and breaking through to adult consciousness, my own goals for the thirties are or were:

_____

_____

_____

Considering Levinson's model of developmental integration of the inner self and social world that includes forming a dream, a mentor relationship, a love relationship, an occupation, establishing a place in society, and working at advancement, my own goals are or were:

_____

_____

_____

Do you have other goals? Clarify them here:

_____

_____

_____

Summary

Although Gould and Levinson have identified the developmental work that is typically done in the thirties, the specific ages linked to the events of this decade are often unclear. It is a period characterized by ambiguous social attitudes, variable individual lifestyles, and—until recently—lack of professional attention.

The early thirties are described as transitional years, by both Gould and Levinson; dissatisfactions with a first adult life structure motivates many people to reconstruct their lives in new ways, as the twenties end and the thirties begin. Levinson has described the early thirties as a time in which adult goals are clearly established, a time for seeking an occupation, a love relationship, and a mentor relationship that will lead us toward what he calls our "dream."

By the middle thirties, stability is a dominant theme in most peoples' lives. Many people experience a period of hard work and striving to get ahead and become deeply involved in work or parenting or both. Gould emphasizes the use of these activities as an avoidance of deeper issues; Levinson is more interested in the dynamics of advancement at this time; and Vaillant underlines the commitment to stability. Gail Sheehy identifies a mid-thirties life survey that is common to many women.

The late thirties often bring a feeling of full adulthood. Life goals are fairly clear, and reality is more clearly perceivable by those who are willing to face it. There is a possibility of being your own person by your late thirties, and there is an awareness of the difficulties that come with that development.

Terms and Concepts to Define

biological aging _____

_____

consolidation (Vaillant's term) _____

_____

dream (Levinson's term) _____

_____

marital conspiracies (Gould's term) _____

_____

maturity _____

_____

psychological aging _____

_____

testimonial woman (Sheehy's term) _____

_____

Experiences

To involve yourself with the concepts in this chapter, try these experiences described in the Appendix.

Alone
8. Lifestyles
26. Cohort Values
46. Planning Strategies II: Realities

With Others
13. Being 33
12. Perpetual Children
32. Thirties Roots

Going beyond the Text

1. Interview a person who has completed his or her thirties, and try to do a developmental reconstruction of the decade.
2. In order to clarify your sense of the potential of the late thirties, make a list of well-known people, your acquaintances, or both who are of that age and are functioning at a high level of productivity, attractiveness, and energy.

Suggested Readings

Sheehy, G. Passages: Predictable crises of adult life. *New York: E. P. Dutton, 1976.*

Rubin, L. Women of a certain age. *New York: Harper & Row, 1979.*

Pellegrino, V. The other side of thirty. *New York: Rawson Wade, 1981.*

7

Getting On with It:
The Early Forties to the Mid-Fifties

When you have finished reading this chapter you should be able to:

Explain the reasons for increasing individual differences in the middle years of adulthood.

Describe the conditions that contribute to middlescence, the mid-life crisis, or both.

Define Erikson's term "generativity," and relate it to Gould's, Levinson's, and Peck's perceptions of the developmental work of the forties.

Discuss the question of sex-role reversals in the. middle years.

Analyze your own potential for reconciling your polarities in middle adulthood.

As we review the life course from this first perspective—the ages and stages point of view—it becomes increasingly difficult to connect chronology to specific life events in the middle years of adulthood. Individual lives may have been in step with each other in the first adult changes of leaving home or entering the work force, but the similarities are soon dropped. Further education (minimal or extensive), marital choices (marrying early or late or not at all), and transitional changes (reentering school, changing jobs, and choosing divorce or remarriage) all differentiate courses of life-event timing in the twenties and thirties. By the forties decade, variability is even more extreme, especially in people from contemporary cohorts; they may be almost anywhere in their family, work, economic, and other social cycles—or re-cycles. People who have experienced the extended period of "youth" may be just beginning; people who haven't had that time-out may be launching young-adult children and anticipating retirement. It seems almost impossible that any age links to development could be found that would hold generally true for all people in middle adulthood.

Yet, if we focus on psychological development instead of on concrete life events, a case can be made for the existence of chronology, even in those years of maturity that might seem to be a long and dull plateau stretching to retirement. Erikson and Peck, Jung and Levinson, Gould and Vaillant all have identified developmental work that is characteristic of the years of **middle adulthood**—a matter of some debate, but approximately 40 to the mid-fifties. In this chapter we'll focus on these developments.

Before you survey the age-linked changes of these years, take a minute to get in touch with your own expectations about middle adulthood. The scale below calls for your responses to the idea of being between 40 and 55. What will this time period be like, or what was it like, for you? Put a dot along the continuum of each line that best describes your feelings about middle adulthood. Then, connect the dots. The connecting line gives a graphic impression of your positive or negative sense of these years.

young	old
creative	destructive
closeness	separation
aliveness	deadness
calm	stressful
growing	static
positive	negative

We'll come back to this chart of your perceptions at the end of the chapter, to see whether the information presented has changed your picture of these years in any way.

In checking your responses to the idea of middle life, you may have found them to be fairly complex. Dealing with the idea of passing 40 may be as complicated and emotional for some people as turning 30. The reasons are similar: negative social attitudes toward aging, a psychological sense that life is diminishing, and an awareness that biological maturity is shading into aging. But stereotypes about the forties only add to the confusion, because by this decade individual differences are becoming more significant.

Bernice Neugarten found in the early social-clock studies (1968a) that self-perception in middle adulthood varies with socioeconomic background, physical condition, and work or family status. Blue-collar workers may describe themselves as middle-aged at 40; white-collar workers or professionals may not consider themselves middle-aged for another 10 to 20 years. Neugarten also has found that feelings of aging may be an issue of body awareness and physical appearance. And, such feelings can be related to a person's progress toward completion of a working career or toward being finished with child rearing. Differences according to sex are another factor in self-perceptions and social perceptions in the middle years: women are often perceived as being older and less potentially attractive than men of the same age (Sontag, 1972). Differences in the perceptions of aging between cohorts are also factors that generate individual differences. With the fading of the cult of youth, and with more affluence and education, the trend seems to be toward an age-irrelevant society where each individual is as old as he/she feels (Neugarten, 1980).

The Forties Decade: An Overview

Although individuals may be becoming more and more aware that age in adult life is mostly irrelevant, life experiences that we have had in the thirties may generate a new awareness in the forties of life's progress. Some of us become uneasy and some desperate as we begin our fourth decade of living.

Long before Sheehy's book *Passages* made the mid-life crisis a cliché, a body of literature in the behavioral sciences was being amassed that describes the troubles of the forties. These troubles range from radical changes of lifestyle that shake careers and families to psychological maladjustments that lead to deep depressions and suicides—in short, they may range over every sort of **mid-life crisis.** All of these problems seem to be related in some way to the biological, psychological, and social changes of this time of life.

Why now? A standard explanation for the upheavals of the early forties has been Elliot Jaques's (1970): that in our early forties we are confronted on the one hand with the inevitability of our death, and on the other hand with the failures of the hopes and dreams of our lives. It's a rare person who has reason to be completely smug at 40. This is a time in which many people reassess their lives—their past failures and disappointments as well as their coming age and death.

The confrontation with life's negatives at this time is most often triggered by external events that many of us haven't faced before. There is a rising number of deaths among people close to us. People in our age group and people we work with die. Friends may die. Our parents' deaths, or their physical failings, underscore our own mortality. If they can die, we can.

We're not only more aware of our deaths, we're more aware of our failures. Small failures or big, they become clear in the reassessments of our forties. The accumulation over the years of tragedies or near-tragedies and losses in the world around us undermine our security. Lack of success at work or in parenting is becoming manifest. By this time we know how far we're going to go in our work situations, and we can see how successful we've been at establishing our families and friendship networks. Life is getting very "real."

Looking the reality of your life in the eye at 40 may be painful, but the outcome isn't all bad. When you've assessed what you've done with your life up to this point, you're in a position to do something positive about your failures, to do something different, something better. With the recognition of the limits that your death sets on your future, you become more willing to value your present, your here-and-now existence. You're more prepared to grow as you increase in years.

Although many people go through deep and difficult changes at some time in the early years of the forties decade, changes that are sometimes compared to the changes of adolescence (and called **middlescence** for that reason), some people experience only mild self-questioning. How rough the going becomes in these years is partly a question of self-perceptions and developmental progress: of attitudes, personality, the accomplishment of developmental tasks, and coping skills. It's also partly a question of your social environment—past events, current experiences, and future expectations.

Although there is a strong possibility of some years of crisis in the early forties, the outcome of the crisis may be a new stage of growth. There is also the probability that, for most people, the greater part of the forties and fifties are experienced as peaceable and productive years.

Several factors in contemporary life make this calmness and productivity probable. Changes in the social setting in the past 20 or 30 years have made work places less dangerous and wearing and have made health services more available and effective, so that youthful fitness and vitality have been extended well into the forties and fifties. New information and new attitudes about sexuality, nutrition, and physical exercise have reinforced this potential for extended prime time. Breakdowns in age-stereotyped ways of dressing and behaving have opened up new freedom to create lifestyles. As a result of these changes, for many people the years between the early forties and the middle fifties are a season of Indian summer. Autumn comes later. Still, in this time of full adulthood, there is developmental work to be done that can be identified with specific time periods. Let's examine them, in sequence.

The Early Forties

Developmental psychologists agree that the early forties are often troubled times. Individual theorists differ, though, on how serious the troubles are and on how age related the mid-life crisis actually is. Gould sees mid-life developmental struggles as being spread over a 10-year period, from 35 to 45. Sheehy also sees mid-life upheavals as spread out, beginning in the mid-thirties for women and focusing around the early forties for men. Levinson finds a clearly age-linked crisis that happens in the early forties. However, Vaillant rejects the "mid-life-crisis" idea strongly while admitting that mid-life changes exist. Davitz and Davitz, whose clinical work on the forties we'll look at in this chapter, find age-linked depression and anxiety in both men and women around the early forties.

The differences may be caused by the differences in the samples on which these theories are based. Gould, Sheehy, and Davitz and Davitz were looking at mixed male and female samples. If women do reassess their lives earlier, on the average, the time spread naturally would be broader in a mixed sample. Levinson's group studies men only, which may be why the age link is so clear even though the sample included men from varied social and economic backgrounds. Vaillant's sample was the most restricted, narrowed to an all-male, all-highly-educated, all-privileged-class group; perhaps, with all those pluses, mid-life despair is indeed the exception rather than the rule. In any case, even Vaillant sees important changes in the early forties.

In Gould's model, the early forties are the last half of a "mid-life decade" that began at 35. The last years of that decade are the conclusion of a 10-year period of turning inward and examining the hidden places of our lives—a striving for authenticity that must be completed if we are ever going to reach full maturity, according to Gould. Our findings from this turning inward, this introspection, are surfacing at a time when parenting experiences may have renewed our own unsolved developmental conflicts, and when age biases from the outer world of work and social life may be pressing strongly on us to complete our "adult-consciousness." But that can only happen if we can reconcile our inner world of childhood illusions with the outer world adult realities. This may be a final stage in our struggle to "own our own life" (Gould, 1978, 1980).

The struggles of people in these middle years are most often, in Gould's experience, around three themes: death, dependency, and destructiveness. Death is often truly confronted for the first time in the mid-life decade, as we are forced to drop our childhood illusion that our parents are immortal. They aren't, and neither are we. Dependence has to be dropped, too, as we lose the illusion that our protectors (first our parents, later our mates) will never leave us. The illusion that we're not responsible for the evils in our lives has to go, also; we must realize our own potential for destructiveness. In other words, we have to see our lives whole if we're going to finish our developmental work and be fully adult. Gould tells us that this time of life is as troubled as the years of adolescence, but with a major difference. In adolescence our basic problem may have been that we didn't know who we were yet. In middlescence our basic problem is not in knowing who we are; our problem is in accepting who we are (Gould, 1978).

Sheehy was familiar with Gould's work when she interviewed couples from the early-forties group described in *Passages*. She shares his perception that mid-life crisis typically extends over the course of a decade, but she finds, as does Levinson (1980), that women tend to begin it earlier and end it earlier. Women seem to reach their time for mid-life reassessment in the middle thirties; men are more apt to experience it in the early forties, the years that Sheehy calls the "age forty crucible." Often frightened by what they are experiencing, or denying realities that eventually have to be faced, many men throw themselves harder into their work lives. Others look for new relationships, often with women who are younger than their wives, to escape marriages that are working badly at this point. And many marriages are working badly.

Marital conflicts are almost inevitable when partners are developing at different rates. For example, when a husband and wife are close to the same age and the wife has gone through her struggles and made peace with her life at 35, she is right in the middle of her new balancing act when her husband starts losing stability. Separated by their different emotional adjustments, different views of life, and different sexual drives, marriage partners can be psychologically unsynchronized in these years (Sheehy, 1976).

One strong factor that can keep marriages together in these years, according to Sheehy, is the tremendous costs of mid-life crisis. There are emotional costs, in terms of love lost and peace shattered. And there are also financial costs, in terms of lost gains in career and in the breakdown of the family economic unit. These costs may be expensive enough to motivate a couple to work on their relationship and solve their problems peaceably.

Dr. Joel Davitz and Dr. Lois Davitz are particularly interested in solutions to the problems of mid-life transition. They have done a descriptive study of the forties based on their experiences as clinical psychologists (Davitz & Davitz, 1976). Their findings are consistent with Gould's: both men and women in their early forties are more complex and are experiencing more change than ever before. And, the Davitzes add, people in this period are "less fun" than ever. It's a time for taking life very seriously.

Both men and women are liable to be troubled with anxieties and with vague uneasiness about beginning to age and beginning to feel mortal. This often is related to a new questioning of identity. Like Levinson, the Davitzes found the identity question shifting from "Who am I?" to "Who have I been?" and "What will I become?"

The men that Davitz and Davitz describe seem to turn to their work for their answers, pushing ahead in their careers while they have time to make some gains. They know that if they don't they will face narrowing possibilities. Home doesn't hold answers for many men at this time; they may doubt that their home life is of any real value, or they may be clearly hostile on the home front.

Personal anxieties are beginning to surface about physical changes, such as baldness or the fear of impotence. It's a difficult time in men's lives. And in women's too.

Davitz and Davitz find that women vary in the sources to which they turn for validation of their changing identity. Married women who are working in the home have to rely on their husbands for comfort from their anxieties and depressions—and their husbands may offer only cold comfort. For those women who have had children, the forties may be years of loss, as children leave home and take away the mother role that has been a primary source of status. Mothers are not subjected only to the physical changes that all women face in these years, they are undergoing a social change, too—from *mother* to simply *wife*. There seems to be a trend, however, for women to view this as a positive change, rather than a negative one (Block, Davidson, & Grambs, 1981; Fortinberry, 1979; Neugarten, 1980).

Married women who work outside the home may, like men, turn to work for affirmation of identity. Single women, too, may turn to work as a more dependable source of validation than their social network. Married or single, this is a time when women are anxious about the loss of youthfulness that in North American society is so often equated with sexual attractiveness and, for women, is equated with personal worth. Lines, wrinkles, graying hair, and pounds gained carry the threat of sexual rejection. "If I'm not a sex object any more, then who am I?" is a puzzle that many women are working through in their early forties (Davitz & Davitz, 1976).

Davitz and Davitz suggest that the early forties are a time of struggles for women, as well as for men. Daniel Levinson, too, feels that mens' mid-life crises are clearly age linked to these years.

Levinson, like Gould, Sheehy, and Davitz and Davitz, recognizes the early forties as a time of inner struggle and a season for dumping old illusions. Unlike Gould, Levinson identifies the years between 40 and 45 as a clearly separate developmental time period. He calls it the "mid-life transition."

Levinson's "mid-life transition" is, like all the transition periods that he describes, a time for reassessing an old life structure, for changing it or modifying it or for creating a whole new structure. This transition is a bridge between early adulthood and middle adulthood; the structure that's being built is the one that will serve the middle years (Levinson et al., 1978).

According to Levinson, the mid-life transition requires that we accomplish three important tasks: we must assess early adulthood and leave it behind; we must start creating a middle-adult life structure; and we must deal with the deep separations of our inner worlds. For the first task we have to look at past life; for the second we have to look to the future; for the third we have to look inside, at our hidden, inner lives.

Levinson doesn't present the first task—looking back—as an exercise in nostalgia or regret. Instead, he sees it as a review of the past from a new perspective, with an awareness of the future. It's a **reassessment** of life as a whole, a pause halfway to see where we've been and what we have to do to get where we're going. It's a time for asking big questions: "What have I done with my life?" "Have my accomplishments been of any value to me? to anyone?" "What do I really want?" "What's happened to my 'dream'? What's happening to it now?" Levinson believes that as we reassess our lives most of us find that much of the life we've been living is based on illusions. (Does this sound familiar? Gould, too, emphasizes that.) Beliefs we have held about ourselves since childhood turn out to be empty of substance. Beliefs about the world we've held for years turn out to be false or only partially true. The forties could be a time of disillusionment and cynicism, but Levinson describes it instead as a time of "de-illusionment." De-illusionment is setting aside our illusions and so seeing more clearly. As we look back over our lives, we come to more complex understandings of our relationships to our world.

Levinson's second task for the mid-life transition—that of considering a new life structure—is also a question of a new look from a new perspective. We look at our occupations and try to perceive how they will go in the years to come. We look at our relationships—marriages, friendships, and extended family groups—and imagine how they'll be in the future. It's a time of reappraisal. It may turn out to be a time of making drastic changes or of creative reworking and recommitment. It may require unwilling acceptance of the parts of our lives that we can't or won't change. In any case, reassessments of the past and future lead us to new self-awareness.

Self-awareness is necessary for the last task, the task of looking inside. That may be the most difficult job of all. Levinson examines this "big task of the forties," the task that all our sources agree is essential, in detail. What he has to tell us is tremendously important to understanding our own internal complexities. Looking inside, in Levinson's view, involves recognizing our inner polarities, a concept he has inherited from Carl Jung.

Like Jung, Levinson believes that we all carry pairs of ideas that are **polarities**—polar opposites. They are the four essential ideas of our inner perceptions. During much of our lives one half of any of the pairs of opposites may have more power than the other half; we may not even recognize that its other half exists. But it does. And to become fully adult, both Jung and Levinson believe, we have to face our inner opposites and bring them into balance with each other. The opposites that we have to integrate come in four pairs:

youthfulness and aging
destructiveness and creativity
masculinity and femininity
attachment and separateness

Both halves of each pair are of equal importance in an integrated personality. Youthfulness and aging must be acknowledged and accepted as parts of our being. The destructive and creative aspects of ourselves must be recognized. Our masculine and feminine qualities must be balanced. And so must our needs to bond with others and to be autonomous. Reconciling these internal opposites may be difficult, but both Jung and Levinson believe that it's not only possible but necessary to reconcile our opposites if we want to become fully adult. This is part of the process of individuation. The possibility of facing these conflicts exists, in the early forties, and it may become a stressful issue.

Vaillant is the only member of this group of developmental psychologists who is reluctant to tie the early forties to stress, perhaps because of his subjects' financial security. He feels that to call this period a "crisis" is an exaggeration. Divorce and depression and disillusionment, he points out, can happen at any time in life. When they happen in the forties they are blamed on mid-life changes; when they happen at other times they are just considered unfortunate events. Vaillant sees most people as quite capable of adapting to the changes of these middle years without serious problems (Vaillant, 1977).

Although Vaillant denies that the changes of the forties are dramatic, he does admit that the changes exist. Like Gould and Levinson and the others, he found that the inner lives of his subjects became much more important to them in these years. People become explorers of their inner worlds in the forties, he says. They begin breaking away from the dullness and conformity of the thirties years of career consolidation. As people recognize their psychological pains, their disappointments, frustrations, hurts, and angers, the inhibitions that they accepted in earlier years may drop away. Sometimes the new awareness causes deep depression. Sometimes self-awareness leads to acknowledgment of a deep need for admiration and love and sexual affirmation. Sometimes the reduction of inhibitions leads to sexual adventures and marital problems (Vaillant, 1977). Crisis or no crisis, Vaillant's picture of the first years of the forties is actually very much like Gould's and Levinson's.

Like Gould and Levinson, Vaillant describes the discomfort of recognizing and adapting to changing relationships with parents and with children. And like Gould and Levinson, Vaillant identifies a sense of taking stock, of facing up to a new identity, and he also admits that *middlescence* is a reality. It's just that he's much more interested in what comes next.

What does come after the early forties and when it actually happens are open questions. As we look at the middle forties we find that some progress is being made toward a less stressful time of life but that many people haven't yet reached it.

The Middle Forties

Moving on to a more self-satisfied time of life is one of the options of the middle forties. According to Erikson, the alternative is to get stuck.

Erikson left the ups and downs of young adulthood in the thirties uncharted in his model of adult life. After the stage of either succeeding or not succeeding at establishing intimacy in the twenties, Erikson identified no new developmental stage until the forties, when he felt that we enter the stage of either succeeding or not succeeding at becoming "generative" (Erikson, 1963, 1968).

Generativity is Erikson's term for a cluster of qualities that involve the ability to give something of yourself to your social environment. **Stagnation** is it's alternative; if you stay turned inward or focused on your own narrow world at this time of life, you stagnate. People who achieve generativity are productive. They're creative.

They can give time, understanding, and guidance to other people. As workers, parents, mentors and leaders, generative people move into positive new relationships with their peers and with younger adults. They make valuable social contributions. People who bog down in stagnation are people who have failed to become generative. Like water that gets murky and stagnant when it can't flow, Erikson believes, lives that don't change and grow become dull and limited. People who stagnate are nonproductive. They are incapable of making creative contributions. Locked into their lives, they become progressively narrower. Stagnation contributes nothing beneficial to their lives or to the lives of other people.

Erikson's stage of "generativity versus stagnation" occurs sometime in the forties decade—Erikson is no more specific about the chronological age. The stage requires a choice between becoming productive and caring or remaining self-limited and self-serving. A person who has a clear sense of identity in his or her inner world and has a strong belief in the value of his or her outer world is able to make the choice for generativity (Erikson, 1963, 1968).

This stage of Erikson's model has been clarified further by Robert Peck (1975). Building on Erikson's work, Peck identifies four issues that have to be dealt with at this point of middle life. The issues involve personal values, relationships, ways of caring, and ways of thinking. Peck tells us that to achieve generativity we must learn a crucial set of new perceptions: we have to learn to value wisdom more than physical power; we have to learn to value social relationships over sexual relationships; we have to establish caring relationships more easily, instead of coming to care slowly; and we have to learn to think flexibly rather than holding beliefs rigidly. To avoid stagnation in the second half of life, in other words, we have to open ourselves to new development. We have to choose to keep growing, and we have to keep on learning how.

Vaillant's work with the men of the Grant Study has convinced him that Erikson is accurate about the timing of the choice between generativity and stagnation and the results of failing to become generative. He finds, however, that not everybody chooses to grow—even men who may seem to be successes. Vaillant describes a number of people who got stuck in the career-consolidation stage of the thirties, which he has added to the Erikson model. These are men who never stopped driving ahead in their careers and who never got in touch with their inner selves. They seem prematurely old, doubtful about the meaning of their lives, and vaguely dissatisfied. What happened to them? The question troubles Vaillant (1977).

Levinson may have one answer for Vaillant's question; Levinson explains an important developmental process that he believes goes on in the middle forties. These years are the peak of coming to grips with our inner polarities, according to Levinson. It might be that people who get stuck are people who never deal with the complexities of their inner worlds.

Facing up to our complex inner selves is part of the process of individuation—the process of becoming fully ourselves. Jung identified it as a process that begins in the forties; Erikson generalized it to mean ego development all through life; Levinson puts these two ideas together, describing individuation as a lifelong process with special importance during the middle years. Remember that Keniston believes individuation is possible in the twenties, given the moratorium of "youth"—a time-out in this decade for self-finding.

Levinson defines individuation as a clarifying of the boundaries between our inner selves and our outer worlds and as a balancing of the polarities of our inner worlds. He describes it as a growing sense of knowing who we really are, what we really want, what the world really is, and how valuable it is to us (Levinson et al., 1978).

Our experience as children, adolescents, and young adults gives us the beginnings of answers for these questions and helps us to know the boundaries between our inner and outer worlds more clearly. The experiences of turning inward and self-assessment in the mid-life crisis, according to Levinson, demand that we go further and clear up the opposing ideas of our inner worlds.

Levinson tells us that, if we are going to get on with our individuation, we have to complete the reconciliation of our internal opposites and to realize that both poles of each pair can exist in the same person at the same time. Each polar opposite is an essential part. We can be both young, in the sense of growing and vital—and old, in the sense of declining. We can be both creative, in the sense of being positive and productive—and destructive, in the sense of being negative and ruinous. We can be both masculine, in the sense of being powerful, active, dominant, and rational—and feminine, in the sense of being nurturant, passive, yielding, and emotional. We can be both attached to other people and dependent on them—and be separate and self-sufficient. Recognizing these polarities and reconciling these opposites bring us into new balance. It carries us to a richer, more confident sense of self. It gives us more choices of ways to be (Levinson et al., 1978).

Generate, individuate in the mid-forties; and the late forties and early fifties may be a fulfilling and fruitful time of life.

The Late Forties and Early Fifties

You know and I know that many people are still miserable people in their late forties, and many people will go on being miserable people as long as they live. Some of us have had such destructive experiences as children and young adults that we don't have any resources—inner or outer—to bring to bear in becoming positive and productive and "fully adult." But there's always hope. Someday life may bring what we need to find our own best selves.

That's Gould's belief, at least. The last developmental stage that Gould identifies is "beyond mid-life," which is any and all of life after the mid-life decade. If the final work of development isn't done in mid-life, it may get done later. If it has been done, a new freedom comes with being more than 45 (Gould, 1978).

Remember that, to Gould, the developmental work of adulthood means dropping the illusions that allowed us to preserve our limited "childhood consciousness." With all the illusions gone, we are finally aware that other people don't own us—we own ourselves. It's the beginning of an inner-directed life.

To be inner directed, in Gould's use of the words, is to be in an unfamiliar situation, for most of us. The framework that we live in for the first half of our lives is one in which we're controlled from outside by what we think other people want from us, by what we think they do to us, or both. The world that we see through our childhood consciousness is a world controlled by power and size. People with power, big people, are the important ones. To jockey for position in that world requires competition and humiliation. Inner-directed "adult consciousness" allows us a new world, a world in which people who seem to have power and status aren't necessarily important in our lives. Inner directedness permits us each our own sense of value. It may also lead us to philosophy or religion, where we find deep and universal values expressed. It's a whole new situation, and it may take time to get used to. With illusions gone and old meanings empty, some people spend years of feeling confused and lost. But, with time, the sense of belonging to yourself alone can evoke a feeling of finally being centered and a sense of being brought to completion (Gould, 1978).

Growing into adult consciousness is no guarantee of a happy life, however. The last years of life are sure to bring their share of losses and sorrows and painful limitations. What adult vision does promise is that you will be able to accept or reject on your own terms whatever life brings. For Gould, arriving at adult consciousness means that you've finally grown up. His model of development could be compared to a "30-and-out" career plan that promises early retirement if you just stick with it.

The other developmental psychologists take the position that growing up takes much longer, and that some of us are never really ready to retire from developmental work. They agree, though, that the late forties and early fifties are a time when life most often levels out and gains a new stability.

Vaillant describes a developmental stage that arrives in the early fifties, after the period Erikson calls the time of generativity or stagnation and before the time arrives for the choice between integrity and despair. Vaillant calls it a stage of **the keepers of the meaning,** a delicate balance between preserving personal values and becoming intellectually rigid. Vaillant's keepers of the meaning find themselves in a relaxed and quiet time of life. Having achieved some degree of generativity, they are not only "keeping the meaning" of their personal values, they're passing them on as mentors and guides. They are actively participating in their social worlds: in church, in politics, and in a variety of organizations. Their senses of identity are strong; they feel ready to take stands on issues about which they have strong beliefs. The only real problem for keepers of the meaning is that they tend to harden their ideas and to hang on to them rigidly. Too much rigidity may push them instead into the state of stagnation (Vaillant, 1977).

Levinson, too, identifies a developmental stage that begins in the late forties and may carry over into the fifties. He sees it as a time of becoming more stable, though, rather than a time of growing rigid. The name he gives this stage is "entering middle adulthood."

What Levinson calls middle adulthood is a new period of stability that is created by the processes of the mid-life transition. It involves a new set of developmental tasks. In middle adulthood we have to make crucial choices about how to live the middle adult years, and we have to give these choices personal meaning and commitment. We also have to build another, more satisfying life structure that fits these new choices (see Figure 7-1).

The choices that you make as you enter middle adulthood can be either positive or negative decisions: you may decide to add some new things to your life, but you also might feel that you have to give up some old things you've valued for years. Giving up old pieces of your life may be hard, but finding new and usable parts for your new life structure may be equally difficult. It takes imagination and exploration, and trial and error too, to put together a comfortable and satisfying life structure in your middle years (Levinson et al., 1978).

Most people seem to get the job done, though. As we look at other descriptive studies of life in these years we find that, with the excep-

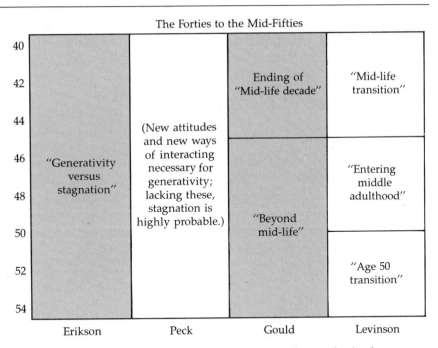

Figure 7-1 Erikson, Peck, Gould, and Levinson all identify the forties as a time of resolving (or not resolving) personal issues, which will determine the positive outcome (or negative outcome) of middle adulthood and later life.

tion of one study's sample, the kinds of changes the theorists describe do seem to be taking place in peoples' lives.

Davitz and Davitz find that after the anxieties and depressions of the main part of the forties decade its ending brings peace and healing. Men who have struggled and rebelled and taken their lives apart in recent years now seem to be concerned with putting life back together. At work they're becoming more integrated, less controlled by their ego needs; in their personal lives they're being reintegrated into their families or into intimate relationships. The Davitzes describe a new degree of self-acceptance and mellowing in men (Davitz & Davitz, 1976).

Women who have lived through years of insecurity, uneasiness, and frustration in their forties now also seem to be finding a new sense of fulfillment. Working women and women at home, married women and women on their own find these years can be a time of easier going (Davitz & Davitz, 1976). Anxieties about unplanned pregnancies become less intense as women come to the end of their childbearing potential. By the late forties, if they have not yet experienced a tubal ligation or hysterectomy, most women will be in the process of the termination of their reproductive capacity, which is **menopause**—the natural end of ovulation and menstruation. In the past, the cultural stereotypes concerning menopause were negative; after all, a woman's reproductive potential was considered all-important, and aging and menopause were synonymous. But informed contemporary women tend to perceive menopause much more positively. The endocrine imbalances that may cause uncomfortable physical responses at this time, such as the common "hot flash," can now be controlled, medically or through natural methods. As menopause is navigated, women are more free and often more stable than ever before (Davitz & Davitz, 1976; Neugarten, 1980).

The Lowenthal, Thurnher, and Chiriboga study (1977) included a group of middle-aged parents, about 50 years old. The men in the sample had developed positive images. Compared to the young-adult sample in the same study, the men at 50 were far more involved in varied roles and activities and twice as likely to be church members. The older men were less impulsive, more self-controlled. They tended to be less anxious and more self-accepting. These people fit the pictures that Erikson, Levinson, and Gould have given us of this time of life quite accurately.

There's a problem with fitting the women of the Lowenthal study into current models, though: they don't fit the profiles featuring generativity, individuation, or adult consciousness at all. The women in the fifties group in the Lowenthal, Thurnher, and Chiriboga study are, like the men, much more involved in varied roles and activities than are the members of the younger comparison-group. But these "empty-nest" mothers, only half of whom work outside the home, are hitting a low point in life satisfaction. They express high dissatisfaction with their mates, their mothers, and, most of all, with themselves. These negative responses may be a function of the women's cohort or their socioeconomic background. However, this sample's negative responses may be attributable to other trends apparent at age 50. One such trend is a tendency toward marital dissatisfaction among women as they lose their accustomed primary role, motherhood. This is a trend that reverses dramatically by age 60, when women often report that they are more happy than ever before (Kimmel, 1974). A second trend is an apparent **sex-role reversal** that is common in both men and women in their postparental phase of life—a reversal that may be a function of the reconciliation of male-female polarities. First identified in the Kansas City Studies

(Neugarten, 1968b), a trend in which women become more assertive, autonomous, and active while men become more nurturant, emotional, and passive has been found in other cultures, as well (Gutmann, 1977). Whether this sex-role reversal is a postparenting release, as Gutmann suggests, or a biological phenomenon traceable to endocrine changes, as Alice Rossi hypothesizes (1980), it seems to be a reality. The possibility of becoming more androgynous—that is, more in touch with all of the qualities that have been socially stereotyped as either male or female, but which may now be seen as both—becomes even more open in these years. As sexual stereotypes drop away we can become more balanced as human beings.

The middle fifties open up other new and exciting options in addition to androgyny. Some people are in work situations that offer early retirement, and more and more people are making that choice. Other people are just shifting into the new perspective of anticipating retirement and its wholly different way of life. In the coming chapter we'll examine some of their concerns.

Before we leave these middle adult years, however, give yourself the opportunity of reworking the scale at the beginning of this chapter. This time use a darker set of dots and a darker line, and see whether any of your perceptions and expectations have changed.

Summary

The period roughly spanning the forties to the middle fifties may be viewed as the prime of life or as the arrival of aging. Either way, it is a time of changes.

The early forties are seen by most developmentalists as the classic time for mid-life crisis—a time for reassessment of life that involves looking back and evaluating the failures and disappointments of the past as well as looking ahead and anticipating the inevitability of death. The crisis may be mild or severe, but it seems to be necessary for continued development.

Gould and Sheehy each see the period of mid-life assessment as spanning the 10-year period from 35 to 45. Levinson and the researchers Davitz and Davitz pinpoint the early forties as the mid-life assessment period. Vaillant admits that an evaluation is taking place in the early forties, but he denies that it's a crisis.

By the middle forties most people are moving toward a new ease in life and enjoyment of it. Erikson calls this productive and positive time the stage of generativity. Levinson sees it as a time of becoming more fully oneself, of individuation. Gould believes 45 to be the most usual age for completing the developmental work of dropping childhood consciousness and becoming truly adult.

The late forties and early fifties seem to be an era for setting life in order and finding it good. Vaillant describes it as a time of firming up personal values; Levinson tells us it's the season for establishing a stable middle-adult life structure.

Descriptive studies, such as those by Davitz and Davitz and by Lowenthal, Thurnher, and Chiriboga, support the theories about middle life that have been noted, for the most part. The exception is the finding in descriptive studies that women seem to hit a low in life satisfaction in their late forties and early fifties—a situation that changes dramatically by 60. A possible explanation for this change in women's self-perceptions is the role changes that many women undergo in these years. The loss of the maternal role and the reversal of sex roles are quite possibly sex-related role shifts in the late forties.

The middle fifties open up the issue of early retirement, or they bring an anticipation of retirement in years to come. Plans for later life become an issue in the mid-fifties.

Terms and Concepts to Define

generativity _____

_____

keepers of the meaning _____

_____

menopause _____

_____

middle adulthood _____

_____

middlescence _____

_____

mid-life crisis _____

_____

polarities _____

_____

reassessment _____

_____

sex-role reversal _____

_____

stagnation _____

_____

Experiences

To involve yourself with the concepts in this chapter, try these experiences described in the Appendix.

Alone
33. Polarities
14. Evil and Death

With Others
15. Being 44
7. Transitions

Going beyond the Text

1. *Do a brief cross-sectional study of people in their early, middle, and late forties and in their early fifties, testing the hypothesis that a mid-life crisis of self-questioning and evaluation is characteristic of this time. Carefully design your questions to avoid communicating your expectations.*
2. *Observe your acquaintances who are in the middle years for indications of sex-role reversal, reconciliation of extreme masculine and feminine role playing, or both.*

Suggested Readings

Block, M., Davidson, J., & Grambs, J. Women over forty: Visions and realities. *New York: Springer, 1981.*

Davitz, J., & Davitz, L. Making it from 40 to 50. *New York: Random House, 1976.*

Levinson, D., Darrow, C., Klein, E., Levinson, M., & McKee, B. The seasons of a man's life. *New York: Knopf, 1978.*

Westoff, L. Breaking out at forty: Finding the skills to find yourself. *New York: Simon & Schuster, 1976.*

8

Getting On:
The Mid-Fifties to the Mid-Sixties

When you have finished reading this chapter you should be able to:
Discuss the contemporary image of what Hunt and Hunt call "new middle age."
Define the characteristics of the group Neugarten calls the "young-old."
Summarize the pros and cons of each of the retirement options possible in middle adulthood.
Describe Atchley's seven phases of retirement.
List the characteristics of people who adapt well to retirement.

In the last chapter we looked at the years from 40 to 55. This 15-year slice of middle life was examined instead of the forties decade alone because the changes that occur during the 15-year span are interconnected: they evolve during individuation, mid-life crisis, the emptying of the nest, and the choice of generativity or stagnation, all of which may thread through the years 40 to 55. Then, after 55, a whole new lifestyle begins to emerge (Levinson et al., 1978; Neugarten, 1978, 1980).

Middle Life: An Overview

In this chapter we're going to explore the 10-year span in which the lifestyle of middle life takes shape. We'll begin where we left off, at 55, but that age is a good starting place for other reasons as well.

The first reason that 55 is a natural starting point is a psychological one. A sense of one's psychological aging is becoming a reality; by 55 most people have adapted some ways to cope with their new perspectives on life as a whole. If adulthood is ever a plateau, this may be it. The outcomes of early adulthood are finally achieved; a lifestyle for full maturity is shaping up. And age 55 brings us to the psychological stage that Levinson and his associates (1978) call "culmination of middle adulthood." This high point of middle adulthood is described in a number of the current redefinitions of middle age, which are a major focus of this chapter.

A second reason for beginning at 55 involves a social factor. Age 55 is also a starting point for an important new social-age category that has been suggested by Bernice Neugarten (1977, 1978, 1980): that of the "young-old." "Young-old" and "old-old" are categories of people that Neugarten has established to sort out accurate and undistorted images of later life. The distinction of these two groups from what has often been considered only one is a helpful clarification of the situation. In the past, information about older people was lumped together in the category of "people 65 years old and older," a practice that is confusing and inaccurate. Mixing data about 65-year-olds with data about 90-year-olds produces the averages that have given us so many misunderstandings about the later years of life. Separating out the young-olds—people from about 55 to 75, and retired—allows us to see later adulthood more clearly.

A third reason why 55 is a pivotal time of life is work related: at 55, early retirement becomes a possibility. With early retirement a possible choice, or, alternatively, later retirement an event close enough to seem a reality, a new set of lifestyle choices opens up. After retirement, social roles change; old work roles drop away and new roles are possible. Retirement brings with it a shift in personal and interpersonal relationships, also. The questions of when and how to retire become crucial issues for the middle-aged and young-olds.

A final reason for beginning at 55 is that biological changes are becoming significant by this time. Surface changes are becoming apparent; these are the years when most people have begun to show the deeper signs of aging: lines have become wrinkles, hair has thinned to baldness, and gravity has tugged everything a few inches lower than it used to be. Deeper changes are also emerging as chronic illnesses begin to take a more serious toll in these middle years (Fries & Crapo, 1981). The majority of people at age 55 are clearly senior adults (Wantz & Gay, 1981).

Beginning, then, with the age of 55 we'll sort out what middle age is all about, what it means to be the young-old, and what retirement can mean as it gets closer. We'll end at 65, which is the traditional social-clock marker for the end of being middle-aged and the beginning of being old (Neugarten, 1968b) and is traditionally the age for mandatory retirement.

The expectation of retirement at 65 is changing, now that new choices are possible: retirement can be either much earlier than that or much later. Pension plans in some occupations that make retirement possible after 30 years have created the trend of leaving the work force as soon as possible; legislation that prohibits forced retirement until the age of 70 has created the countertrend of staying in the work place as long as possible. Again, we have a changing social setting that allows more personal flexibility. This flexibility extends the issue of retirement over a time span of almost 20 years. But, by the age of 65, most people will have made their own decisions about retirement and will have established their lifestyles for their later years. By the late sixties, new issues become more pressing; middle adulthood comes to an end, and late adulthood begins.

The "Middle-Aged"

By the time we've reached our mid-fifties, we're deep into middle adulthood, a time of life that is often called *middle age*. What, exactly, does *middle age* mean to you? Define it for yourself. Then describe what it's like to be a middle-aged man and a middle-aged woman, in terms of what they experience, how they look, and what they feel.

Middle age is _____

_____

_____

To be a middle-aged man is to be _____

_____

_____

To be a middle-aged woman is to be _____

_____

_____

You probably have a fairly clear understanding of your own concept of middle age. There's a strong possibility, though, that your idea of it is somewhat different from the ideas of other people. *Middle age* is an ambiguous term in our culture, and concepts of middle age vary widely. Your sex, your age, and your social and economic background all affect your perceptions of this period (Bengtson, Kasschau, & Ragan, 1977; Neugarten, 1968a).

Even the specialists in adult development have trouble agreeing on exactly what middle age is. They tend to set different chronological limits on the period, and this automatically affects their descriptions of what it's like. For example, Havighurst places middle age between 30 and 60 (1972). Jung says middle age starts somewhere between 35 and 40; he doesn't identify the end (1971). Levinson and his associates call it "middle adulthood" and place it at 40 to 60 (1978). Erikson's "generativity versus stagnation" stage begins at around 40 and ends at around 60 (1968). Gould calls the period the "middle years," occurring any time after 45 and before "old age" (1978). And Bühler describes a reassessment stage between 45 and 65 (1968). This lack of agreement on the chronology of middle life is fairly confusing. Neugarten has attempted to bring order to this confusion by shifting the concern away from chronological age and toward a social perception of middle age. She surveyed a group of 400 men and women between the ages of 35 and 55 for their perceptions of middle age and found that, at least for members of this cohort sample, it is a matter of "position in life" rather than an age in years. Position in life is a matter of the social tasks that are accomplished before one is middle-aged. The respondents described it as a period of time after youth and before old age (1968b).

In a positional time frame, then, being middle-aged is being in the middle. It's a bridge between early and late life. Women with children tend to define it in terms of the family cycle; it begins when their children are full grown. Women who have been child free are also apt to define their middle age in terms of the ages of children they could have had. Men, on the other hand, are more apt to define middle age in terms of their work cycles; they're middle-aged when they have achieved their highest level of advancement. This relationship between the family and work cycles and the awareness of middle age explains some of the wide variations in time estimates: people who have children early or who work at jobs with little room for advancement are "middle-aged" while they're still quite young; other people, who have children late or who have wide possibilities for getting ahead, don't get "middle-aged" until they're older (Bengtson et al., 1977; Neugarten, 1968b).

How can you tell when you're middle-aged? What is it like? It's changing, as social expectations and individual perceptions of the middle years change. In the 1960s, the women in Neugarten's survey described it as a time of freedom. With less work to do in maintaining their families and their homes, these women finally began to find time for themselves. The men in the survey experienced it as a time of pressure. With little time left for achievement in their careers, and with younger men competing for their jobs, men have less opportunity to relax. But they aren't terribly anxious. Both men and women describe feeling middle-aged as feeling competent, on top of the day-to-day tasks of living. They feel that they've reached self-understanding. Psychologically they're more aware of their inner worlds, more able to cope with their outer worlds, more sure of both. Both men and women are beginning to balance out sex-role behavior; the women are becoming more assertive, and the men are allowing themselves more gentleness and openness. Physically, they're more aware of their bodies. Neugarten calls this new awareness of body functions **body monitoring.** It's not only the habit of "listening" more carefully to what the body is saying, it's also the practice of using protective strategies to keep the body functioning well. A focus on physical health is a natural outcome of another change that the subjects of Neugarten's survey describe: they have shifted their points of view on time. Instead of seeing life in terms of the number of years that they've lived since birth, they have begun looking at it in terms of years until death, a new perception of time called "time-restructuring" (Neugarten, 1968b).

Neugarten's work on the perception of middle age frees us to some degree from chronological limitations, but it does characterize middle age as a certain way of being, in the middle years of life. Like Neugarten, Vaillant, too, has found that middle life has its own special quality. His analysis of the Grant Study identifies many of the characteristics of Neugarten's "middle age" in his subjects at the age of 55.

In the 1970s Vaillant found that the men in his sample in their middle fifties were finding systematic ways to monitor their bodies, as Neugarten described, in order to maintain both physical and mental performance. They were learning to deal realistically and competently with their work lives. They were becoming more gentle and nurturant. These men, Vaillant feels, confirm Neugarten's descriptions of middle age (1977).

Both Neugarten and Vaillant were dealing with samples of "well-placed" individuals at mid-life. As a result, their image of middle age is quite positive. But that positive view need not be limited to the segment of the middle class that is materially well-off. A new version of middle adulthood as autonomous, assertive, free of age and sex stereotypes, growing, whole, and individuated is emerging in our culture in general (Neugarten, 1980).

This updating of attitudes about middle adulthood is illustrated in a cultural analysis of life between 40 and 65 in contemporary America by Bernice Hunt and Morton Hunt (1974).

The Hunts describe the "new middle age" that has emerged in recent years as an outcome of modern technology and of longer life spans, in contrast to the "old middle age" that existed in the past as a product of negative attitudes toward aging in Western culture. The **old middle age** concept was inherited from classical Greece and Rome: it tells us that life is short, and time is flying, and that the world belongs to the young and the strong. Although life is longer now, and a long period of years between youth and senescence has become a reality, those negative attitudes from the past have hung on. They are the basic ideas behind the "old middle age."

Hunt and Hunt (1974) describe "old middle age" as a time of gathering dullness. People feel that they're slowly losing their grip at work, in their social lives, and in their sexual lives. Women, particularly, feel that they are losing their sexual and family roles and beginning to decline. Both men and women of "old middle age" **think old,** to themselves and out loud, blaming their ages for their problems. And they **think sick,** relating all their physical problems to age. Thinking old and thinking sick become self-fulfilling prophecies in a process Ashley Montague has called "psychosclerosis." By this means, one creates the very physical conditions that are expected, in many cases (Montague, 1981). That's the "old middle age." It really isn't necessary any more, according to the Hunts.

In contrast, **new middle age** is a time of renewal, a mid-course correction in peoples' lives. For many couples it's the first opportunity to take time and to spend money for leisure and pleasure. For women, it's a time of new freedom and new directions. For men and women both it's time to "think fit," exercising their bodies regularly, and to "think healthy," taking seriously nutrition and medical prevention. That's the "new middle age." For some people, it's already a reality; for the rest of us it can become a realistic goal (Hunt & Hunt, 1974).

Positive thinking about the later years of middle adulthood isn't just an inevitable result of technological progress and extended life spans, however; on the contrary, modernization—that is, "Westernization"—of agricultural societies that are simpler than North American societies has seemed to reduce the status of older people (Cowgill & Holmes, 1972). In many non-Western societies, it's always been understood that wisdom and balance come with age—so older people have been the leaders, the decision makers. It's a question of attitude; and contemporary North American attitudes about the middle years seem to be shifting from negative attitudes toward more positive perspectives. Middle age can be defined by a cluster of the social expectations held about role changes as well as the personal expectations, the biological changes, and the psychological attitudes held about crossing the bridge to late adulthood. Perceptions of oneself as middle-aged may be developed early in the middle years or late; and they may be positive or negative. Either way, they create a **self-fulfilling prophecy:** what we expect to happen will probably happen.

The "Young-Olds"

Levinson identifies the last years of the fifties decade as "the culmination of middle adulthood." Because the men in his study hadn't yet lived these years, Levinson has little to tell us that's based on research data. Nonetheless he does have something interesting to say about cultural attitudes toward the years of middle age: the forties, the fifties, and the sixties. In the conclusion of *The Seasons of a Man's Life*, Levinson states his hypothesis that the age stages that he describes exist not only in the lives of American men currently alive but in the lives of people in all societies now and within earlier cultures as well. As evidence, he presents materials from Confucius (a philosopher of ancient China), from Solon (a statesman of classical Greece), and from the Talmud (a Hebrew text from Biblical times), as illustrated in Figure 3-1. Confucius and the Talmud share a positive point of view on the fifties and the sixties, considering these decades of deeper understanding and acceptance. But Solon describes the function of the fifties in more negative terms, and he sees the sixties as the beginning of the end (Levinson et al., 1978).

It's interesting that in the recent past, Western culture, which is based on both classical and Biblical attitudes, has been more in agreement with Solon's negative assessment than with the Talmud's developmental perspective. It's even more interesting that we seem to be finally coming around to the positive point of view. And we do seem to be. Like most of the developmental philosophers of ancient times, modern developmental scientists generally agree that the years of the fifties and the sixties can be a time for personal growth and social contributions.

Martin Puner has written a positive and helpful description of the fifties, the decade that he claims is the most ignored period of adult life (1977). He describes the fifties as a special time "between." In the fifties people are between starting out and finishing up, between being the "elderly young" and "newly old"; between Erikson's choices of generativity or stagnation and of integrity or despair; between adult children and aging parents; and between the challenges of the forties and the conservatism of the sixties. Puner uses Havighurst, Neugarten, and Tobin's (1968) picture of the fifties as a time for creating a new lifestyle for the later years while hanging on to the valuable parts of earlier life. People in their fifties, says Havighurst, are learning to deal adaptively with doubts. To deal with doubts about physical aging, they may be stepping up physical activity with exercise, controlling weight with a healthier diet, dressing more attractively, and paying more attention to grooming. To deal with social doubts, they may be making efforts to fill out their networks of friends and getting involved with community organizations. To deal with doubts about intellectual changes, people in their fifties may be learning new systems for organizing information and may be replacing action with thought as a method of coping (Puner, 1977).

These "elderly young" and "newly old" may perceive themselves as middle-aged; in some cases they may also be perceived as the "young-old." Neugarten's term "young-old" is, like middle age, localized at a general chronological period, but it is much more a matter of social perception than of the number of years that have been lived (Neugarten, 1978). Between the years 55 and 75, depending on individual lifestyle, a person may move into the category of the "young-old." Rather than a value judgment, this designation classifies a person's age in years, social roles, and age status all at once.

"Young-olds" are, first of all, old enough in years to retire from work; most of them probably retire early. Physically, they are still young enough to be relatively healthy and active. However, because they are retired, "young-olds" have given up the social roles that are identified with employment. They are free from many social responsibilities, but they still have a number of social roles left over from earlier life. Many are tax-paying citizens; 80% of them are still living in their own homes. Many are still husbands and wives; 80% of the current "young-old" men are still living with their wives, and more than half of the women who have married still live with their husbands. In many ways, early-retired "young-olds" are much the same as they were when they were younger. But they are also considered old. Their age status has changed. When a person retires and is no longer an economically productive member of society, his/her social status is different from what it was when the person was employed. Instead of carrying economic responsibilities, the retiree has become an economic dependent. The "young-old" person occupies a hard-to-define social position that, in our society, still may carry a slightly negative status—in spite of attempts to change the image with such terms as "golden ager" and "senior citizen" (Neugarten, 1978).

The stereotypes are changing, however. Neugarten finds that the present cohorts of "young-olds" are very different from the negative stereotypes of aging people. Compared to older cohorts, they have had more years of education, they are politically more informed, and they are more socially active. This is a trend that should get stronger as cohorts with more education and a history of political activism become "young-old." They not only will reflect the social world that formed them in the past but will have a powerful influence on the social world of the future (Bengtson & Haber, 1975; Neugarten, 1978).

With the wider range of retirement options that are available, including early retirement, late-life career changes, late retirement or no retirement at all, "young-old" will be an increasingly useful term for defining a special group of older people. However, with the wider range of life patterns that are available in later years, it also will become a slightly less specific term. We *are* apparently moving toward an **age-irrelevant society**: a society in which chronological age has little influence on the choices of later life, including work choices, social roles, and age status (Giele, 1980; Neugarten, 1978).

Compare the items below with those in your own definition of middle age and with your statements of what it is to be a middle-aged man and middle-aged woman, at the beginning of this chapter. Check off the items here that you included in your own descriptions. Middle-aged people in their late fifties and early sixties are:

_____ not young, not old, but in between
_____ finished with parenting
_____ at the highest rung of their career ladders that they will reach
_____ free for leisure, pleasure, and relaxation
_____ busy with last-minute attempts to be more successful
_____ probably more self-aware than at any earlier time
_____ reversing roles; women are more assertive and men more gentle and perceptive
_____ "body monitoring"; keeping close watch over their health
_____ more focused on the time that's left than they are on the time that's past

People in their late fifties and early sixties may also be "young-old." Check off any of these items that you included in your own descriptions:

_____ still healthy and active and socially involved
_____ still living as couples, in most cases
_____ still living in their own homes, in most cases
_____ retired

Do you find that your perception of these middle years has expanded—at least slightly?

Preretirement and Retirement

Retirement is an issue that separates the middle-aged from the young-old. For some it's the dream of a future of leisure; for others it's the nightmare of being pushed out of productive living. It can mean finding yourself or losing yourself. How and when retirement proceeds is a very personal issue.

Retirement itself is a fairly recent human invention. And an invention is what it is; retirement is not a natural life stage. Perhaps exactly because it is artificial, retirement is a troubling life issue for many people—and more difficult for some cohorts than for others because of their attitudes toward work and leisure, toward independence and dependence (Foner & Schwab, 1981).

Deciding when you are going to retire is a complex decision, and it's a choice that's available as a function of our technological society. The technologies of improved health care and means of dealing with chronic disease have extended life expectancies significantly. Now average lifetimes are long enough that people continue to live for many years after they move out of their work roles, but this has been the case only in the last half of this century. And, now there's enough economic surplus to support a large nonworking population of older people—which also is a new development (and one that may not continue far into the future). At the moment, a person in the middle years has a number of options about retirement. One is **early retirement,** an option that requires a comfortable economic base. Another option is **gradual retirement:** slowly phasing out a career or shifting to a new, less demanding one. Then there is the **traditional retirement**—that beginning at age 65. **Late retirement** begins at the now-legal age of 70. The final option is **nonretirement,** which is quitting only when death ends your work. These choices are available to more and more people. An individual's choice should reflect personal needs and capabilities and life circumstances (Foner & Schwab, 1981; Levinson et al., 1978).

There are some simple and obvious pros and cons that go along with these choices, but before we discuss these it's important to have a total picture of retirement as a part of life.

Robert Atchley (1976) has analyzed the retirement phenomenon from three points of view: as an event in life, as a social role, and as a process that is integrated with the life structure.

From the first point of view, retirement is just an event, a social milestone. It's a passage from the world of work to the world of leisure, the occasion for a party or a gold watch, time to play golf or go fishing. But that's an oversimple and surface point of view.

From the second point of view, retirement is a social role; being retired affects the way you see yourself and the way others see you. It's a sort of "roleless role" in that it carries very few expectations. However, it's a role that you can anticipate, accept, learn, master, and eventually give up. Your changing relationship to the role of retiree is one of the processes of life.

The point-of-view of retirement as a process is Atchley's particularly useful contribution to our understanding of the ways that retirement is built into our life structures. He describes seven phases of retiring (see Figure 8-1). The first is the "remote" phase; at first retirement is a vague idea, and we feel fairly positive about it. We may try to find information about it from many sources. A second phase is named for the time when retirement is "near." As friends and mates retire, we recognize that retirement is a reality, and we may come to feel rather negative about it. We tend to deal with it in

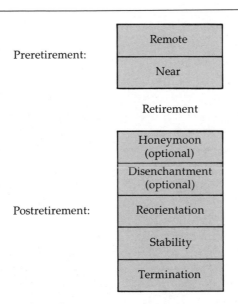

Figure 8-1 Robert Atchley has identified seven stages in the retirement process. Some are optional, and some are highly probable. (*From* The Sociology of Retirement, *by R. Atchley. Copyright © 1976 by Schenkman Publishing Co., Inc. Reprinted by permission.*)

terms of fantasy rather than the information available. Some people, after they actually retire, experience a brief high: the "honeymoon" phase of retirement. After retirement, or after retirement plus the honeymoon phase, some people feel bored, depressed, lost, or a combination of these responses. This phase Atchley calls "disenchantment." Although some retirees skip the honeymoon or disenchantment phases, or both, all have to eventually reorient their life-styles to fit retirement. In the "reorientation" phase people learn to restructure their choices and create new ways of life. When life settles into new routines, retirement is in its "stable" phase, which lasts as long as retirees are healthy and active. Eventually, through disability or death, retirement ends; this is the "termination" phase, the last phase, when active life is no longer possible.

The phases of retirement can coincide with any of the periods of middle or later life. When you are in your late fifties and early sixties, you may see your own retirement as remote or near. Or you may be in the honeymoon phase or be disenchanted; or you may be stabilized in retirement.

Early retirement—the first option—is possible in many occupations. People choose it for a number of reasons: boredom with their work, failing health, or the desire for leisure. The most crucial factor in the decision, though, is money.

In order to retire comfortably at any age, you have to have enough money in savings, pensions, and investments to give financial security; the rising costs of living can be disastrous when you have a fixed income. One good aspect of early retirement is that it allows a large percentage of the population to look forward to 15 years or more of leisure living before they die: they have paid their dues and have time for enjoyment. One bad aspect of early retirement is that it removes from the labor force a larger percentage of the mature populace than would otherwise be unemployed. This leaves a smaller group working to support them—an imbalance called the **dependency ratio** (Sheppard & Rix, 1977). It costs a lot to retire, and the rising costs of retiring may make later retirement preferable.

Another retirement option, gradual retirement, may lighten financial problems at the same time that it relieves boredom, provides more leisure time, or permits fewer working hours for a person whose health is not optimal; any of these reasons might otherwise have caused early retirement. Gradual retirement may consist in shifting from full-time to part-time work in your occupation (Butcher, 1978), changing occupations and beginning a career that's more compatible with later life (Sarason, 1977), or retiring from your occupation and working at part-time odd jobs (Butcher, 1978). Gradual retirement keeps the majority of active and able people in the work force and so relieves financial strains. However, it doesn't allow years of great freedom in later life.

Retirement at age 65 and at 70 have been a long time in becoming options. Before the Age Discrimination in Employment Act (**ADEA**) of 1968 and the amendment to it that was passed in 1977, forced retirement at the age of 65 or earlier was routine. Now **mandatory retirement** is prohibited until the age of 70 in private businesses, and it is prohibited in federal jobs at any age (Butcher, 1978). One advantageous effect of the ADEA is that it allows people to work as long as they want to. However, choosing late retirement is not without drawbacks—particularly that, if you're male, you may never live to enjoy it. The average male life expectancy will have to advance several years before retirement at 70 can be a common choice.

Age as measured in years is not a valid way to determine retirement readiness. Variations in the timing of the other major events in life produce variations in readiness for retirement. Also, differences in functional age create differences in the appropriate age for retiring. Remember that your functional age is a result of the body you were born with and of the life experiences that your body has undergone. It's a product of both genetics and environment, affected by mental attitudes and social attitudes, by general health and physical fitness. Only when senescence limits your functioning to the point that you can't work do you really have to retire. This, incidentally, has been the criterion by which airline pilots have been retired for years; some wash out at as young an age as 40; some are still functionally competent in their sixties (Sheppard & Rix, 1977). People who retire only when senescence limits their ability to function can be economically productive and socially involved for most of their lives, which may be important for their self-esteem. However, if many people choose this option, fewer job openings will exist for young people.

Fortunately, choices that provide satisfactory retirement situations for many different people are opening up. Whatever your choice, you can begin at least tentative retirement planning in early adulthood and pick the option that best fits your own lifestyle. If you set the date later than you really want to, your last working years may

be simply a matter of putting in time, barely tolerating your job (Butcher, 1978). If you retire too early, you may find yourself with too little money and nothing to do with your time. Almost a third of the people who retire have trouble adjusting (Atchley, 1976). Those people who adapt well are those who plan ahead, who are independent and realistic, who have positive attitudes, who are financially comfortable, and who have a wide range of leisure activities (Atchley, 1976; Butcher, 1978; Lowenthal, 1972; Reichard, Livson, & Petersen, 1968).

By the age of 65, most people probably have found their answers for the retirement question. But life hasn't stopped bringing new questions to answer, new problems to solve, and new lessons to learn. We have more growing to do.

Summary

The period between 55 and 65 seems to be a level time of life, with many of the psychological problems of earlier years resolved. Levinson describes it as the "culmination of middle adulthood" and the high point of middle age, but it can also be seen as the beginning of the retirement era and later life.

Middle age itself has been given many chronological boundaries— it may begin as early as age 30 and may end as late as 65, depending on which theorist is describing it. Instead of attempting to define the period chronologically, Bernice Neugarten has defined it descriptively. What she calls "middle age" is a stage between youth and old age. It is often connected with the end of the family cycle or the high point of the work cycle. It may be a time of new freedom or of gathering pressures, but it's most often a time of feeling capable and self-aware. In Neugarten's "middle age," coping techniques for dealing with the present are supplemented with techniques for dealing with the future: "body monitoring," for example, and "time restructuring" that is geared to the future rather than the past. Sexual stereotyping is dropping away, also.

Vaillant's study supports Neugarten's description; in the Grant Study, the men at 55 illustrated all of the characteristics that Neugarten theorized are typical of middle age.

Bernice and Morton Hunt have explored the positive potentials of middle adulthood in contemporary society—of a "new middle age," free from negative traditional stereotypes. They describe "new middle age" as a time for leisure, pleasure, and self-maintenance. The Hunts include the forties, fifties, and sixties in this period.

For the group now in their mid-fifties, there is a possibility of a shift occurring in age categories. Bernice Neugarten has developed a new descriptive category—the "young-old"—for people who retire early, are healthy, socially active, and often still married and still living in their own homes. The young-olds are different from the middle-aged only in the fact that they have retired.

Retirement may be a positive or a negative experience. One of the ways to make it a positive experience is to choose the retirement option that fits one's personal lifestyle the best.

Robert Atchley has described the phases that most people experience during preretirement ("remote" and "near") and postretirement ("honeymoon," "disenchantment," "reorientation," and "stability"). Knowing that these phases must be worked into our life structures helps us formulate our retirement strategies.

Each retirement option has its advantages and disadvantages. Early retirement promises extended leisure but causes both personal and social economic strain. Gradual retirement is more socially productive and less financially disruptive than early retirement, but it limits leisure in later life. Late retirement allows people to remain productive and involved throughout life, but it will eliminate having a period of leisure years for most people unless the typical life span increases dramatically. Retirement at senescence is another possibility that allows a full and productive life, but if many older people choose that option, it may have the effect of limiting job opportunities for young people.

Early planning, realistic goals, positive attitudes, stable finances, and broad leisure interests all help make retirement a positive experience and make young-old living a satisfying time of life.

Terms and Concepts to Define

ADEA _____

_____

age-irrelevant society _____

_____

body monitoring _____

_____

dependency ratio _____

_____

early retirement _____

_____

gradual retirement _____

_____

late retirement _____

_____

mandatory retirement _____

_____

new middle age _____

_____

nonretirement _____

_____

old middle age _____

_____

self-fulfilling prophecy _____

_____

to think old _____

_____

to think sick _____

_____

traditional retirement _____

_____

young-olds _____

_____

Experiences

To involve yourself with the concepts in this chapter, try these experiences described in the Appendix.

Alone
16. Retiring
17. Getting There
48. Exploring Alternatives I: Widening Your Goals

With Others
34. Middle Age
9. Social Norms
4. Autobiography

Going beyond the Text

1. *Create and evaluate your own retirement scenarios, choosing at least two options and examining their pros and cons. In addition, you should read some material about retirement planning, finding out what you could be doing in the present to ensure satisfaction in retiring.*

2. *Interview at least three retired people on their experiences in adapting to retirement. What characteristics seem to lead to positive reorientation in their cases?*

Suggested Readings

Foner, A., & Schwab, K. Aging and retirement. *Monterey, Calif.: Brooks/ Cole, 1981.*

Hunt, B., & Hunt, M. Prime time: A guide to the pleasures and opportunities of the new middle age. *New York: Stein & Day, 1974.*

Puner, M. Getting the most out of your fifties. *New York: Crown, 1977.*

9

Getting Older:
The Mid-Sixties to the Mid-Seventies

When you have finished reading this chapter you should be able to:

Discuss the dynamics of the sixties from the points of view of Bühler, Erikson, Jung, Peck, and Levinson.

List the role decrements and other losses common in the decade between ages 65 and 75.

Explain how sociogenic aging and hypokinetic disease promote self-fulfilling prophecies about unproductive aging.

Describe the four sociological adaptive strategies for positive aging discussed in the text.

All of us begin getting older the moment we're born. Aging is a lifelong process. However, by the time we're 65 the effects of aging are strong enough to be taking our lives in a new direction. In the decade between 65 and 75 we may still be in the "young-old" category—we may be vital and active, though retired—but we're moving more quickly than before toward old age. The largest part of adult life is over, and our style of life is certain to change.

More Middle Life

At 65 many options are still open for maintaining the lifestyle of the forties. We may still be working, married, active, and healthy. At 65 we may be doing most of the same things that we have done for most of our adult lives, and in the same ways. There's a possibility that we can go on in much the same patterns or in a new but similar lifestyle for another 20 years. But at some time between 65 and 75 there's a strong statistical probability that one or more of these factors may change.

Work? Few people are still working at 75. Some may have been retired for 25 years by then. Marriage? Fewer people are still married in this decade. Many lose their mates during these years and few remarry. Health? By 75 many people have some physical problems that restrict their mobility. The social world is getting a little bit smaller.

As social life diminishes, what happens to personal life? There seems to be agreement that, in the late years of life, as the social world becomes smaller, the inner world becomes progressively more important. Bühler and Jung, Erikson and Levinson, Havighurst and Neugarten all describe an important new turning inward in the sixties. However, in this new transition, when again many people turn to their inner worlds, the balance between self and environment is different.

The outer world that was so important to handle in the twenties, to master in the thirties, to manage in the forties, and to maintain in the fifties is beginning to come apart in the sixties. As pieces of it are lost—work and family roles, social status, friendship networks—the outer world may seem less relevant. What is becoming relevant now is the inner world of our personal history; everything we have been and known and done is preserved there. The coping skills that we've learned and the patterns of our personalities are clearer now. We are becoming more and more our own selves.

In coming to a new balance, with the inner self beginning to be more central and the outer environment becoming less vital, we are apparently coming to new developmental tasks whose outcomes will determine how we live our remaining years. In the earlier transitional stages of life, the tasks that must be accomplished involve either finding appropriate ways of dealing with the outer world or fitting together the inner and outer worlds in adaptive ways. In contrast, the developmental tasks of later life are basically inner tasks; they demand adjustments in thinking and feeling, and they call for honest self-evaluation, compassion, and acceptance.

In this chapter we'll look at the most universal choices, the most common losses, and the most useful adaptations in the transition to senescence and "old-old" age.

Choices

In the sixties, people begin work on the final structuring of life. The structures being completed in this period are the ones they'll live with for the rest of their lives. The work leading to this completion is noticeable on the outside: lifestyles may change obviously. In fact, the mid-sixties have been seen traditionally as the starting point for a final stage of life—and this was the traditional view even when adulthood itself was considered relatively unchanging (Erikson, 1968). The work becomes noticeable from the inside, too: a new self-concept, a sense of a completed self, seems to be forming from a combination of old personality patterns and life events and new conditions of living (Levinson, 1980). Developmental theorists have described the changes of the sixties as not only starting points but turning points, with outcomes that determine the future life span.

Jung presents the sixties as the product of his version of individuation, a time for finally reconciling our internal polarities and arriving at a state of inner balance and peace. In Jung's view, these years of resolving inner conflicts are a time of gradually reworking and changing earlier choices in our inner lives (Jung, 1971).

In Bühler's analysis of her biographical studies, she found a less gradual, more clear-cut pattern of inner decisions that lead to later directions in the outer life. Until the age of 60 or 65, Bühler says, we are involved in reassessing our pasts. We measure our accomplishments against our original goals. These reassessments will determine how we live our lives from 65 onward. Those who have at least partly achieved what they wanted to when they've reached 65 can be expected to go on striving for fulfillment in an active late life. However, if you assess your life as a failure you'll either give up in resignation or go down in defeat, depression, and despair (Bühler, 1977; Bühler & Massarik, 1968).

Erikson would go along with Bühler's description of the dynamics of this period. He describes a tension between integrity and despair that begins to emerge in the early sixties—the beginning of late adulthood. In Erikson's model, this turning point is the final outcome of all the stages that have gone before. His terms encapsulate the struggle: to the extent that "identity" has won out over "diffusion," "intimacy" has crowded out "isolation," and "generativity" has rolled over "stagnation" in earlier adult life, "integrity" will triumph over "despair" in late adulthood. If these achievements haven't been made before, now's the time to work at them (Erikson, 1968).

"Integrity," or **ego integrity,** as Erikson sometimes calls it, is more than just the completion of identity; it's also the ability to go beyond the limits of identity, to recognize that you may be more than ego. Beyond the recognition that you are someone unique lies the recognition that you are nobody special—a fully human being. Erikson's concept of "integrity" is a sense of wholeness within yourself and a feeling of connectedness with all humanity. It requires a willingness to live in the present, the here and now. It means knowing that, whatever life has been, it cannot be changed now, and must be accepted. You have lived as you have lived. Acceptance is everything.

Self-acceptance is the heart of Erikson's "integrity," and rejection of oneself is the basis of "despair." Despair is the feeling that nothing in your life has worked out, that nothing has any meaning or value. When you opt for despair in late life you are rejecting your remaining life, and you are liable to resent your inevitable death. You've lost faith in yourself and in all humanity. The struggle to reach acceptance and wisdom—to reach integrity—is the last great developmental task (Erikson, 1968).

Robert Peck, working from Erikson's model, has defined three specific issues in this developmental transition of the sixties to old age. The issues are social, physical, and psychological self-acceptance. Self-acceptance on a social level means perceiving your own values as more important than society's; it requires separating yourself from former social roles and social status and finding new satisfactions when work and parenting roles drop away. Peck calls this role-free social self-acceptance **"ego differentiation** versus work-role preoccupation" because, with self-acceptance, the ego is free to be unique, freed from work-role identity. Self-acceptance on a physical level means realizing that your body is only one of your sources of satisfaction in life; it means learning to pay less attention to your physical functions and more attention to personal creativity and interaction with other people. Peck's term for this acceptance of an aging body is **body transcendence.** The psychological level of self-acceptance Peck perceives is more demanding than the social and the physical levels. This psychological self-acceptance in old age requires recognizing that your life is only a small fragment of human history and requires identifying instead with a greater whole, which will continue after you're gone. Psychological self-acceptance depends on an acceptance of death as inevitable yet as no great loss; this is what Peck terms **ego transcendence** (1975).

To be able to think about your own death as nonthreatening, as a new experience or a further stage of growth, you probably have to reach a deep philosophical understanding of the relationships between beginnings and endings, life and death, youth and age. Levinson's speculations about the "late adult era," beginning at about 60 and ending at perhaps 85, are mostly about this sort of understanding. The developmental tasks that he identifies for these years can be seen almost as one: to integrate youth and age and to carry a new form of youthfulness into old age. When Levinson uses the word *young* he uses it in Jung's sense, as a symbol for beginnings—births, sunrises, and seeds sprouting. It evokes such qualities as energy, growth, and self-renewal. And to Levinson *old* means endings—deaths and sunsets, wisdom and completion (Levinson et al., 1978). As the young and old aspects of ourselves come into a new balance in later life, the major polarity they create is often resolved in personal images of rebirth and renewal and immortal life, a perception that gives many of us a sense of meaning for our existence. An awareness that our lives leave behind a legacy of acts and memories, which live on after we die, is part of this resolution. So is the understanding that youthfulness can be psychological (as in the associated qualities of curiosity, interest, and enthusiasm) rather than just physical (as in beauty, strength, and quickness). We can choose to integrate youth and age in later life or to live in fear of loss and sickness and death.

Loss and sickness and death can be the realities of later life, even as early as the sixties. They are the central themes of at least half of the developmental tasks that Robert Havighurst has listed as the work of late maturity. In Havighurst's view, after age 60 our responsibilities shift from contributing socially to achieving personal adaptations (Havighurst et al., 1968): adjustments to reduced strength, to less dependable health, to doing less work outside the home or none, and to having less money. Adjusting to the loss of a mate, relating more closely to friends and age mates, learning new roles (or altering old ones), and finding an environment that is comfortable—all these are additional, more personal adaptations. The first four of these tasks require changes in our personal lifestyles; the second set of four tasks is directed toward changes in our social involvements.

Making the adaptations—the positive changes—that Havighurst suggests, or even anticipating them, may require formulating whole new strategies for dealing with life. The first four can be handled fairly passively—what they call for is the ability to endure limitations and losses. But relating more closely to people and assuming new roles in society require active effort. Whether or not we make that effort may be a function of our personalities, a function of our social settings, or a function of informed choice. Gerontologists have studied the problem of adaptation to the losses of later life with mixed conclusions. It's an interesting issue, but before we explore it, let's examine the losses more specifically.

Losses

By the time you reach this point in later life, what have you got to lose? A lot. The decade between the mid-sixties and the mid-seventies may bring losses that are both social and personal, and it often brings them at close intervals. Life changes may follow each other in what seems to be a chain reaction.

The social-role losses that characterize this period are serious. These losses of a number of roles are called **role decrements,** and they may lead to insecurity and confusion. First of all, without familiar roles it's hard to know just who you are. Second, role losses lead to nonconformance with social norms, which makes it difficult to know how to act. Third, without roles or conformity to norms your status in society is unclear, so you lose your social status, too (Bengtson & Manuel, 1976). For example, when you outgrow your role as a sex object, who are you? How do you act toward people of the opposite sex? And how do you establish a new social status? But that's a minor role loss, compared to some others.

The most inevitable of the social losses that you can expect in these years is the termination of any possible paid work role. People who retire early in their fifties still have the option to go to work again or take a part-time job if retirement gets dull or money gets tight, but early retirees tend to be people who don't value their work roles highly to begin with. If you are a person who cares intensely about your work role, you will want it to last as long as possible. Yet it does end. And the end of paid work can be the end of a vital part of your life. Mandatory retirement may be upsetting even at 70, and, at that age, options for even part-time work are rare (Atchley, 1976). Loss of paid work is a significant life change.

Loss of the work role is accompanied by a loss of applicable social norms. What do lifelong workers do when they're not working? How do they structure time? How does an unwilling retiree behave? This is another life change to deal with.

Along with the loss of work there is a consequent loss of social status. Most people may regard you as having little value when you can't work, and you may accept that. There's a loss of the sense of belonging. Low self-esteem and a sense of isolation are reported by many retired people (Butcher, 1978). Loss of status is another life change. Not only is work status lost, but social status, through recognition by acquaintances and friends, is diminished. Loss of friends, through death, accelerates in these years. As you draw nearer to the average age of life expectancy for your cohort, maintaining a friendship network of your peers is harder. Friends who haven't died in earlier years are increasingly liable to die as life progresses. Funerals become the social rites of later life.

Again, with the loss of friendship roles, comes the loss of norms for social interaction. A lack of social interaction may lead back to a feeling of lost social status. Who are you important to now? Maybe the closest friend that you have left is your mate. To your mate, at least, you are a valuable person! Still, every marriage made ends either in divorce or death, and in late life death is the far more usual end. If you are a woman, the chances are high that you'll be widowed in this decade. Age 65 is close to the average age of life expectancy for men, and after 65 death rates accelerate. Widowhood for women doubles, rising from 20% in the 10 years beginning at age 64 to 42% by age 74. Men are widowed twice as fast as before also, but in much smaller numbers; in the same 10 years, widowhood for men increases from only 4% to 8% (U.S. Bureau of the Census, 1980).

As the husbands of other women in their age cohort die, married women develop a number of strategies—unconsciously and consciously—that help them adjust to possible loss. They may increasingly "body monitor" their mates, controlling their diets and encouraging them to get preventive medical care. Women often begin to show the assertiveness and independence of sex-role reversal in these years, too, and begin to replace their social dependence on their husbands with social dependence on a friendship network. Bernice Neugarten, who has described these changes, has called them **rehearsal for widowhood** (1968b).

Widowhood, for either a man or a woman, is both a personal loss and a social loss. The social roles in being husband and wife, head of the household, or a homemaker no longer apply. Therefore, norms for behavior in the social world don't apply, either. The last stage of being a family unit is finished, and so is status as part of a family. The typical outcomes of this process for men and women, however, seem to be quite different.

A woman who has accepted the social role of wife or of wife and mother as her full identity may experience a painful identity crisis when her husband dies. She may have had little or no experience in making decisions or dealing with financial matters, and she may be faced with managing her own life for the first time. Whether a woman's lifestyle in the past has been basically dependent or independent, her role becomes a new one on the death of her husband— she becomes a widow. The widow role involves participating in a friendship network that will probably include many other single women; it may involve active membership in church or other organizations. Family ties with in-laws may become weaker; family ties with blood relatives may become tighter. Men who are widowers tend to be more socially active than women who are widowed; an extra man seems to be more in demand socially than is an extra woman. The chances that a woman widowed after the age of 50 will marry again are very slight: only 5 out of 100 find a new spouse. Men are much more likely to remarry. In fact, most widowed men under the age of 70 do marry again, usually choosing women who are younger than 65 (Troll, Miller, & Atchley, 1979).

On the personal level, widowhood may be the most difficult life change. It is hard to generalize about the trauma of losing a spouse and describe it adequately. As Ledford Bischof has remarked (1976), the only real experts on widowhood are the people who have experienced it. Depending on the quality of the relationship that a couple has had in their marriage, the survivor will have to deal with a level of grief ranging from mild to intense. Grieving absorbs time and energy. And then there are all the many large and small details of life, beginning with the funeral arrangements, that the living partner must now handle, or handle differently. Needs that have been met in the marriage aren't being met any more. In their place is a universal sense of loneliness. On a scale of significant life changes that Holmes and Rahe researched (1967), it's not surprising they found the death of a spouse to be the most intensely difficult of all adjustments.

Holmes and Rahe's Life Change Scale is a product of their extensive research into the relationship between the stress caused by significant life changes and the physical illness and accidents that often accompany it. They have found that there is a significant correlation between the degree of life change one experiences and the physical breakdowns of one kind or another that occur in the following year. Gerontologists are now aware that the predictable effects of radical life change may be a source of the physical decline that begins to take its toll in the late sixties and early seventies (Weg, 1976). That is, the loss of roles, mate, or friends may itself be a catalyst for more loss, which is experienced physically.

Physical losses may be the effects of diagnosed diseases, borderline or hidden diseases, biological aging, or personal attitudes (Butler & Lewis, 1977; Kart, Metress, & Metress, 1978). Whatever their causes, for most people physical problems are more significant in the decade between the age of 65 and 75 than they have been before. Losses and limitations of body function are liable to directly affect lifestyle in later life. An estimated 20% to 25% of all people currently between 65 and 75 have to limit their major activities because of some physical problem (Neugarten, 1978).

Chronic diseases become more common in later life than they were earlier—perhaps because organ systems have had more wear and tear and more time to break down. Infections have a better chance to attack, also; the immune system works less well. And in many people the respiratory system and the cardiovascular system are less efficient. When we look at the physiology of aging later on, we'll see that there are some changes over time in every area of body function. There is not just one senescence, there are many senescences (Atchley, 1977). The biological decline that is caused by aging alone, however, is very slow; any rapid changes are more likely related to disease (Kart et al., 1978).

It is important to understand that aging and disease are two very different causes of decline. If you expect physical losses as a natural side effect of time's passing, you'll be less motivated to get regular checkups to spot and treat diseases. Biological losses caused by lack of medical attention become a question of attitude and expectation.

Two aspects of aging that are closely related to the phenomenon of self-fulfilling prophecy are sociogenic aging and hypokinetic disease. **Sociogenic aging** is aging that is literally caused by social expectations; in other words, if you expect your body to become progressively impaired, it will. A number of gerontologists take the position that many of the losses of function that we have assumed to be caused by biological aging really have social origins. People do succumb to the pervasive "act-your-age," social-clock pressure. A person who thinks that he or she should be old at 65 will act old at 65. And as we act old, we physically decline—fulfilling our own prophecy (Butler & Lewis, 1977).

Hypokinetic disease is a common result of sociogenic aging. *Hypokinetic* means too little movement. When we get no regular exercise, all of us, even the very young, experience a decline in heart rate, respiration, oxygen use, and muscle size. Three weeks of bed rest can cause such profound decline and can make even a healthy young body functionally "old" (deVries, 1975; Kart et al., 1978). Your expectations and your attitudes may quite possibly influence your biological aging. Certainly your attitudes and expectations will influence how you adapt to losses in later life.

Adaptations

Let's say that you're now 70 years old. Within the last 5 years you have retired, lost your spouse, and you have developed a major physical ailment that keeps you from driving a car. How are you going to deal with all that? Fantasize for a minute about possible solutions.

I'm not able to work at all any more. I've coped with that loss by

_____

_____

After I got over the immediate grief I experienced when my husband/wife died, I adjusted by

_____

_____

Now that I can't drive a car anymore, I have adapted by

_____

_____

How did you adapt to these changing situations? Are your coping strategies a function of your personality or of your social learning?

Whether adaptive responses are due mainly to personality or to socialization—whether they should be primarily active or passive—has been the focus of much of the research on the adjustments of later life. The developmental understanding of personality as the product of both inner shaping (your drives, goals, experiences, and ways of thinking) and outer shaping (your roles, the norms, your status, and ways of coping) suggests that adaptive growing through time can be the natural outcome of the interaction between these inner and outer forces. But growth isn't inevitable. If the inner shapers are too strong, consistent personality patterns will hold; the personality will become locked into patterns that are rigid and non-adaptive. For example, if you have a very excitable personality and refuse to modify it, when you come up against the restrictions and losses of later life, you won't adapt and the stresses caused by the inability to adapt will make you miserable. Or, if the outer shapers are too strong, the loss of one of them—perhaps a role or status level—may leave you without a personality structure you had considered your own. For example, if you have always been a "good spouse," a "good parent," or a "good worker," when you experience the "rolelessness" of later life you won't adapt, and you'll be lost. Adaptation to life is a process. It involves changes in personality that are the product of inner choices and that are fostered by stimuli from the outside—by outer-input (Lazarus, 1976).

The stage theorists, such as Erikson, Gould, Levinson, and Vaillant, take the position that the inner choices are the key to aging that is adaptive. There are a number of social theorists, however, who argue that the "outer-inputs" provide an equally useful key.

Sociologist Irving Rosow is one theorist who sees an advantage in manipulating the outer environment. He has suggested that a whole socialization process could be provided to teach more adaptive late-life aging. New social roles and norms, new rites of passage, and new segregated environments could be created. Lost roles could be replaced by new ones. Norms offering only vague guidance could be supplemented with clear-cut social expectations. Low status in a society that devalues its older members could be dealt with by removing the elders to communities that are designed to provide different social networks and, consequently, different self-images in its members (Rosow, 1974).

What's useful about the adaptive strategy Rosow has suggested?

_____

_____

_____

What are its drawbacks? _____

_____

_____

How do you feel about this adaptation for your own life? _____

_____

Another outer solution to the adaptation problem is to educate everyone in how to grow old (Birren, 1978; Fiske, 1978). Through training for life-course development in our social and educational institutions and through the emergence of positive role models for a new kind of aging, the entire population could be encouraged to upgrade and clarify its attitudes about later life.

What's useful about the strategy of education to further adaptation?

_____

_____

_____

What are the strategy's drawbacks? _____

_____

_____

How do you feel about this adaptation for your own life? _____

_____

Ronald Ramsay and René Noorbergen propose a third method of adaptation to the many concrete and symbolic losses in life. They have developed a therapeutic technique called Guided Confrontation Therapy (GTC), in which the client is guided through a process of remembering and exploring all the events, thoughts, and emotions connected with a loss, with the goal of extinguishing the negative associations to the loss and thus freeing the person to get on with life creatively (1981).

What's useful about the GTC strategy of adaptation? _____

_____

_____

What are its drawbacks? _____

_____

_____

How do you feel about this adaptation for your own life? _____

_____

_____

A fourth way to further social adaptation to the losses of later life is suggested by Bengtson and Manuel (1976): it's simply to promote positive attitudes about losses before they occur. For every loss in life there's a potential gain. For example, the loss of roles and of conformance to norms creates a new freedom from outside pressures and a new opportunity for inner development. Loss of work, friends, a mate, and even body parts can stimulate people to relate to themselves and their worlds in creative ways. People can find new ways to cope and find strength as well as finding loss in life changes. Bengtson and Manuel suggest that this adaptation can be encouraged by working for social changes that allow older people to be self-reliant and responsible, as well as by strengthening their personal coping skills.

What's useful about Bengtson and Manuel's strategy of encouraging adaptation by promoting the opportunities that losses offer in order to strengthen people's coping skills before the losses occur?

_____

_____

_____

What are the strategy's drawbacks? _____

_____

_____

How do you feel about this adaptation for your own life? _____

_____

_____

Of all the outer world solutions to the issues of aging that we've looked at, Bengtson and Manuel's is the one most closely aligned to the general developmental point of view, which suggests that the new environmental situations related to growing older require new personal orientations—positive new perceptions of experiences that you have always seen from the other side (from the point of view of youth) as being negative. This is the choice of integrity or despair, in Erikson's terms; it's continued striving for fulfillment, from Bühler's point of view; Peck would call it social, physical, and psychological self-acceptance; Levinson would see it as integration and self-renewal. In simple terms, choosing to perceive the losses and stresses of later life as positive challenges creates a further commitment to growth.

Some people commit themselves to personal growth early in life. This commitment is the central characteristic of the type of person that the psychologist Abraham Maslow has identified as "self-actualizing." **Self-actualization** means fulfilling one's fullest human potential for awareness, creativity, understanding, autonomy, and other qualities. Maslow believes that self-actualization can begin at any time in life if one's needs for physiological and interpersonal security are met and if emotional and self-esteem needs are filled (Maslow, 1971).

It is quite possible that in the freedom of later life a person may begin to self-actualize for the first time. At least this is the opinion of John McLeish, who calls self-actualizing older people **"Ulyssean adults,"** in memory of the Greek hero Ulysses. Ulysses refused to stop adventuring in his old age, and McLeish feels that this is a possibility for all of us. Getting in touch with our own creativity is the beginning of becoming **Ulyssean adults,** which also calls for opening our minds in curiosity and courage and self-exploration (McLeish, 1976). What McLeish is suggesting is strongly in line with one contemporary point of view on successful adaptation to

aging, which is called "activity theory." In the next chapter we'll explore the activity theory as well as some other theoretical points of view about positive adaptations to aging.

Summary

After age 65, aging may become a more significant factor in everyday life. Although lifestyle may not change radically in the decade between 65 and 75, there is a high statistical probability that some basic losses will occur.

Work, marriage, and physical freedom may be lost in these years, through retirement, being widowed, and physical decline. As the outer world shrinks, the inner world may expand. Jung, Bühler, Erikson, Peck, and Levinson all see this as a time for possible inner growth and integration, even in the face of apparent outer losses.

The losses that can be expected during these years are the losses of accustomed social roles, applicable norms, and status, which accompany the end of work, of marriage, and of youth. In addition there are the personal losses in the deaths of friends and mates and with the decline of physical functions. These losses may cause reactions that have been interpreted in the past as the effects of aging, but that are seen now to be symptoms of social or personal disorientation or of low-level and/or stress-related disease states.

The effect of positive or negative socialization to late-life losses must also be considered if we are to understand these years. Adaptive responses to these losses may be a function either of a person's maturity and integration of personality over time or of appropriate socialization. The developmental theorists whose work we have surveyed so far in this text emphasize the personality factor. Sociologists of aging tend to emphasize instead socialization and adaptive skills. One suggestion that has been made for fostering social adaptation is to isolate the old in structured social settings that provide new roles, norms, and status, as well as supportive social networks. Another suggestion is to reeducate society, which would encourage role models that are favorable to the old. Finally, providing guided confrontation therapy may promote the ability to adapt to past and future losses in old age.

Whatever the solutions to negative aging, it seems obvious that a personal commitment to positive aging is at the heart of any successful adaptation to later life. Growing through time may involve continuing self-actualization, in Maslow's terms, or a conscious effort to reactivate personal growth, as McLeish suggests. Both of these concepts are clearly related to the "activity theory" of adaptive aging, which will be discussed in Chapter 10.

Terms and Concepts to Define

adaptations _____

_____

body transcendence _____

_____

ego differentiation _____

_____

ego integrity _____

_____

ego transcendence _____

_____

hypokinetic disease _____

_____

rehearsal for widowhood _____

_____

role decrements _____

_____

self-actualization _____

_____

sociogenic aging _____

_____

Ulyssean adults _____

_____

Experiences

To involve yourself with the concepts in this chapter, try these experiences described in the Appendix.

Alone
17. Getting There
18. Ego Transcendence
35. Losses

With Others
19. Ageism
36. Disengagement versus Activity

Going beyond the Text

1. *Research and evaluate support systems in your community that are available to the widowed. Such services may be provided by churches and by mental-health and other organizations, public and private.*

2. *Check the* Reader's Guide to Periodical Literature, Psychological Abstracts, *and the* Social Science Index *for reports of the effects on the elderly of socially engineered retirement communities.*

Suggested Readings

Comfort, A. A good age. New York: Crown, 1976.

Dangott, L., & Kalish, R. A time to enjoy. Englewood Cliffs, N.J.: Prentice-Hall, 1979.

Ramsay, R., & Noorbergen, R. Living with loss. New York: Morrow, 1981.

10

Getting There:
The Mid-Seventies and Later

When you have finished reading this chapter you should be able to:
Describe the "old-olds."
Define ageism.
Discuss the myths about aging that lead to the stereotypes on which ageism thrives.
List the common adaptations to senescence that are made in these years.
Summarize the predictable events of the final developmental period: the terminal stage.

In the future it may become inappropriate to describe all people over 75 as experiencing their last life stage, which includes senescence and death. If, eventually, sociogenic aging and hypokenetic disease are brought to an end—along with drug and alcohol abuse, smoking, chemical pollution, and obesity—another decade or so of healthy late life may be the normal expectation. If medical research eliminates the chronic and life-threatening diseases of old age, and if life-extension research slows or reverses cellular aging, the odds for living extra years will be greater yet. Perhaps then new stages of adult development will appear. Even now, there are rare individuals who maintain their bodies and their spirits into their nineties and beyond. The annual televised International Senior Olympics gives us a glimpse of the possibilities. Although, for the majority of people living now, *75 plus* is an appropriate designation for the final stage of life, future cohorts may have developmental periods that must be further differentiated.

At the age of 75, you might be very near the end of your life, or you might still be relatively young—you could live another 20 years or more. The 75-and-over group is a fast-growing population (Butler & Lewis, 1977), and more and more of us are likely to make it to our 100th birthday. There were almost 1200 centenarians in the United States in 1979, and the numbers are increasing (U. S. Bureau of the Census, 1980).

How do you feel about this future stage of adult life? What might you be like when you're 100? Write a brief description of yourself and your life then.

_____

_____

_____

_____

_____

How does it feel? What you wrote isn't the point of this exercise; it doesn't matter if you wrote anything at all. The important thing is that, as you confront the possibility, you get in touch with your feelings about truly being old.

Some people have positive feelings about the coming of age. Most don't. If you hate the whole idea, you have plenty of company. There are a number of reasons for our discomfort about age; we have touched on them in earlier chapters. A pair of major reasons is that Western culture carries negative attitudes toward aging, and urban industrial lifestyles have exaggerated these attitudes (Cowgill & Holmes, 1972; Gruman, 1978).

Another reason we may feel negative about aging is that contemporary North American culture has been predominantly a youth culture for the past 20 years, with its attention and its commercial focus centered on the "baby-boom" cohort. As a result, mass media and advertising have exaggerated youth, causing those of us no longer young to feel devalued (Toffler, 1970). Considering adulthood to be equivalent to aging, which it is in one of our cultural myths, is part of this valuing of youth and rejection of maturity.

Perhaps the most important reason that we contemporary North Americans might confront our own old age with dread is that the stereotypes we have of aging are so threatening. We may feel that to be old is to be stripped of personal power, attractiveness, independence, strength, even sanity. Is that what you thought of when you described your old age? Pitiful, crippled, weak, helpless, senile—these attributes describe some degree of the reality for some people who are now aged, but they are only part of the reality and are in most cases wrong. Your cohort has the potential to age quite differently, because now enough is known about the aging process for informed people to avoid their worst fantasies. In your lifetime, further discoveries may allow your last years to be your best years. Those who are aged now are not so lucky.

People who are now 75 and older are people who have been caught in a cultural time lag. They didn't expect to live this long; nobody else expected so many to be still alive. They have an extra 15 or 20 years of life that weren't planned for. As a result, to be old now is to have problems that could have been headed off, had people known to anticipate them (Butler, 1975). The problems of members of the older cohorts and the solutions to those problems are issues that are important in the study of aging. They are also important in your own life.

In this chapter we will examine some of the situations connected with aging, and as we do, you may be looking your future in the eye. Two dimensions of the issues of aging are involved in the examination process: a perception of aging as it is now (because that's the origin of our information) and a projection of the way it can be in your lifetime (because that's where the information can be put to use). Rather than being a brave confrontation with the hard facts, understanding the issues of aging can be a positive experience in your own development.

Robert Butler, who was one of the most influential gerontologists of the 1970s, has said that each human life is a work of art that isn't finished until death (1975). John McLeish's concept of the "Ulyssean adult" conveys essentially the same point (1976). And in this chapter, as we follow life through to the end, we'll find that even individual human death can be understood as a further stage of growth, the final touch to the work of art that each of us creates.

This is the chapter in which we meet the "old-olds." It's about ageism, the cultural and personal bias against especially those in old age. It's about the choice of senescence or senility and the choice of disengagement or living to the end. And it's about the end itself: death. When we reach the end of the chapter, we'll have covered all of the adult life span from the perspective of chronological stages. From this first thorough overview of adulthood, beginning with early adult life and ending with old age, you'll be able to see your potential life span as a whole. Once you can do that, you'll be in a position to make each stage the best it can be (Erikson & Erikson, 1978).

The "Old-Olds"

Most people who are 75 plus fall into Neugarten's category for people in their final season of living—the **old-olds.** "Old-olds" are different from "young-olds" in having experienced more losses and more life changes. Their health and strength are declining, and they are losing their abilities to be completely independent. The "old-olds" are aged people who require social services that will meet the needs that they, as individuals, can't handle anymore: for food, transportation, and medical care. "Old-olds" often need special environments where their lives are safer and less difficult, in terms of daily function; environments such as well-designed apartment complexes, group facilities, or, eventually, nursing-care settings (Neugarten, 1978).

The majority of those who are old-old now were born early in the 20th century; many were born in rural environments. They may have experienced years of undernutrition during the Great Depression; they may have undergone traumas from four wars; they may have worked under stressful and dangerous conditions for years. Most have a lower level of education than the population as a whole and had a lower level of intellectual stimulation in early life. Women among the old-old may have played passive and dependent female roles all their lives. Both men and women are liable to have lived sedentary and unhealthy adult lifestyles. The changes of modern life have left many of them "future shocked." But not all of them. Changes in the lifestyles of the old-old are already under way. Today's young-olds—tomorrow's old-olds—are far more healthy, active, educated, and socially involved than their predecessors (Blau, 1981; Neugarten, 1978).

The "new old people," like the "new middle-aged," will influence the styles and images of aging in the future; individuals who have found positive adaptations to aging can become role models for a growing population of older people (Bengtson & Haber, 1975; Birren, 1978). Instead of being a long and empty time of waiting to die, late life can be a full time of living, for those of us who are prepared for it (Fiske, 1978; Fries & Crapo, 1981).

Ironically, the difficulty in fostering comfortable, productive late lives may be in getting people in the frames of mind to prepare themselves for it. Many people aren't willing to face their own old age even in their imagination. They would rather face that "problem" when they come to it. Old age is indeed a problem, even a bad joke, for most of us (Butler, 1978); we're all infected to some degree with **ageism.**

Ageism is prejudice against any age group, but it's expressed particularly against the aged and against aging (Butler, 1975; Gruman, 1978). It's based in a cluster of negative stereotypes that we turn against all older people, even against the older person we each harbor inside. Ageism breeds isolation and disgust, rejection and self-hatred. Fortunately, it's a prejudice that's beginning to crack. The end of the 20th century is seeing the beginning of a revolution against ageism.

There are enthusiastic activists in the struggle—for example, a group that calls itself the Gray Panthers has become a powerful pressure group. More conservative, but still active and powerful, the American Association of Retired Persons (AARP) has also lobbied for changes in conditions for older people. One of the first big victories in the battle against ageism was the legislation that moved the mandatory retirement age up to 70 in the private sector. More gains are occurring as young-olds push for social supports on many levels (Butcher, 1978).

The courts are only one ground on which the revolution against ageism is being waged. Changes in the social setting can be legislated, but changes in social attitudes can't be. Education and mass media are primary resources for attitude change. The National Institutes of Health have a special National Institute on Aging, now, and a National Advisory Council on Aging has been formed. A primary goal of these agencies is to explode the myths and negative stereotypes of aging.

Dr. Robert Butler, the Director of the National Institute on Aging, has been one of the most effective voices in the attempt to open up attitudes. Butler was one of the first people to publish research demonstrating that what most people believe about old age is not true at all.

In 1975, Butler was a member of a National Institute of Mental Health (NIMH) research team that began the first study of mentally and physically healthy older people; earlier studies had tapped only the population that was institutionalized. The subjects in this study of the healthy aged were all men, with an average age of 71. All of them lived in their communities rather than in institutions. The NIMH study was longitudinal, with 5-year and 11-year follow-ups.

What Butler and the other researchers found, to their surprise, was that none of the stereotypes of older people were supported by their data. The brains of Butler's subjects were functioning well, with no slowdown of cerebral blood flow. Performance on cognitive tests was good, although the subjects seemed to need more time to think than do younger people. The tests indicated clear interconnections between good health, being active, and positive thinking. In the follow-ups, the men who lived longest were found to be nonsmokers, with less arteriosclerosis and more positive attitudes than those who died during the span of the study. The survivors were the people who lived well-planned, socially integrated lives (Butler, 1968).

That study was one of many to suggest recently that the stereotypes of ageism are seriously misleading overgeneralizations. Butler and others have come to describe being old as a social role, which we may or may not choose to play (Butler & Lewis, 1977; Comfort, 1978). The role consists of a number of characteristics that are based on cultural myths. One such myth is that chronology controls aging. A second myth is that to be old is to be senile. A third common myth is that the old are inactive and tranquil. The myth that to be old is to be unproductive and the myth that the old resist change also are part of the old-age role. None of these beliefs is supported by research. In fact, research suggests that many of the negative factors of later life exaggerated by the myths can be prevented. If they're not prevented, they may be reversible. Activity and integration rather than withdrawal may be the images of aging of the future (Atchley, 1977; Butler, 1978; Erikson & Erikson, 1978; Fries & Crapo, 1981).

Where did the myths come from? Ironically, the field of gerontology was responsible for some of them. The myths were embodied in a concept called *disengagement*, which suggests that the final developmental task of the last years of life is to withdraw from active living in order to get ready to die.

Living to the End

In 1961, a team of gerontologists created the **disengagement theory** to describe the withdrawals from active life that are so common in the stereotypes of ageism. Disengagement theory holds that older people progressively withdraw from society, stop caring about things and people, and become increasingly self-concerned as a natural outcome of aging. The theory also holds that society withdraws progressively from older people as a mutual part of the same process (Cumming & Henry, 1961). A positive adaptation to old age, from this point of view, is to stop actively participating in the world long before you die.

Some aspects of disengagement theory are related to the developmental trend toward increased self-awareness and autonomy. Psychologists have noticed a turning inward that begins as early as the forties and increases in the sixties. Sociologists have noted that social withdrawal often goes along with retirement. These disengagements from the outer world may be productive for some people, but for others disengaging may be neither natural nor adaptive.

Disengagement may be positive or negative, depending on the person and the situation. To give up attachment to material things and dependence on human relationships and to focus on transcendent and eternal values is often presented as the highest form of human wisdom. Disengaging to some degree is part of becoming wiser at any age; for the wise, it is easy to be nonattached. The rest of us—the vast majority—feel a need for activity and affection and familiar places and things. To be forced to disengage from the things we care about is to be pushed into hypokinetic disease and living death.

In a way, disengagement theory was essential to a more contemporary view of aging, because it stimulated the research that eventually proved the theory to be inappropriate in many cases (Mussen, Conger, Kagan, & Geiwitz, 1979). The research that was designed to support disengagement as the most productive strategy for aging didn't support it. In fact, the results have been either mixed or supportive of the need for activity, not for disengagement, in later life. The Kansas City Studies, for example, indicated that some people do disengage; but disengagement often was correlated with low morale. Some of the data seemed to support both disengagement and its opposite—activity theory—according to the personality types of the subjects. People who used activity as a defense against depression were better off active; people who were passive to start with were comfortable disengaging; people who had integrated personalities could choose whatever suited their condition. A single pattern for everyone obviously isn't suitable (Havighurst et al., 1968; Neugarten, 1972).

Rather than a developmental task of late life, disengaging may be a strategy that can be appropriate in any period. As life situations change you may choose to drop pieces of your former life, roles that are better left behind. Changes in energy and health may lead to some kinds of letting go; changes in attitudes and self-perceptions may lead to others. You may choose to disengage selectively from aspects of your previous lifestyle. Disengagement may be adaptive and may create life satisfaction for passive or self-protective people, or it may be a natural response to the stresses and losses of later life, but it is not a universal solution to the difficulties of aging (Lowenthal, Thurnher, & Chiriboga, 1977). In fact the contrary may be true; current research suggests that a high level of physical activity and social integration combined with controlled nutrition can result in healthy and active later life. This is the point of view called **activity theory** (Atchley, 1977; Butler, 1978; Luce, 1980).

Can we stay relatively healthy and young as we live out the farthest reaches of our lives? Contemporary answers to that question all begin with "It depends." It depends on the level of physical fitness that we maintain during our lifetimes, especially in maturity. It depends on our individual genetic programs for aging. It depends on the degree to which we avoid both infectious and chronic diseases. It depends on planning ahead for the styles of life that best suit the last years of our lifetimes. Remember that, after all, the effects of biological aging are only loosely related to increasing age. Because of variability and the factors that cause the variability in aging, within limits, senescent changes over time are not inevitable. This is the concept of **plasticity of aging:** until the last limits of life are reached, the effects of aging can be mitigated to permit vital living (Fries & Crapo, 1981). Certainly, if we are going to live well in late life, we need to inform ourselves about how we should live in the meantime.

In the Meantime

Only 5% of the people over 65 in America are living in institutions for the elderly, which leaves 95% living as part of their communities most of the time (Butler, 1978). But as chronological age increases, physical fitness does decline, and the genetic factors that control the onset of senescence can be seen to take effect. The percentages of people who need institutional care or some other special setting increase. It's been estimated that as many as 25% of the elderly spend some time in nursing homes or other long-term care facilities. Although not many people take up residence in institutions, almost a quarter of the aged population dies in institutions (Kastenbaum & Candy, 1973). There may be better places in which to end our lives. Unless an appropriate setting for late life is planned ahead of time, living conditions during the last years can be a problem. The big consideration is finding an environment in which it is possible to maintain self-respect and have the best chance of living a good life. What are the options?

There are three typical solutions to the problem of finding a non-institutional setting for late life. The most satisfactory choice seems to be to live in the community as long as possible, relying on community day-care or support systems; the other two alternatives are to either move in with family members or to find an environment that's been specially modified for older people, allowing autonomous life with access to services.

The first solution has some important benefits: living in your own place, among your own things, limits the life changes that you experience in later years. Your setting remains a familiar one. There is no loss of freedom; on your own, you can still function as an autonomous adult, with your own lifestyle. There is no change in social network, either, if you have friends and acquaintances in the community to enrich your social life. Because community living is such an advantageous solution, many communities that are sensitive to the needs of older people supply some of the requirements basic to maintaining life there: food services, transportation, recreation, and home medical care. These provisions can make it possible for an older person to manage an autonomous lifestyle for years. Living this way seems to be the best choice for most people, but it does have limitations.

The biggest limitation on maintaining life within the community is financial. To be an older person in the present is to be a poor person, in many cases. Because of inadequate financial planning in the past and rising economic inflation in the present, a majority of the elderly have a hard time making ends meet. Older people are often forced to find low-rent housing in dangerous neighborhoods. They sometimes can't afford to buy nutritious food, or to heat their homes adequately, or to get good medical care. Transportation and recreation may become too expensive to even consider, if the community doesn't provide them. Poverty, like disease and loss, creates serious problems for our aged people (Butler, 1975).

Disease and loss, however, are problems for almost everybody in the late years, poor or not. Living in the community becomes more difficult with the passage of time, as older people gradually experience physical decline. The daily tasks of keeping a home may become too demanding to manage. Eventually, many people have to accept a new condition of dependency.

Late-life dependency is most often taken care of by family, especially when money is a limitation. As an older person, you may have the option of getting rid of most of your possessions and moving into the home of one of your children—a solution that is more likely (according to the statistics) if you have a daughter and even more likely if she's unmarried (Troll et al., 1979). In 1975, 98% of American women over the age of 80 and 72% of the men either lived with one of their children or lived within 10 minutes travel time of one of their children's homes (Atchley, 1977). A small percentage of the elderly live with younger brothers or sisters—you could do that, perhaps, if you're sufficiently compatible with one of your siblings. However, in many cases such family solutions turn out to be unfortunate for everyone involved. Parent-child power struggles and conflicts from the past may be reactivated (Knopf, 1975), new parent-child role reversals are often resented on both sides (Atchley, 1977), and complications in new roles in which children become the "parents" and a parent becomes the "child" may disrupt the family balance (Troll et al., 1979). Americans value independence very highly and resent its loss, which often makes late-life dependency painful for everyone involved, as recent media articles on "parent abuse"—the mistreatment of parents by their children, the corollary of child abuse—remind us.

A far more appropriate setting for the last years of life is beginning to fill the wide gap between autonomy and dependency: the planned environment. High-rise apartments, clusters of cottages, and living complexes in various other configurations are the new environments for the aged. Physically safe settings that offer privacy but also quick and easy access to medical care, social support, food service and recreation are becoming more common as a way to meet the needs of later life. Although the first settings of this kind have been expensive, as they become part of the social programs for the aged created by communities, churches, unions, and other organizations, they should become less expensive and more available to everyone. As supportive settings for late life, they seem to offer maximum opportunity to stay active and socially integrated in the years of senescence. If senescence progresses to the point that individuals need continuous care, institutionalization still becomes a necessity, in most cases. Aged persons then must place themselves in a hospital or nursing home or be placed there by others. Of these two possibilities, voluntary admission promotes more positive morale, but even the voluntary decision to "give up" may create a morale problem. In a study of three groups of old people—one group on a waiting list for an institution, one already institutionalized, and one still living in the community—the people on the waiting list were more often anxious and depressed than those already living in the extended-care facility (Tobin & Lieberman, 1976). Adaptation to a new "family" grouping in small and responsive institutions with little staff turnover may be a positive and satisfying experience in the last stage of life; isolation in large and impersonal institutions, on the other hand, may increase disability and speed senescent changes.

Senescence, like adolescence, is a phase of life that dramatically affects our inner and outer worlds. Like adolescence, it's a physical process that has social and psychological implications. Adolescence is the passage into adult life; senescence is the passage beyond adulthood. Senescence is the final stage of life. It's a combination of deteriorative biological processes that accelerate in later life. It occurs in people of varying chronological ages, and it varies in both the parts of the body it affects and in its timing once the stage has begun. The rate of your senescence will be influenced by a number of factors: your genetic inheritance, the environments you have lived and worked in, the degree of physical fitness you have maintained, the kinds of food you have eaten during your life, your responses to stress, the medical care that you've received, your cohort experience, and the results of life-extension research that are made available to you. All of these contribute to the pace and timing of your biological lifetime (Fries & Crapo, 1981; Kalish, 1975).

There is an important distinction between senescent decline and senility. *Senility* is a word that is often associated with the effects of aging, but it is a condition that is very different from senescence. Senescence is not a disease; senility is. At least, some forms of senility are disease related.

Senility is a catch-all term that has been used to label any cognitive or emotional disorder in the aged. It's a label that has often been used inaccurately and destructively, because it confuses treatable and reversible problems with untreatable and irreversible problems. The treatable and curable problems that are often labeled *senility* in older people are episodes of depression, anxiety, confusion, or forgetfulness. They may be caused by eating habits that don't supply adequate nutrition, drug doses that are too high for a slowing body, too many life changes in too short a time, too much alcohol, or shock from an illness, such as congestive heart failure. If these causes are identified as the source of a person's "senility," they can be taken care of appropriately. If they're not, the disorder may never be reversed (Butler, 1978).

In addition to the reversible and treatable problems the elderly may suffer, there are also forms of mental disorder that can't be cured. The irreversible and permanent disorientations of later life have symptoms similar to those of the forms that can be helped, but the causes are very different. Permanent mental disorders in later life are most often caused by organic brain syndromes: about 5% of the very old suffer from these organic conditions, which are caused by insufficient blood and oxygen supply to the brain because of arteriosclerosis or deterioration of brain cells, called Altzheimer's Syndrome, recently identified as a disease state that is most likely a slow-virus infection (see Chapter 11). These conditions require institutionalization or constant care (Torack, 1981; USDHEW, 1978).

However, most of late life, for most people, can be a good time of life. The potential is there, but it's not always fulfilled.

In exploring the social forces in later life, Atchley has explored some of the possible adaptations to aging. The less life enhancing adaptations to aging involve escape from the reality of being aged. Suicide, for instance, is the ultimately effective escape. The rate of suicide is extremely high among those in their later years, especially among white males. The number of suicides in all groups increases dramatically after the age of 75. Indirect forms of suicide, such as drug and alcohol abuse, are other ways in which those older people who don't find any other way of adapting manage to numb their pain (Atchley, 1977).

More life-enriching ways to be old involve modifying lifestyles to fit new life conditions. Maintaining involvement in work or family to the end is one form of adaptation; another approach is minimizing involvement, drawing into a "loner" or "closed couple" style that is satisfying. Living fully is the best possible adaptation, says Atchley; whatever that means for each of us, it seems to be a valuable goal. Satisfaction in late life is clearly correlated with positive attitudes, high self-esteem, courage, energy, and a sense of accomplishment (Atchley, 1977). However, this form of adaptation may call for modifications in personality to fit the situation.

Can a passive or a negative person go through positive changes in late life? Can personality still change? There's evidence that it does (Butler & Lewis, 1977). A number of characteristics emerge in people in old age that may never have surfaced before. Butler has described some of the possible changes in orientation in later years. For example, older people often come to value the quality of their time, rather than its quantity. They may develop a sense of the life cycle unfolding. And an orientation toward review and reinterpretation of life termed **reminiscence** may develop. This "life review" behavior in later years has such positive effects that it is often used in therapy with older people. A desire to leave behind a legacy of some kind is also common in these years, often as the outcome of a new orientation toward giving up personal power. There may be a change toward a feeling of consummation and fulfillment, and a sense of even further capacity for personal growth may also emerge. The last item may surprise you. Although late life is not ordinarily perceived as a time for growing, some people are indeed deeply committed to continuing their growth until the end (Butler & Lewis, 1977).

The Terminal Stage

Life can end at any age; in a sense, living itself is terminal. In this and the preceding chapters that have traced the chronological stages of life, the assumption has been that you'll live out your full life course and die of old age, although for many of us that's inaccurate. Life can end at any time. It's hard to truly deal with that during most of our life span. It may get a little more believable as we get older.

After dealing in childhood with personal concepts of death that may be confused and anxious, most people tend to assume unconsciously in their adolescent and early adult years that they're immortal. Deaths, when they occur, are experienced as shocks, as mistakes. Intellectually, we know that death exists, but our comprehension of that seems to stay fairly limited in early life. By the forties, death becomes more threatening. Much of what contributes to mid-life crises is related to realistically confronting the facts of aging and death at a deep emotional level. In the fifties and sixties, death is more common in most people's lives, and more expected. In the seventies and eighties, people's expectations of death seem to become tinged with acceptance.

Fear of death diminishes in many but not all older people, and it seems to be related to their experiences in the course of life. Over the years, we are socialized to the fact of our own deaths as we experience the deaths of other people. Our own deaths become gradually more expected, as we live out the later years of life; when many of our peers are dead and we're still living, we become more aware that our time also will soon be up. A sense of limitations on our future and a sense of diminishing ego importance seem to also make death a little less threatening. Religious convictions may or may not be a help; a review of the relevant research suggests that strong belief or disbelief is comforting, while half-hearted religion is not (Kalish, 1976).

Still, no matter when we die, the end of life is difficult to deal with. Alive, it's hard to imagine being not alive (Imara, 1975). So much is lost in dying. Death is the end of our physical experiences, our social interactions, our psychological self, our legal existence, and our personal growth. Yet even the act of dying holds the possibility of personal development (Imara, 1975; Kart, Metress, & Metress, 1978; Kübler-Ross, 1974). Dying can be the furthest stage of human growth. At least that's the belief of a number of specialists in the psychology of dying, a field called **thanatology.**

In the 1960s Elizabeth Kübler-Ross, a psychiatrist at the University of Chicago, became a leader in the movement to "repossess" dying as a human experience. Her work in the psychology of death and dying began in 1969, with interviews of over 200 dying patients. In their conversations, she identified a pattern of changing attitudes toward death that suggested five progressive stages of acceptance (Kübler-Ross, 1975). The stages that she identified have become widely accepted, although she warns that there are individual differences and that each person has a unique experience in facing death.

The stages of emotional development that often precede dying may begin with denial, based in shock and rejection of the possibility of death. As denial weakens and acceptance strengthens, the dying person may enter a stage of anger and frustration, often directed at other people as well as at death. Often, when anger has been ventilated, the person goes through a bargaining stage, in which there is an intensive search to find a way out, to make some kind of deal that will prolong living. The patient who recognizes that death is inevitable may experience a stage of depression, grief, or both that needs to be expressed and communicated. The final stage is a state of peace and acceptance. These stages may occur in any order, and movement back and forth is usual (Kübler-Ross, 1975). Sometimes people stay in one stage to the end. It is possible to help a dying person move toward acceptance, however (Imara, 1975; Levine, 1982).

It is also possible to be hurtful rather than helpful by misusing the stage approach to dying. There are many individual differences in attitudes toward death, and attempts by medical personnel or friends and relatives to push a dying person through the stages constitute misuse. Support for the terminally ill person consists in being open to his-her expression of feelings and being accepting of the feelings expressed. If the person is more comfortable with denial of death, acceptance should not be forced (Kübler-Ross, 1975).

Acceptance is probably an important stage to reach, if a good death is going to be a final time of growing in a good life. A good death is probably different for each one of us, though. Our attitudes toward what we feel is an appropriate way to die and be "put to rest" are shaped by ethnic background, religion, social class, cohort, and individual personality. On any of the issues associated with death and dying, a diversity of attitudes is possible. If we don't communicate our own preferences in these matters, the decisions will be left to others who may not share our values. Where one should die—at home, in a hospital, or in some other facility for the dying—is an issue. The degree of control over death that should be allowed—euthanasia, limited life support, heroic measures, or just plain waiting for death—is a controversy. And the disposal of the body—cremation, expensive or simple burial, donation of the body for transplants—also must be determined. What constitutes a good death to each of us requires some thought. Consider it for a minute.

When would you want to die? _____

_____

Would your "good death" be slow and anticipated, or quick and painless? How long a dying process would be your ideal?

_____

_____

Would you want to have a personal choice in the time and the place and the conditions of your death?

_____

_____

Where would you want to die? _____

_____

Who would you want with you? _____

_____

What would enable you to accept your death? _____

_____

Responding to these questions may have been an uncomfortable experience, but it is not without value. A basic premise of the psychology of death and dying is that confronting death allows us to fully experience life and to experience our own deaths in a creative way. Although there is much about death that we can't control, we can control the quality. To make death the best possible end to life, there are many things that can be done.

The preceding questions suggest that you have a number of possible choices about your death and that these choices can make a difference. In more and more cases, the choices that do make a difference can be made. Recent legislation in some states has provided the option for terminal patients of signing a **living will**—legal permission for health-care personnel to withhold or withdraw life-sustaining medical care. Like the experience of childbirth, the experience of dying is being reclaimed as a human rather than a medical procedure. More people are choosing to consciously experience their own dying, to learn to let go of attachments to living and to use meditative techniques to control terminal pain (Ram Dass, 1977). Centers called hospices and centers for conscious dying, in which a terminal patient can experience an appropriate death in a supportive environment, are becoming more widespread (Ram Dass, 1977; Saunders, 1967). Under the new conditions of dying, life can be sustained long enough for a terminal patient to deal with unfinished questions, before being allowed to die naturally. We have some degree of control over several factors in the death process, and that degree is increasing.

Time is an important factor in dying. The time spent in the death process is called the **trajectory of dying.** Awareness of certain death is the beginning of the trajectory. A person with a long, slow trajectory has time to work through concepts and feelings about terminating life and perhaps to come to the acceptance of death as a relief. There is time to deal with the last details of life and to set affairs in order. A quick trajectory—a sudden death—may leave much unfinished business behind. Time may be too short for reaching resolution (Pattison, 1977).

Place is another important factor in death. The place of one's death may be determined randomly, but in America life often ends in modern, impersonal hospital surroundings. However, as thanatologists have raised the national consciousness about the depersonalized death experience that modern hospital settings impose, new options in place of death have been made possible. A person may choose to die at home or in a hospice or center for conscious dying maintained by a religious group, experiencing the end of life in a warm and supportive place.

People are a third factor in a good death. Just as people who care about us help us create a good life, they can help us experience a good death. In the final social role, that of "dying person," interactions with other people are crucial. Appropriate and caring social and emotional support may allow a fuller awareness and a more self-sufficient acceptance of the last big life experience. Family members, friends, religious professionals, and health professionals trained in thanatology can grow with us, at the end.

Courses in death and dying have become more widespread in colleges and universities, and, because of their influence, more medical and lay personnel are better equipped to support human rather than institutional death. The tendency in urban industrialized society to depersonalize dying, to deal with it in technical language, and to handle it as much as possible with sophisticated technology is slowly giving way to a more genuine and compassionate acceptance of death as a natural end to life. This attitude is as helpful to the living as it is to the dying.

The bereaved survivors are also supported and helped to work through acceptance of loss by professional thanatologists and non-professionals who recognize that grief work is an essential in adaptation to loss. Therapies for dealing with extreme reactions to death have been developed to help fully work it through. For example, there are "re-grief" therapy in which grief work is reexperienced (Volkan, 1972); "re-creating the past" in order to release it (Arkin and Battin, 1975); and "grief confrontation therapy" (Ramsay & Noorbergen, 1981). For less extreme mourning reactions, self-help groups such as "Theos" and "Widow to Widow" are available in many communities. Talking about death openly and coping with loss creatively are finally becoming acceptable ways of dealing with the end of life.

Life ends with the termination of our biological, social, and psychological processes in this world. Biological death occurs when the electrical activity in the brain stops and the body systems cease their functions. Social death can come before or after biological death; it happens when social interactions no longer take place, when conversation and interaction with others end. Psychological death occurs when awareness of experiencing terminates. The time of psychological death has become an open question in recent years: interviews with people who have been apparently biologically dead but have recovered suggest that awareness of psychological experiencing continues after vital signs have ceased (Sabom, 1981). When the psychological, social, and biological processes do end, however, our growing through time—on this plane of experience, at least—is done.

Summary

The last stage of life is often perceived negatively in American culture. Modernization, industrialism, contemporary youth-culture attitudes, and a traditional bad stereotype of late life are all responsible for this perception.

People in their last years fall into Neugarten's "old-old" category. Contemporary old-olds are badly in need of social services; today's planning may make the lives of tomorrow's old-olds less difficult.

Prejudice against the old and the process of aging is called *ageism*, and, like all prejudices against minority and disadvantaged groups, it is currently under attack—legally and socially.

Current research on the characteristics of healthy people in late adulthood has indicated that the stereotypes of ageism are based mostly on myths. The myths of chronological aging, senility, disengagement, and the alleged uselessness of the aged are being dispelled, although they are still capable of creating self-fulfilling prophecies.

Although in advanced age people may withdraw selectively from the social world and focus more strongly on their inner lives, social integration and physical activity have been identified as the most successful adaptations for the elderly.

Only 5% of the aged population in America is institutionalized, but other, more ideal living conditions for late life are still in the early stages of development. Community living is often too expensive and too stressful for older people; living with children may be less expensive, but it's often quite stressful, too. "Planned environments" seem to be a far more functional solution to the living problems of late life, and many organizations are sponsoring them as settings for the declining years.

The decline of senescence in late life is inevitable. The rate of senescence is affected by life experiences and genetic factors. The dreaded psychological aspect of senescence—mental disorder, usually called *senility*—has recently been reappraised, and many types of it have been found to be reversible. Only a small percentage of the aged population experiences irreversible brain disorders.

Adaptations to senescence vary: "escape," lifestyle and personality changes, and recommitment to personal growth are all possible ways to adjustment. And older people are apparently quite capable of achieving what in other times has been called *wisdom*, before they die.

Acceptance of death, no matter when in the life span it occurs, requires a further stage of personal growth. Contemporary research in the field of thanatology has generated a new understanding of the death process as well as new environments and supports for the dying.

Terms and Concepts to Define

activity theory _____

_____

ageism _____

_____

disengagement theory _____

_____

living will _____

_____

old-olds _____

_____

plasticity of aging _____

_____

reminiscence _____

_____

senility _____

_____

thanatology _____

_____

trajectory of dying _____

_____

Experiences

To involve yourself with the concepts in this chapter, try these experiences described in the Appendix.

Alone
18. Ego Transcendence
20. Biological Aging
49. Exploring Alternatives II

With Others
36. Disengagement versus Activity
28. Seasons
19. Ageism

Going beyond the Text

1. *Visit several institutions for the elderly in your community and evaluate them in terms of size, activities, individualized care, and general attitude toward residents.*

2. *Find out what hospice facilities or other support situations exist for the dying in the hospitals in your community.*

Suggested Readings

Kastenbaum, R. Growing old: The years of fulfillment. *New York: Harper & Row, 1979.*

Levine, S. Who dies?: An investigation of conscious living and conscious dying. *New York: Anchor Press/Doubleday, 1982.*

Rattison, E. M. The experience of dying. *Englewood Cliffs, N.J.: Prentice-Hall, 1977.*

PART FOUR

A Perspective: Developmental Processes

Part Four is a second thorough survey of the life course, this time from the point of view of individual processes—processes that are biological, social, and psychological. Process perspectives emphasize the continuity of changes, presenting development as a continuous unfolding rather than as a series of age stages. In everyday life, in which individual differences and cohort changes make each life history unique, process points of view are perhaps more useful than age-linked guidelines.

11

Life Cycles: Biochanges over Time

When you have finished reading this chapter you should be able to:

List the factors that may affect the timing of any person's biological clock.

Discuss why sorting out the effects of biological aging from the effects of other changes that occur over time is difficult.

State the three criteria for identifying changes as the effects of biological development.

Discuss the maxim "If you don't use them, you lose them" as it relates to body function.

Describe the effects of aging on the neurosensory, cardiovascular, respiratory, skeletomuscular, endocrine, and immune systems.

One point of view on adult development is the perspective of development as essentially a biological process. The biochanges of adult life—completion of maturation in the early adult years, slow aging over the long middle years, and final senescence in late life, clearly underlie the social and psychological processes that are common to most adults. For example, the social roles that involve working, being a mate, being a parent, and other social functions are attained through maturation, are ripened in the aging process, and are released during senescence. Psychological adaptations of the personality to new situations that maturation, aging, and senescence bring create the potential of growing psychologically, also. To become aware of the powerful role of biology in all the processes of adult growth and change, all we need to do is imagine a situation in which no biological changes would occur after the age of 25, in a normal human life span of, say, 80 years.

If you experienced no changes in physical appearance, reproductive ability, physical strength, or endurance after the age of 25, how might that affect your life course in the areas of education, relationships, parenting, recreation, economics, and life planning?

_____

_____

_____

_____

You might have responded to that question in many ways; and almost any answer would reflect overwhelming variations from adult development as we know it. There are researchers in the field of life extension who believe that biologically unchanging adult life may become a real possibility in the imaginable future. For our purpose, however, the realities of the present are more relevant. We will examine the realities of biological change, but first we will review some basic biological considerations.

Biological Considerations

In Chapter 4 several concepts were introduced that are important to keep in mind as we survey the biological processes of the life course. These concepts help to remind us that biological processes vary significantly as a function of the person in whom they occur.

The first concept we need to recall is the clear distinctions made among the biological changes of maturation, aging, and senescence. As a biological system, organ, or tissue reaches its peak of development, it becomes mature; as it begins a gradual decline in efficiency, it is aging; and as it declines rapidly in the last years of life, it is senescent. Aging begins very early in some biological systems: the visual and respiration processes are already aging by mid-adolescence. Senescence begins very late in most systems, unless disease induces it prematurely. (Comfort, 1978).

The notion that the three types of biological change differ from each other brings us to a second central concept of biochange—that individual rates of maturation, aging, and senescence are controlled by an internal biological clock. Genetic inheritance, physiological health or disease, environmental stress, lifestyle choices, and personality patterns all seem to be components of the biological clockworks that determine individual biochanges and their timing.

Individual biological change and its extreme variability are at the core of the third concept: *functional age*. Functional age is a description of aging in terms of the efficiency of a person's functioning rather than in terms of years lived. People who are of the same chronological age may be years apart in terms of how well their bodies function. And various systems, organs, tissues, and cells within the same person may be of different functional ages. Biological processes are highly individualized.

Taken together these concepts allow an important understanding about the changes over time in adult bodies: each person's biological clock times his or her functional age—the rate of maturation, aging, and senescence. The biological life course is universal: all people grow, mature, and, if they live long enough, reach senescence. But we each do it in our own way, contrary to the common myths and stereotypes.

Until recently, biological changes usually have been considered to be correlated with chronology. Most gerontologists supported this idea, researching and establishing "average" ages for age changes. In the 1960s, however, such researchers as James Birren, Robert Butler, and Alex Comfort began to turn around the thinking in their profession in order to emphasize the realities: adults develop at different rates and in different ways, and many of the processes that were thought to be the effects of aging are really the effects of disease.

What biologists term *age* is, in fact, what social scientists call *functional age*. As people mature, chronology becomes less and less a significant determinant of the aging process. Biologically speaking, chronological age is a useful indicator of maturation only in prenatal life and in the early years of childhood. The size and development of a fetus are closely time related, and the skills and capabilities of a small child are fairly correlated with age. But, by puberty, chronological age begins to be more questionable as an index of development. There is a six- to seven-year "normal" time span during which puberty can begin (Katchadourian, 1976). The classic illustration of this fact is a classroom full of early adolescents: 14-year-olds can be apparently undeveloped little girls and boys, obviously developing adolescents, or seemingly full-grown men and women. The correlations between chronological age and maturation after puberty weaken progressively, and full biological maturation of any bodily system may occur at any time between the ages of 20 and 35, with no clear indicator of when it has taken place (Timiras, 1972).

When living things stop growing, they begin to die—except in the case of some very simple, one-celled life forms. And when human systems arrive at full maturity, they begin to age. We all mature at different rates as the result of the interaction of our genetic programming and our environment—the two broad determiners of our biological clocks. We decline at different rates for the same reason. Racial, national, and family patterns of aging apparently have some basis in our genetic codes, but these patterns of aging may be strongly modified by the environmental factors of geographical location, social setting, level of physical activity, quality of nutrition, availability of medical care, and the degree of environmental stress mentioned earlier. The bottom line on all these influences on our individual rate of biological change over time is that we age when we age, and in our own special ways (Atchley, 1977; Finch & Hayflick, 1977; Kart et al., 1978).

Chronology is even less useful in the assessment of aging than it is in assessing maturation. The 7-year variability in puberty mentioned above, for example, becomes at least a 10-year variability by the time of menopause (Kart et al., 1978). Differences in individual biological function create extreme individual differences in the later years of life.

Assessment of age in terms of functional age is actually a widespread, if often unconscious, concept. You probably rely on functional indicators most of the time to assess the ages of people you meet, if you don't have any other information. When you assess a person's age, how much do you rely on appearance? behavior? attitudes? performance? How much of your perception of age depends on skin texture, facial expression, posture, speed of movement, accuracy of response, strength, or endurance? These are all characteristics of functional age that we unconsciously or consciously consider as we assess age in others. More sophisticated measures are used by physiologists to test functional levels of performance, but the criteria assessed are the same (Sheppard & Rix, 1977).

Suppose you were to assess a person's age. In the list that follows, jot down a percentage on each line to indicate how much of your assessment would depend on each of the items. (Remember that your answers shouldn't exceed 100%.)

texture of skin	_____	facial expression	_____
posture	_____	quickness of movement	_____
accuracy of response	_____	strength	_____
endurance	_____	attitudes expressed	_____
dress and style	_____		

Even within the framework of functional age, there are a number of difficulties in sorting out the actual effects of biological aging in adult life. It is very difficult to separate changes in efficiency of functioning that are caused by disease from changes due to aging. It's difficult to tell whether a biological change is caused by disuse (which results in hypokinetic disease) or by aging. It's often difficult to determine whether changes pinpointed by research are caused by the cohort effect in cross-sectional studies, or by genetic characteristics in the subjects of longitudinal studies. And it's also difficult to decide which research findings are valid, because results of studies often contradict each other (DeVries, 1975; Finch & Hayflick, 1977; Weg, 1976).

Having recognized all these biological considerations, we can now review the findings about the biological changes that have occurred over time in cohorts from the past. A loose relationship between chronological age and changes in the functioning of body systems and organs has been established; we will refer to it, but keep in mind that individual variability is the rule.

Biological Development

Biological development encompasses the processes of maturing, aging, and senescing; it includes growth and decline; it is the natural unfolding of the human body in time. The real effects of biological development, ruling out disease, are the effects that are universal, progressive, and predictable (Finch & Hayflick, 1977).

Some general changes that fit these criteria have been identified. For example, biological growth progresses over time quite predictably in most people. Between the ages of 25 and 30, most of your systems and organs are full grown, but some—like the ears and nose—will keep on growing until you die. Your skull will grow cumulatively thicker until your eighties; and the lenses of your eyes also are thickening as time goes by. Biological shrinking, even though it is the opposite of growth, is equally universal, progressive, and predictable. Cells shrink; as a result, tissues shrink; and it follows that organs get smaller, too. Skin cells, muscle cells, bone cells, and nerve cells all may grow measurably smaller—but the changes are so small that in most cases they aren't important (Finch & Hayflick, 1977). In contrast, the universal, progressive, and predictable changes that result from wear and tear are much more noticeable. Skin wears out from continuous movement and from exposure to sun and weather, and so it gets wrinkled. Cartilage wears out from heavy use and loses its stretch, so backs and knees and joints generally stiffen progressively (Finch & Hayflick, 1977). Organs get worn out, too, from use and abuse (Kart et al., 1978). Growth, shrinkage, and wear and tear are the essential changes of adult development.

Changes that occur in the body at any one level—at the systems level, the organ level, or the cellular level—eventually affect other body parts. The systems of the body—the nervous system, cardiovascular system, respiratory system, skeletal and muscular system, digestive system, excretory system, immune system, and endocrine system—are all interrelated and interdependent. So faltering systems, the worn-down organs that form the systems, or diminishing cells in the organs inevitably lead to inefficient functioning of the whole.

In spite of the interdependence of the body's systems, they mature and decline at varying rates. Everybody is aware that by the age of 25 most of us have biologically mature bodies; all the systems are working nearly at their peaks. Most people aren't aware that long before 25 some of our systems may have already begun the very long, very slow decline that will continue through our years of maturity. It is a decline that won't become rapid or obvious until late adulthood.

Our interrelated body systems are made up of interrelating organs. Organs also develop and peak and decline at different rates. When an organ is damaged or wears out, it naturally affects the function of its system. When the system declines in its function it affects the function of the other organs within the system; it also changes the performance of all other systems.

Naturally, each of the body's systems is essential to the health of the body overall. However, the health of some systems is more integral than the health of other systems to survival. One, the nervous system, keeps all the others going.

Neurosensory Development

The brain, the nervous system, and the sensory organs make up the **neurosensory system,** one of the first body systems to mature. Its central organ is the brain, which is 90% complete in size by the age of 6 (Sagan, 1977). Your brain is the center of operations for your entire nervous system and for all of your sensory organs: eyes, ears, skin senses, everything. It also controls the vital functioning in all other body systems, so the neurosensory system is all-important.

The brain's early development makes for a parallel early slowing of function—a loss of nerve cells that begins in childhood and progresses all through life. Luckily, there are so many neurons in the brain to begin with that we don't even notice the decrease. After age 25 the size of the brain decreases slightly, and its electrical activity slows down a little, most noticeably after age 50. One result is a slowing down of reactions to stimuli; this is a loss of perhaps 17% in speed of reaction between 25 and 40 (Bromley, 1974).

Probably the most serious changes over time in the brain are caused by problems in another system, the cardiovascular system. If the heart and blood-supply system are operating inefficiently, they bring less blood and oxygen to the brain. The long-term effects of reduced oxygen are tissue destruction and slowed activity. This is one of the conditions of later life that is a matter of disease, rather than of aging itself (Birren, 1964). There are a number of cardiovascular-system abnormalities that may cause damage to the brain in later life. If the blood-supply system remains healthy and intact, the brain will function efficiently until death. Brain death, as a matter of fact, is death—legally. When the brain dies, all nerve activity stops (Butler & Lewis, 1977; Kart et al., 1978).

The nervous system can be pictured as a series of complicated networks of electrical fibers that reach out from the brain to every part of the body, controlling all our sensory and motor processes. All conscious and unconscious physiological activities—breathing and digesting, tap dancing and TV watching, any process that you can name—depend on messages that pass along nerve networks to and from the brain. The speed of these messages depends on the efficiency of the networks, and as the nerves gradually shrink, decrease, and decline in function, body responses gradually slow also (Finch & Hayflick, 1977; Kart et al., 1978). Fortunately, we do have more neurons than we'll ever need; the decrease begins at birth and continues thereafter, but even so we lose a maximum of only 15%, and most of that loss happens between birth and biological maturity (Weg, 1976).

Skin, which is our largest sense organ, illustrates the consistency of nerve efficiency. Skin is full of nerve endings that are sense receptors for touch, temperature, and pain. All these skin senses actually increase in sensitivity up to somewhere around the age of 45; only then do they begin a minimal decline, which isn't significant until the last stages of senescence (Ludel, 1978).

Like the brain, the skin runs into trouble when there are slowdowns in the cardiovascular system. When the blood supply isn't circulating strongly, the skin loses capillaries through atrophy and, as a result, loses its oxygen and nutrient supply and its waste-disposal ability. Skin functions also suffer from decline in the endocrine system. This system modifies oil and sweat production in the skin and also may control pigment production and the synthesis of new collagen, which connect the cells together. The production of collagen, or connective tissue, ends at about age 18; wrinkling, as the result of wear and tear on brittle collagen, begins by the twenties (Kart et al., 1978). The changes in our skin over time illustrate both the decline of the organ singly and the interdependency of body systems.

Unlike the skin, the eyes are an example of sense organs that in most cases decline because of organic defects, rather than because of breakdowns in whole systems. From the age of 10 on, the eyeball progressively loses flexibility of shape, causing farsightedness. By age 60 most people are farsighted to some degree. Sharpness of vision peaks in the twenties, stays fairly constant until the forties, and then begins a slow decline. Some loss in visual clarity is due to yellowing and thickening of the lenses; some is because of shrinking of the pupils, which then let in less light (Kart et al., 1978; Troll, 1975). There also seems to be a slowing in adaptation to changes in light intensity during the late years.

Ears may start to lose sensory function in the early twenties, but usually hearing loss is not serious until late adulthood. Even then, deafness isn't common. Rather than an effect of aging, a significant loss of hearing seems to be associated with exposure to loud sounds, such as loud music, noise in the work place, and the noise pollution in cities. Unless such exposure has occurred, most older people only have trouble with some pitch levels (Kart et al., 1978).

Taste buds begin to diminish in number in infancy. Except in the case of heavy smokers, however, people maintain taste discrimination into their sixties. In late adulthood, many people do have a dulled sense of taste, which affects their eating habits (Kart et al., 1978). The sense of smell, too, may decline, but the results of studies on this contradict one another—which is the case with work on a number of the sense organs (Kalish, 1975).

Balance and kinesthetic sense are at their peak of function between ages 40 and 50, like the sense of touch (Kart et al., 1978). After that, they begin a slow decline that may be related to changes in other systems—the skeletomuscular system, for example, or the cardiovascular system.

Cardiovascular Development

All the senses rely on the **cardiovascular system,** the heart and its blood-circulating network, for the oxygen and nutrients that keep the sensory cells alive and carry off cellular wastes. The cardiovascular system is as essential as the neurosensory system for maintaining life. However, hearts, unlike brains, break down quite commonly.

The heart is the central organ of the cardiovascular system. Hearts reach their peak of function before the age of 20, in both their maximum rate of speed and the maximum volume of blood they pump with each beat (deVries, 1975). But even before age 20, even in early adolescence, many Americans show signs of loss in heart efficiency from **atherosclerosis,** a clogging of the arteries (Kart et al., 1978). Among the common cardiovascular diseases are hardening of the arteries (**arteriosclerosis**), fat-clogged arteries (**atherosclerosis**), blood-clotted arteries (**cerebral thrombosis**), and broken arteries (**cerebral hemorrhage**). By the age of 40 in men and 49 in women, diseases of the cardiovascular system are reaching their highest frequency; by 65, they have become the most common causes of death. Atherosclerosis may be related to diet, disease, or genetic predisposition. Unfortunately, at present it seems to be almost universal, as well as being a progressive and quite predictable effect of aging in America (Butler & Lewis, 1977).

There is a strong possibility that some of the factors in the heart's decline are related to lack of physical activity. Losses of size and muscle strength in the heart between the ages of 20 and 70 are probably more the effects of hypokinetic disease than the effects of aging. Loss of elasticity of heart tissue, on the other hand, is more apt to be age related (deVries, 1975; Kart et al., 1978).

Veins and arteries, which make up the circulation network of the cardiovascular system, also gradually lose elasticity over time. But actual hardening of the arteries, arteriosclerosis, may be considered a disease condition rather than an inevitable change with age (Butler & Lewis, 1977). Because capillaries, the tiny veins that feed body cells, diminish as cardiovascular function slows down, oxygen supply to the cells becomes limited. And as oxygen supply is limited, all body systems suffer.

Respiratory Development

The **respiratory system,** which is the oxygen-exchange system that serves as the blood's source of oxygen, is a vital system for sustaining life on all levels. The amount of oxygen that the lungs supply affects all other body functions. The amount of oxygen they supply peaks at about age 17; it begins to decrease significantly between 20 and 40 (Bromley, 1974). After 40 it may begin a decline that, by age 75, leaves people with from 66% to 50% of the oxygen intake they had in youth (deVries, 1975). This loss isn't due to shrinkage; in fact, lung size may continue to grow during the whole life span (Finch & Hayflick, 1977). But ironically the increase in size is accompanied by a decrease in lung function that limits the actual oxygen exchange. The oxygen loss stems from reduced elasticity and number of functioning oxygen-exchange cells—both kinds of reduction the effects of aging—but most of all it comes from inactivity, and from smoking and other forms of air pollution (deVries, 1975).

The decrease in oxygen supply affects metabolism, slowing down cell efficiency at every level. The skeletomuscular system shows these effects most clearly.

Skeletomuscular Development

The changes in the **skeletomuscular system** with age are visible earlier in muscle tissue, later in bone. Muscles can be developed effectively until the fifties, but maximum muscle strength peaks between 25 and 30. Strength declines very slowly, with a loss as small as 10% if conditioning is maintained. However, with age even strong muscles tire more easily and take longer to recover from stress (deVries, 1975). Loss of endurance rather than of strength is characteristic of aging. Activity and good nutrition are the key factors in maintaining flexibility and endurance.

Bone strength, like muscle strength, is at its peak at age 30, and it remains stable until middle age. In later years, however, some people—especially women—experience calcium loss in their bone tissues, causing progressive weakening of the bones. This condition, which is called **osteoporosis,** used to be considered a normal effect of aging; now it's thought to be a disease state caused by nutritional factors, inactivity, hormone deficiency, or a combination of these factors (Kart et al., 1978).

Hormone deficiency can be the effect of poor nutrition or emotional factors on another essential body system—the endocrine system. Or the changes in the endocrine system, about which relatively little is known, may be regulated primarily by the body itself.

Endocrine Development

The **endocrine system** may be the system that's ultimately responsible for all the age changes that have been described. This system includes the glands of the body and brain and their production of hormones—of all the body systems, perhaps the most delicately balanced. Endocrine connections with the timing of biological events (such as puberty and menopause) and with the management of reactions to stress (short-term emotions and long-term adaptations) have made the endocrine system a focus of aging research. Yet, because of the system's complexity, much remains to be learned. One of the current theories of cellular aging is that senescence may be the effect of hormone messages from the pituitary gland. (The theories about why we age are elaborated in Chapter 15.)

Puberty is brought on by the endocrine system when, with the pituitary as the trigger, it increases its hormone output. The increased estrogen production in women and testosterone production in men maintains the sexual and reproductive functions of adulthood (Katchadourian, 1976).

Menopause—the end of the menstrual cycles—is the effect of a reduction of estrogen production in women, and it, too, is timed by the pituitary. At menopause a pituitary hormone is released that signals the ovaries to slow their ovulation and estrogen production, and, eventually, to stop them. Without the estrogen the ovaries had produced, a new hormone balance must be established, relying on the smaller amount of estrogen that the adrenal glands produce. Reproductive ability then ceases, although sexual responsiveness is relatively unaffected (Butler & Lewis, 1977).

Some women experience physical or psychological problems while the hormonal balance is being reestablished in menopause. Hormone imbalances may cause such physiological discomforts as temporary "hot flashes," headaches, and dizzy spells, but these symptoms can be treated with estrogen replacement therapy or by a combined nutritional and exercise approach (Kart et al., 1978). Women's psychological problems connected with the changes of middle life have traditionally centered on mood swings, depression, and confusion. These may be physically caused in some cases, but they are often connected with a fear of losing a sexual role. Therapy focused on self-acceptance is often helpful. Mid-life despair in some degree is understandable in a youth-oriented, sexist society. But, as separate from reproduction, sexuality is not necessarily affected by menopause. Physical fitness and positive attitudes allow most contemporary women to experience menopause as a freeing experience, an end to the complications in their lives brought on by concern over unplanned pregnancies. The postmenopausal years may be more sensual, more calm, more physically free than any other time in women's lives (Butler & Lewis, 1977; Neugarten, 1977). Successful adaptation to menopause is often a question of understanding bodily change and interpreting it positively.

In men, as well as in women, the changes of middle life are broadly termed the **climacteric**. The climacteric in men is more gradual and is spread out over a longer time period than it is in women.

Men can continue procreating into late life. Hormone production in the testes may decline slightly between late adolescence, when it peaks, and the early thirties, but then it levels out, further decreased only by such uncommon conditions as disease, drug abuse, dietary deficiency, or lack of sexual activity. However, although hormone levels remain steady, neural slowdowns and circulatory limitations may cause mild reduction in the intensity and efficiency of penis function by the late thirties. These changes may be perceived by men as threatening and may generate anxiety about sexual perform-ance, causing men to limit sexual expression and communication. Alternatively, the changes may be dealt with adaptively; they may be integrated into a more leisurely sexual lifestyle. As with women, men's interpretations of the changes they experience in middle life are influenced by the clarity of their understanding and by their willingness to adapt (Butler & Lewis, 1977; Finch & Hayflick, 1977). Therefore, the social and psychological aspects of changes in sexual-ity, which are discussed later in the chapter, greatly modify the impact of the endocrine system.

Besides the regulation of reproductive changes, endocrine func-tions have other far-reaching effects, including control of the speed of metabolism and changes in the biochemistry of the blood, both of which affect the growth, maintenance, and decline of almost every cell in our bodies.

Even hair growth is related to levels of hormone production. En-docrine changes can cause thickening, thinning, coarsening, or just plain disappearance of the hair on our heads. Hair loss may begin in the twenties, especially in men. By the fifties, most men are at least partially bald; women's hair thins, but balding is rare (Kart et al., 1978).

The Immune and Other Systems

Although there are minor changes in the digestive and excretory systems over time, these changes do not necessarily result from mat-uration or aging. Diet and exercise are far more influential in main-taining both systems. There is, however, a body system seldom con-sidered by most of us, yet with functions as crucial to our staying alive as those of any other system, that does indeed decline with age. This vital part of our bodies is the immune system.

The organs of the **immune system** are the thymus gland, the spleen, the lymph nodes, and the bone marrow. These organs produce cells that attack and destroy the viruses, bacteria, and fungi that enter our bodies, and they even control cancer cells, which attack from inside our bodies. As long as the organs of the immune system do this well, we're protected against disease. However, over time the immune functions decline, with the result that the older we get the more vulnerable we become to disease. If the immune functions stop entirely, we soon die (Finch & Hayflick, 1977).

Considering the immune system's central importance, it's not surprising that much of the current research on aging is centered on ways to stop decline in immune functions. Some researchers even feel that the whole process of aging may be a question of becoming immune to our own bodies. Certainly, immunity to our own body cells is a kind of self-rejection that we could happily do without. It's self-acceptance that we need—ironically, perhaps acceptance by our bodies as well as of them. Self-acceptance and our attitudes toward aging generally are a strong factor in the consequences of the changes we experience in aging.

Biological Consequences

Biological aging over the adult life span turns out to be a slow-motion process—actually a cluster of slow-motion processes. Growth blends into maturation and maturation shades into senescence. There isn't any point at which we suddenly "get old." As we grow older gradually, the consequences of the accompanying changes are manifested at varying times.

Quick changes in biological well-being can occur if disease or accident or wear and tear damage organs or whole systems. In late adulthood, such damage is aggravated by the weakening of our immune systems over the years and the consequent slowing of our recovery rates. Otherwise, however, in late life we have more or less the same responses to physical problems that we have had earlier in life.

Alex Comfort makes a tremendously important point about aging. It is so simple that it is lost on most people, other gerontologists included. Comfort's point is that you are the same person when you are older that you were when you were younger. You have merely been here longer and experienced more. You look a little different and you may have more physical problems. But a biological change affects you at 70 in more or less the same way as it would have if it had happened when you were 20, unless you accept society's negative stereotype of age and so play out the myth that to be old is to be sick (Comfort, 1976). Assuming that we're free from the expectation of disease, just what can we expect from the body changes that accompany aging, when they're taken together? What are the real consequences to our minds and bodies?

Over the years, the brain shrinks and the nervous system loses neurons—both quite minimally, and both very slowly. At one time, because comparative cross-sectional studies showed significant losses in IQ as people aged, it was assumed that aging brought a loss in intelligence. Actually, the cohort effect of the cross-sections had distorted the reality. Older people with little early education and simple lifestyles were being compared to younger, more educated people who had lived in far more complex environments for most of their lives. In actuality, very little intellectual decline or no decline at all is found when the same people are measured in longitudinal studies (Butler & Lewis, 1977). In surveys of the research literature on mental functions, there seems to be little or no age change in cognitive flexibility or in visual problem solving. There are age-related increases in experience-based intelligence, in social awareness, and in the ability to generalize. In a study of healthy older men of average age 71, James Birren and his associates found a difference in the peak frequencies of brainwaves of the older men, but the slowing of EEG waves wasn't apparently connected with mental functions (Birren, 1964). Brain decrements—reduction of the number of brain cells—in healthy people don't seem to affect cognitive functions significantly. Only visual and motor flexibility, short-term memory, and reaction times decrease with age (Atchley, 1977; Kart et al., 1978). As we get older we take longer to learn new tasks, but nevertheless we can achieve mastery, which is what performance is all about. Over the adult years we have plenty of time to develop strategies for dealing with slower response times or shorter memory.

The first consequence of aging after maturation, then, is that we just generally slow down. The slowing in response time that studies report is quite possibly an effect of minor losses of electrical activity in the brain and nervous system (Woodruff, 1975), but the slowdown may also be related to decrements in reception by the sense organs.

Loss of up-close vision in the eyes and the slight thickening and yellowing of corneas eventually make vision less sharp. And, because picking up enough visual cues to form images takes longer as time goes by, responding to the images also takes longer. Uncertainty in what's heard also may slow down responses. Fortunately, vision and hearing can be easily modified at any time in life with the right glasses or the right hearing aid. The slow decline in the neurosensory system is most significant in the effects that it has on the slowing in other systems; on its own, it gives us few problems.

The cardiovascular and respiratory systems are more problematic. Together with the skeletomuscular system, they are the keys to our physical performance and our continuing good health. The essential thing to keep in mind about these three interlocking systems is that they are at their peaks only when we are physically active. Commitment to lifelong physical conditioning is essential for lifelong functional performance. Circulation, oxygen supply, and muscle reaction are all interdependent.

Heart, lungs, and muscle are probably at their natural best when we are in our early twenties, losing peak performance after 30 but only slowly—if we maintain consistent levels of activity. Remember the effects of hypokinetic disease? There is a direct relationship between heart/lung/muscle activity and heart/lung/muscle capacity. Exercise physiologists have found that three weeks of bed rest can cut heart/lung/muscle function by 30% in young, well-conditioned men; this is a percentage higher than that considered to be caused by aging in 70-year-olds. Further, it's been demonstrated that older men and women who exercise can improve their cardiovascular, respiratory, and skeletomuscular systems, modifying and even reversing the decreases in fuctioning that are identified with aging (deVries, 1975). "If you don't use them, you lose them" is a maxim that applies to all aspects of human capacity.

"If you don't use them, you lose them" applies classically to sexual functions. Sexual arousal is directly tied to neural and endocrine activity, as well as to physical fitness, but in human beings there are also two far more important factors operating. These are the social factor and the psychological factor.

Social attitudes reflect an increasing recognition that we are sexual from birth and will be sexual until we die. But until recently American society was united in a massive denial of adult sexuality during middle and late life. While there has been an intense focus on sexuality in young adults, mostly for commercial and entertainment purposes, the idea of sex in the middle years and in old age has been considered ridiculous—considered only in terms of the "dirty old man/lady" syndromes. Men and women could choose either to accept the prevailing social stereotypes of sexless aging or to stay in touch with their sexuality while feeling that they weren't quite normal (Masters & Johnson, 1974). Contemporary research suggests that neither option is necessary. There seems to be a continuity in our individual levels of sexual response. The gradual slowing of body systems over the years may lead us to limit our sexual function, but this limitation is a matter of choice, not of biological senescence (Kart et al., 1978).

Sexual function can be discussed in terms of quantity or in terms of quality. Quantity of sexual activity is the most age-related aspect, apparently; the average rate of a little more than three acts of intercourse a week for marital partners between the ages of 18 and 24 does drop—to fewer than three times weekly between 26 and 35 and to twice a week between 35 and 45 (Hunt, 1974). It's important to be aware that most frequency data is cross-sectional; it is quite possibly distorted by the social attitudes of earlier cohorts that have been mentioned. After 45, however, frequency of sex apparently reaches a plateau, and the rate maintained thereafter depends on the patterns of sexual activity that have been set in earlier years (Butler & Lewis, 1977). Quality of sexual activity may be related to both social and personal habit. It may also be strongly influenced by psychological responses to biological changes.

An example of psychological interpretations of physiological changing and some quantitative and qualitative outcomes is found in male reactions to body changes that may occur during the thirties or forties. As mentioned earlier, by the end of early adulthood most men experience some changes in penile response during intercourse: maximum erection may be less fully erect and may take longer to attain than at age 18; ejaculations may become less forceful and orgasms less intense. If a man interprets these changes as a loss of sexual powers, he may become anxious and develop problems with psychologically based impotence, or he may initiate sex less often, and, as a result, limit his physiological functions even further.

However, if he is aware that these are natural changes and that penetration and ejaculation are only some of the possible activities in mutual pleasuring, he may interpret the changes as a gain in his potential for lovemaking, since they allow him to delay ejaculation and take more time for intercourse, extending his physiological capability. A man can thereby extend his sexual functioning into late life (Butler & Lewis, 1977; Masters & Johnson, 1974). The changes in men's sexual functioning in mid-life may also have the advantage of relieving "performance anxiety," since lovemaking becomes more relaxed and less structured.

Another example of psychological interpretations of sexual changes is in female reactions to menopause. By the early fifties, most women have experienced some menopausal changes that may affect their sexual response: for example, less vaginal lubrication or more clitoral sensitivity, either of which may cause discomfort in intercourse. If a woman interprets the end of her potential for child-bearing as an end to her sexuality, she may use these changes as an excuse for ending sexual relations. If instead she interprets menopause as a release from anxiety about unwanted pregnancy, she may see the potential for freedom that these changes offer and may deal with the minor difficulty of increased irritation constructively. Deficiencies in vaginal fluids are relieved simply by using water-soluble lubricants, while more serious sensitivities can be treated medically with estrogen-replacement therapy (Butler & Lewis, 1977).

Freedom from performance anxiety, a genuine desire to share intimacy, and a consistent pattern of sexual activity make sex an activity at least into the eighties—and the future may hold even more potential for sexual expression, as social attitudes become increasingly positive and good biological conditioning is more widespread.

Barring accident or illness, in the years before senescence there need be only minor losses in biological well-being. James Fries and Lawrence Crapo, of the Stanford University School of Medicine, have recently synthesized the current information on biological aging and pointed out that the losses occurring over time are, for the most part, loss in **organ reserve.** *Organ reserve* is the term for the body's back-up capacity. Most of our organs have at least four times more functional capacity than they need under normal conditions. So losses in organ reserve are barely noticeable in daily function. and, Fries and Crapo (1981) tell us, given a personal commitment to disease prevention and to maintenance, vitality is possible until our reserve is depleted. Only then, sometime around the age of 85, will the body go into the rapid decline of senescence, followed by natural death. **Natural death** can be defined as a death that occurs at the end of an individual's biological life span, the final phase of senescence.

All in all, the biological consequences of life-span development are changes that can be absorbed smoothly into any individual pattern of growth over time. Increased (rather than decreased) physical exercise, appropriate nutrition, and positive attitudes toward being the most we can be should make our later years as good as any we've lived (Butler, 1978; Leaf, 1975). Disease—extreme destructive change in body functioning—has to be dealt with on its own terms: prevented when possible, healed if it can't be prevented, accepted if it can't be healed. That sounds easy, but we know it's not.

If all we had to do were to keep our bodies strong and healthy, we could make a full-time occupation of it; but we have to do more than that: we have to be a part of the world we live in. The stresses of our social world complicate the job of biological maintenance. In the next chapter we'll review some of those social forces.

Summary

Biological changes in adult life underlie both social and psychological change. The processes of biological change are extremely variable. An individual biological clock controls the rate of functional aging as an individual progresses from maturation through aging and senescence.

Until the 1960s biological aging was equated with chronological aging; currently, biological age is considered to be more a question of function. Chronology is not a useful indicator of maturation after childhood, because there is such a wide potential age span for puberty. And as an indicator of aging, chronological age is even less helpful. Functional age is a far more useful concept.

Disease, disuse, genetic idiosyncrasies and the usual problems of generalizing from cross-sectional and longitudinal studies make identifying the actual effects of aging difficult. Only those effects that are universal, progressive, and predictable—such as the continued growth of some tissues, the progressive shrinkage of others, and the cumulative wear and tear of most—can be considered the changes of biological development.

Changes occur at the cellular level, the organ level, and the systems level. The neurosensory system in general experiences a gradual slowing and dulling of its functioning over time. The cardiovascular system is subject to breakdowns but responsive to efforts to maintain and repair it. The respiratory system, too, responds to conditioning, especially conditioning in the form of rhythmic breathing exercises and general activity. The skeletomuscular system may slow down in function, but an adequate level of response, flexibility, and strength nevertheless may be maintained over the life span. The relationships of the endocrine and the immune systems to the aging processes remain puzzling; research is increasing in these areas.

The consequences of the slow losses of efficiency aging brings are similar to the consequences of the same losses at any time of life. Over time, people develop strategies to deal with the growing limitations in the speed of their response time. Such devices as glasses and hearing aids can counterbalance sensory deficits. Physical exercise will maintain effective and efficient body functioning: if you use your body (and don't abuse it), the effects of aging can be minimized. This holds true for sexual as well as other functions.

All together, adulthood's biological changes—barring those from disease—are slow, and they are only gradually limiting.

Terms and Concepts to Define

arteriosclerosis _____

_____

atherosclerosis _____

_____

biological development _____

_____

cardiovascular system _____

_____

cerebral hemorrhage _____

_____

cerebral thrombosis _____

_____

climacteric _____

_____

endocrine system _____

_____

immune system _____

_____

menopause _____

_____

natural death _____

_____

neurosensory system _____

_____

organ reserve _____

_____

osteoporosis _____

_____

respiratory system _____

_____

skeletomuscular system _____

_____

Experiences

To involve yourself with the concepts in this chapter, try these experiences described in the Appendix.

Alone
20. Biological Aging
37. Body Systems

With Others
34. Middle Age
36. Disengagement versus Activity

Going beyond the Text

1. Scan newspapers and periodicals for accounts of individuals who have maintained remarkable biological functioning well into late life.
2. Develop a personal plan for improving your present cardiovascular and respiratory functions. Create a detailed schedule, incorporating both increases in activity and decreases in smoking, overeating, and other inappropriate behaviors.

Suggested Readings

Kart, C., Metress, E., & Metress, J. Aging and health: Biologic and social perspectives. *Menlo Park, Calif.: Addison-Wesley, 1978.*

Butler, R., & Lewis, M. Sex after sixty: A guide for men and women in their later years. *New York: Harper & Row, 1977.*

Fries, J., & Crapo, L. Vitality and aging. *San Francisco: Freeman, 1981.*

12

Life Patterns: Social Changes over Time

When you have finished reading this chapter you should be able to:
List at least five widespread family forms.
Describe the developmental role changes of men and women in the nuclear family.
Discuss the current trends in the working careers of men and women.
Explain why education has become a continuing process in contemporary life.
Summarize Keniston's theoretical description of interpersonal development.

In adult life, the processes of social change are just as essential as the processes of biology—and sometimes the two are causally related to one another. We're deeply rooted in our social world. It can be fundamentally either a source of stress or a source of support, depending on how well the patterns of our society fit our personal lives.

In changing times the fit is not always comfortable. Social patterns that were formed in the past to deal with the social processes of adult living are often based on an economy, a technology, and a social setting that no longer exist. We live, today, in a tangle of these patterns for living. Some of them have been left over from the past and some are being created now to cope with new conditions. Traditional life patterns no longer fit many of us. Different and innovative patterns may be more individually comfortable, but they may also be in conflict with the patterns of family or society. Much of the time we're caught between cultural traditions and contemporary trends.

Social Processes: An Overview

This chapter is a review of some of the social processes of the adult life course. These are the developmental processes of moving through a life history of family, work, education, and friendships. Each of these processes has at least three levels of existence: as a social myth, as a past reality, and as a reality that is being created in the present.

Dealing with each process separately allows us to isolate the myths, the traditions, and the trends. It also allows us to untangle the developmental relationships among family, work, education, friendship. Like the systems of the body, these systems of the social world are deeply interdependent and delicately balanced. A change in any one area affects some or even all of the other aspects of living.

Because changes in the social world may lead to serious complications, it's not surprising that societies create built-in structures to resist change. We have identified in Chapter 4 the two major restraining forces: the social restraints of norms and roles. Social norms establish standards of behavior; social roles dictate ways of acting in specific situations. Changes at any level affect other levels: if we violate norms and roles, relationships change and, eventually, the whole social environment changes; if the environment changes, so do relationships, and norms and roles. Changes may turn out to be productive, but they cause social confusion for a time.

Social confusion is fairly widespread these days. We may be confused, in the first place, because some social norms have changed and other related norms haven't: sexual norms in America have changed radically, for example, but our marriage norms have changed very little. In the second place, we may be confused because some people have shifted their social norms and other people haven't; acceptable behavior varies across age groups, socioeconomic groups, and geographical locations. It's confusing. And then there's a third problem: we may have accepted a considerable shift in one norm but none at all in a corollary to it. For example, a person may accept contemporary standards of sex before marriage but nonetheless feel strongly about requiring virginity at marriage.

If we need to be clearheaded about any one social process, the developmental process of marriage and family is that one. It's central, in that it affects all of the others in very important ways. Let's see what _marriage and family_ has meant traditionally and what trends are evolving.

The Concept of Family *Defined*

Before we can really discuss how families are changing, we need to define what, specifically, they are. *Family* is a concept that can be defined in a number of ways, many of them unhelpful in understanding the family process developmentally.

To illustrate the difficulty of pinning down what's meant by *family*, try doing it the easy way—describing it.

List the members of your family.

_____

_____

_____

_____

_____

Describe the kinds of expected behaviors that connect the members of your family. What do they do to one another? What do they do for one another? What do they do together?

_____

_____

_____

_____

_____

Describe your family's part in your social life.

_____

_____

_____

_____

Describe your family's part in your emotional life.

_____

_____

_____

_____

_____

Now read over your descriptive definition. Is it sufficient? Did your attempt to define your family pose complications? It should have. One complication might have been deciding who should be included. Did you limit it to mother and father, sister and brother, or did you extend it to grandparents, aunts, uncles, cousins, their mates, and on and on? A second complication might have been limiting or even recognizing all the kinds of mutual behaviors in family interaction. Becoming aware of your family's rules, responsibilities, and rituals isn't easy because they are often so subtle and so embedded in your perceptions as "the way things are." Social and emotional questions can be extremely complicated, too, if you think about them deeply enough. The whole function of family in your life is actually difficult to subjectively assess.

If it's hard to find an adequate subjective definition of *family*, it's even harder to establish a single objective definition—there are so many ways of defining it. Biologically speaking, a family is a group of human beings who are genetically related: people who are connected in some way by blood ties. The problem with that approach is that it leaves out legal kinds of family relationships, such as marriage and adoption. The sociological definition avoids that problem by defining *family* as a set of rules, rather than as a group of people—to a sociologist, *family* means a social institution based on rules that control mating and the socialization of children, among other functions. That's an interesting approach, too, but it isn't particularly helpful for discussing our relationships with the real people who are our families. Psychological definitions are more adequate for discussing the family developmentally; psychologically, the family may be defined as both a group of related people who interact intimately and as an internalized set of rules about the ways in which related people interact (Laing, 1969; Minuchin, 1974).

For our purposes, we can integrate the three concepts and define *family* in a developmental sense as a group consisting of two or more people who have direct biological, functional, or legal ties to one another that endure over time. Such a broad and clear definition is necessary for discussing the American family as it is now, because it exists in so many forms.

Let's consider some fairly common family forms. A formerly unrecognized form, the (unmarried) **cohabiting couple,** who might be heterosexual or homosexual, with or without children, has become such a prevalent family style that it is legally recognized. Many young people have used cohabitation as a way of learning how to be in a relationship that has a strong resemblance to marriage. Many older people choose cohabitation for its economic benefits. Married couples without children represent a second, more stable form that may continue as a **childfree couple** or—with the addition of children—may be transformed into a third form, the **nuclear family.** When we speak of a family, in our social setting, we're usually referring to the nuclear-family unit. Escalating divorce rates are changing that, however. The family form increasing most rapidly is another type—the **single-parent family,** consisting of one divorced or never-married parent and one or more children. Divorce and remarriage create the aggregate family or **blended family,** including children from former marriages in a new family unit. A form that is more traditional, especially in ethnic family groupings, is the **extended family,** in which a couple, their children, and other relatives live together; a similar situation, in which members live separately but remain mutually dependent, is called the **modified extended family.** Another grouping, this one strictly nontraditional, is the **group marriage,** also called a "multilateral marriage," in which three or more men and women are married to all members of their group. And, finally, there are families in which a group of people with mutual commitments live together as a **communal** family—perhaps in a commune or in a group-home setting (where people in need of social supports live in a family-style setting, also called institutional families). Some of these forms are very common and some are relatively rare, but they all exist in contemporary America (Toffler, 1980; Troll, Miller, & Atchley, 1979). (Figure 12-1 lists all the types of family groups we've discussed.)

Traditionally, the modified extended family seems to be the most common American pattern, but, in terms of the developmental process of family life, the form that is most influential is the nuclear family (Troll et al., 1979).

Family as a Process over Time

The developmental process of family life involves a series of socially expected phases of family participation. The process begins when young adults who have been living with their nuclear families of origin marry; they are then a "beginning family." If this new couple has children, a nuclear family is founded. When the new generation of children is mature, it is "launched," and its members, too, marry. As the older members reach advanced age, the family process may involve reestablishment of the earlier nuclear family, when the older parents move into the homes of their middle-aged children.

Social expectations for family process are deeply embedded in cultural myth. The mythical nuclear-family process goes like this: when we are ready to marry, we find a perfect mate; soon after marriage we have some lovely children of the appropriate sex and number (first a boy, then a girl—two in all). Everybody is happy, and everybody loves everybody else. When the children are grown, they find their own perfect mates, and so on through the generations. Everybody lives happily ever after. So goes the myth.

Cohab-iting couple	Child-free couple	Single-parent family	Nuclear family	Blended family	Extend-ed family	Group marriage	Com-munal family

Figure 12-1 Any group consisting of two or more people who maintain direct biological, functional, or legal ties with one another can be considered a family group.

The actual traditional nuclear-family process has been an attempt to approximate the myth. Sometime in young adulthood most young adults find mates; not always perfect mates, unfortunately. Children may begin appearing very soon after marriage (sometimes disconcertingly soon), creating the nuclear family, which develops through a number of substages that have been identified as phases of the family process: the early childbearing family, the preschool family, the family with teenage children, and the launching center for young adults. When the children are launched, the nuclear family shrinks to an **empty-nest family,** eventually becoming a family in retirement and even a family in old age, if both spouses live long (Carter & Orfanidis, 1980; Troll et al., 1979).

Each of these traditional nuclear-family substages is quite different from the one that preceded it, resulting in **developmental role changes:** changes in roles and relationships between husband and wife and between parent and child. In courtship and in marriage before any children are born, the roles played are male/female, husband/wife roles, and the mates' interaction can be expected to focus intimately and emotionally on one another. In early child rearing, there is a shift to mother/father roles, and the emotional focus may move away from a mate, to the infant. Sometimes the addition of the mother/father roles strengthens the parents' relationship; however, sometimes the playing of parent roles weakens the mates' relationship and introduces conflicts. As new perceptions of parenting change the traditional parental roles, new conflicts may emerge. For example, as the role of fathers becomes clearer, new expectations of fathers will arise (Appleton, 1981).

During the school years, the emerging personalities of a family's children add to the complexity of family interactions; children's school years particularly are a time when partners can either strengthen their mutual commitment to parenting or be pulled apart by family conflicts. The teen years often are even more wearing. When families deal with the sensitive issues of sexuality (of children and of parents) and of autonomy (again, that of everybody concerned), the struggles within the family are especially stressful. These struggles are relieved only when children leave (Schenk & Schenk, 1978). For some parents, the return to being an intimate couple after children have left is a second honeymoon, as partners return to sexual rather than parental roles. For other parents, the change requires a new struggle to establish a relationship that works. Recognizing the developmental role changes that occur in families is a key to understanding the problems the contemporary marriage partners face over the span of their life together. Smooth transitions from courtship and husband/wife roles to mother/father roles, and later on to new husband/wife roles, is difficult, unless both partners are aware of what is happening and are willing both to share their expectations about the roles and to reach some agreement on how the roles will be acted out. Most people are not aware of the role changes that are shaping and reshaping their relationships when the first child is born or when the last child leaves home. So couples have problems.

Add the confusions of a changing social setting and of changing sex roles to the problems of the traditional family cycle, and you have a clearer understanding of the situation that exists now. The evolving social environment has affected the timing of the family process; it also has made such breaks in the cycle as divorce and remarriage much more common. Cohorts of the present are creating new trends in the family that may become the norms of the future. For example, Ellen Galinsky (1980) has described a contemporary model of parenthood based on a continuous process of separation of the child from the parent. It begins with a "blended" phase during pregnancy and extends through the issues of authority in early childhood and in adolescence, culminating in the final autonomy struggle and the offspring's departure.

The timing of the family process is held relatively steady by the social and biological clocks, which will probably keep it fairly stable in the future as well (Neugarten, 1977). But there are a number of trends away from the traditional timing of the cycle—and even a trend away from participation in the cycle—that may have significant future effects.

The traditional timing of the social clock sets parenting within a 15-year period between the late teens and the middle thirties, although it's biologically possible for women to give birth in their early teens (and earlier) and, at the opposite extreme, for men to father children in their seventies (and later). Early in the 20th century and in the depression years of the 1920s, people married relatively later, on the average, and they parented later than the cohorts in the middle of the century (Neugarten, 1977). By the 1950s, early marriage and parenting in the economic boom years had caused a speedup in the timing of the family cycle. The end of the century, with its economic problems on one hand and its effective family-planning technology on the other, seems to be shaping the family cycle differently. The cycle begins later in many people's lives; but small families keep the cycle short (Hansen, 1977).

Age at marriage is moving upward, with the average age of first marriage 21.2 years for women and 22.9 for men by 1978; their ages at the birth of their first children are moving upward also (Lopata, 1978). There also seems to be a trend among people in the early years of marriage to delay having children. Instead, both partners work to establish an economic foothold. The fact that more women are postponing marriage and, even after marriage, are taking their education and work lives seriously seems to be one factor in these changes. A tendency toward smaller families is another factor; the U. S. average is now 1.9 children (U. S. Bureau of the Census, 1980). As a result, couples tend to spend a longer period of time as a beginning family—that is, without children. And adults are apt to spend fewer years as heads of nuclear families, because couples have fewer children to bring up and launch; correspondingly, the couples spend many more years in the postparenting stages of marriage than did the generations preceding.

The current pattern of the family process seems more appropriate for the realities of women's involvement in the contemporary work world than is the traditional pattern of early marriage and or parenting that both begins earlier and lasts longer. The reality is that many women are not only full-time workers in their early years—before marriage—and in their late years—after parenting—but they often spend most of their adult lives in the work force. In 1979 over 49% of all U. S. women were employed in the work force; more than 47% of all married women worked outside the home, and more than 50% of all women between the ages of 25 and 34, the usual child-rearing years, were in the work force (U. S. Bureau of the Census, 1980). These figures indicate an increasing trend away from the traditional roles of women as full-time homemakers, wives, and mothers, and toward women as performing all those roles plus the role of full-time worker. With this development and others, it's not surprising that the family is an institution in a state of change.

Another trend in the family cycle that is becoming increasingly noticeable is divorce. Divorce has been a solution to marital problems for centuries, but it hasn't been as socially acceptable as it is in present-day America. Aside from a peaking of divorce rates after World World II, in the mid-1940s, divorce has never been as popular as it is today. And the number of divorces is increasing steadily, with a U. S. rate of 50% in 1978 (U. S. Bureau of the Census, 1980). As divorce becomes almost a social norm in contemporary life, the forms of family life are altered. Couples who marry, have children, and then divorce are contributing to the rising number of single-parent families. Couples who marry, parent, divorce, and then re-marry are creating the growing number of aggregate or blended families, made up of the partners' children from former marriages and often the offspring of the new couple as well. The family process grows more complicated. Divorced men tend to marry women who are younger than their former mates, so an aggregate family may be at the same time a launching stage for older children and a child-rearing family in its early stage. Understandably, conflicts aren't uncommon in blended families.

The high statistical probability of divorce has another effect on the family, as well; rather than inviting a future of troubling family forms, such as being single parents or part of blended families, some people are choosing to remain child-free, opting out of the nuclear-family structure and its variations completely. Some individuals, recognizing the growing transience of marriage, experiment with group marriages and communal families as ways of achieving stability in family life with children. Other people just don't marry at all.

A small percent of the population never marries. Currently the figures on single adults are somewhere around 16.4% of American women and 22.5% overall of American men (U. S. Bureau of the Census, 1980). They leave the nuclear family formed by their parents, usually, but never establish one of their own. They form the core of a group of adults that is a growing population in contemporary society: singles. Singles may be involved in families as single parents, or they may be isolated from family life completely. Single people may be never married, not yet married, or previously married. They may be single by choice or from lack of opportunity. They may be "swinging singles," involved in active heterosexual lifestyles, or they may be "gay singles," with active homosexual social lives. Or they may be neither, having instead sparse social lives and little sexual interaction (Kimmel, 1974). They may even choose religious celibacy, a way of life that also is on the increase (Fracchia, 1979).

The baby-boom cohort of people born between 1947 and 1957 seems to have generated more singles than any former cohort. There are a number of explanations for this new singles factor. The years required for pre-occupational training have been increased. Also, cultural emphasis on self-expression and living one's own life has increased, and there has been a decrease in emphasis on work and reproduction as life's central activities. In the resulting social climate, being single isn't as likely to be perceived as being deviant as it was previously (Sheehy, 1979). Further, as birth technology produces new options for people to manipulate their life patterns, and as work cycles shift into a more central position in the lives of both men and women, family patterns will likely change even more.

Right now, where are you in your family development? And where are you in your work process? Mark the appropriate block in each column with an X. (Note that the stages of family development shown here reflect the "typical" family.)

Family Development

In parents' nuclear family
Launched but single
Married and child free
Parenting a nuclear family
Launching your children
Empty nest
Retired

Work Development

Training
Experimenting in career
Career commitment
Career progress
Career's high point
Preretirement
Retired

Draw a line from the block that you marked on your family cycle to the block that you marked on your work cycle—the blocks may or may not be parallel. If they are parallel and you are a male, you are quite traditional. If you're a female and the levels of your boxes match, you're very rare, unless you are still on the first or second squares. Most women and many men who have moved past the fourth square will come up with diagonal lines, unless they have retired. At the same time that family forms have been shifting, changes have been occurring in the life patterns of working.

Work as a Process over Time

To keep work changes out of a discussion of family changes as a developmental process is impossible. Especially the effects of changes in the work cycle on family life must be considered with respect to the life patterns of women. The family has traditionally been considered women's only career. Now, with more and more women choosing the two-career life of raising a family and working outside the home, the relation between the two spheres is a dynamic one (Van Dusen & Sheldon, 1977).

The mythic form of the developmental process of work life is that women work in the home and men work outside the home, as do "career women" who are unmarried. A man is committed to a permanent career before marriage; he spends the greater part of his adult life climbing up a career ladder, and he gets to the top sometime in his middle years. As retirement approaches he loses interest in work, and at some appropriate age he retires. A married woman, meanwhile, is thought to be deeply involved in homemaking and child rearing; eventually she turns to grandparenting. Her unmarried sister has a life pattern that resembles the pattern identified with men. That's the myth.

The traditional work patterns of 20th-century men have reflected the myth to some degree, although with significant exceptions: many men never make a permanent career but move in and out of varied jobs; many men have no "careers" because their jobs offer no career ladder; some men view retirement as social death and never retire. The traditional work patterns for 20th-century women have differed from the myth increasingly as women have become an increasingly larger percentage of the permanent work force outside the home. As procreation has become less the absolute center of women's lives, the work patterns for men and women have become more similar (Van Dusen & Sheldon, 1977). But there are some important differences.

Development in the sphere of work, like development in the family, is described as a continuous sequence of stages. The first stage is the preparation and training of early adulthood; the skills gained then will be put to use in future work roles. By the end of early adulthood, after experimentation with kinds of training and of work, there is a stage of commitment to an occupation, which for most people endures until retirement. In many occupations there are substages by which a person can move up a career ladder of status, pay, or both during his/her middle years. In middle age comes the last stage—phasing out and retiring (Atchley, 1977; Peters & Hansen, 1977).

Men are likely to experience their working history in just the order described, but women, because of their childbearing potential, have increasingly evolved variations on it. Nine out of ten women now work at some time in their lives (Kline, 1975). A fairly common work pattern for women has become the sequence of a very brief period of preparation; a few years of work, often in a service occupation such as sales, nursing, or office work; a time-out period for child rearing; and, as children get older, reentry in the workforce, (Hansen, 1977). As women have gained more opportunities for education and have resisted traditional stereotypes that present women as passive and emotionally nurturant but rationally incompetent, they have prepared themselves for more extensive careers. Variations in the female work cycle accompany these new work patterns.

Gale Sheehy (1976) has described some of the variations in the work lives of women. They can choose not to marry, not to have children, or both. They can integrate marriage, parenting, and career in their twenties; they can defer either parenting or career until their thirties; and they can come and go from the work force as the need arises. The choice of never marrying allows women to experience a career pattern very similar to the pattern common to many men; a long period of preparation without conflicting responsibilities is more likely for women who don't marry, and so are the abilities to move freely from job to job and to focus attention on a career. Choosing to integrate traditional family roles with new work roles permits women to develop in their work lives, along with men; however, women often experience complications when the mother or wife role conflicts with job responsibilities. **Deferring a role** is a much easier solution than combining roles. By deferring either maternity or career, women can handle one demanding job at a time, parenting and working outside the home at separate times in their lives. Many women are handling social transitions in the female roles by returning attention to their own educations when their children go to school, preparing ahead for skilled occupations in the work force when the parenting tasks become lighter. This way women can avoid having to juggle two "careers" at the same time.

Many women, however, still have to juggle. In 1979, 57.2% of all married women in the U. S. with school-age children and 41.6% of women with preschoolers worked outside the home, primarily for financial reasons (U. S. Bureau of the Census, 1980). The modern family consumes far more goods and services than it can produce, and earning two paychecks is often the only way to maintain an adequate standard of living. As the economy grows tighter, both men and women are increasingly involved in lifelong work outside of the home.

In addition to the overwhelming trend of women participating in the work force in increasing numbers and in varied occupations, a number of other current trends affect traditional work patterns. One is the trend toward longer preparation, especially in technical areas. Automation is phasing out many unskilled occupations, and the new jobs that are appearing require more training. Many service occupations, too, now demand more training and higher credentials than they did in the past. As the result of extended years of training for any given job, more young adults are reaching their late twenties with little or no opportunity for job experimentation, except in unskilled labor (Schenk & Schenk, 1978). And the shift to jobs requiring longer preparation may have the direct effect of postponing family cycles.

Another trend is an emerging pattern in the work cycle of **second careers.** In addition to the housewives retraining and reentering the work force are more and more men who find second careers a necessity (Sheppard & Rix, 1977). A second career may be required because an earlier one has been phased out as the result of economic or technological change. Or a second career may be a renewed attempt to find a fulfilling work role after years spent in an unsatisfying job. It can also be a way to restructure life after retirement from a first occupation. Awareness of the second-career option is increasingly important, as career choices multiply and young adults are pressed by parents and schools to make commitments while they're still not sure what they want to do with their lives. The message to them probably should be to choose a promising direction and plan for alternate careers that require similar skills. As the baby-boom cohort moves into an already tight job market, flexibility in work roles is even more necessary for social and psychological survival (Sarason, 1977).

Learning as a Process over Time

One process of development that is clearly tied to both family and work is formal education. Like family and work patterns, educational patterns are shifting.

The educational myth of this century has been that formal education is the key to occupational and economic success. Part of the myth is that if you finish high school, and especially if you finish college, you will be prepared for life. At mid-century, when the economy was booming, this was almost true. But by the 1970s it was becoming obvious that an education doesn't guarantee employment. Another part of the myth is that once you have completed your education you're educated completely, for all time. But in a period of rapid technological development the fantasy of an end to learning can never be true for technical workers. And in a time of considerable social change it becomes less true for everyone. By this century's end, lifelong learning is the educational probability (McClusky, 1978).

Traditionally, the process of education moves through a number of levels. The levels at which people stop their educations determine their positions in the work force. The first level is a grade-school education; this limits job choices to unskilled labor, for the most part, unless a person can find an apprenticeship of some kind in a trade or is a gifted entrepreneur. The second level, a high school education, has been the traditional level of qualification for most trades and for clerical and industrial jobs. But as technical and service jobs have become more complex, another level has developed to extend education further—the 2-year college. Two years of college provides a basis for more demanding occupations, and 4 years of college takes a person even further, potentially. College graduates form another level in the work force. The professions and many technical fields demand an additional level—graduate school. Traditionally people have entered their educational cycle in childhood and stayed in it until they reached their maximum level of education. Then they were finished—usually in the late teens or early twenties. This is not true any more.

Education is changing to reflect the changes in the social environment. New trends in work and family cycles have created an educational situation in which people may drop in and drop out of educational institutions as new needs arise in their lives. People may begin and end their educational development for any number of reasons. Perhaps the most common reasons for renewing the educational process are the following: for further education or training, for updating of a previous education, for reeducation in a new career, for obtaining academic credentials, and for enrichment of intellectual life. On-the-job training programs are offered in many academic programs, integrating education into work life. Businesses may offer educational opportunities for off-the-job adult education as a fringe benefit, to motivate an employee's preparation for advancement or to help retrain employees whose jobs have been eliminated. Individuals, too, increasingly integrate further education into their plans for family and work commitments. A growing number of people have found that continuing-education programs can be sources of entertainment, recreation, and personal expression. As **adult education** becomes an expected and accepted institution of adult life, it may outlast both work and family as sources of life satisfaction (McClusky, 1978).

In both its traditional and contemporary forms, the educational cycle has a function other than to provide learning. The school supplements the neighborhood and the work place in providing opportunities for another important developmental pattern: that of friendship.

Friendship as a Process over Time

When people come together in educational or work settings they already have two of the three main criteria for friendships that research on interpersonal attraction has isolated. The first of these is propinquity; the second is perceived similarity; the third is establishing mutuality and compatability (Clore, 1975; Fiske & Weiss, 1977). Propinquity, the opportunity to meet and be together for some time, is the first stage of any interpersonal encounter. Friendships begin when people meet and recognize that they have a common bond for interaction, whatever the bond may be. Similar backgrounds, attitudes, and interests all stimulate relationships, but the most important similarity is mutual attraction. Positive mutual feelings are a basis for trust and compatability. When a person we like in turn likes us, we know that we have a friend. Shared experiences over time can build and consolidate friendly relationships until they become central to our social lives.

Unlike the other formal life patterns—family, work, and education—committed friendships guarantee acceptance, social stimulation, and affection. Friends catch us when we fall through the cracks in the other kinds of life patterns. Recent research has identified some coherent, lifelong patterns in the search for friendship, which seems to be an unfolding process of creating social-support systems. The overall developmental pattern the research reveals may parallel the patterns of family and work development that have been identified.

The history of our friendships is based in the intensity of our needs for intimacy. Our less intimate friendships supply surface social needs for belonging; more intimate connections fill our deeper needs for love. Several studies indicate that the degree of intensity of people's friendships and intimate relationships seems to increase and decrease during the life span (Bensman & Lilienfield, 1979; Block et al., 1981; Fiske & Weiss, 1977). And there is some possibility that the intimacy needs of men and of women may reach their peak intensities at different times (Fiske & Weiss, 1977).

Sexual difference doesn't necessarily create different kinds of friendship; the difference is in degree. Both men and women need the same things from their friends—someone to talk to openly; someone to help, when that is needed; and someone to share food and entertainment. But men are socialized to avoid intimacy, especially with other men (which might be perceived as homosexual) or in a manner that could reveal vulnerability. In general, male friendships are less intense than female friendships (Fiske & Weiss, 1977; Parlee, 1979).

Both intimate relationships, with lovers and mates, and casual relationships, with friends from work and social groups, are involved in the adult-friendship sequence. It begins in late adolescence and early young adulthood, when the future is particularly uncertain, with a strong need for intimate friends or lovers who will provide social support. The existence of this phase is itself strongly supported, incidentally, by Erikson (1963), who identifies the task of these years as one of establishing intimacy versus isolation. In courtship and early marriage, friendship needs are often met by one's lover or spouse, and other friends may drop away. The later years of young adulthood seem to require friendships that are less intimate, as individuals involve themselves in work or family or in both. Friendships with other young couples are most often based on shared interests, consumption of goods and services, and parenting activities. Often divorce causes difficulty in friendship ties; shared friends are lost. The middle years are for many people a time of more socially formal and less open friendships, based on shared interests and activities. Retirement reduces social competition and once again permits more intimate interaction. The very old seem to be more open to friendly exchanges than people in any other time of life (Bensman & Lilienfield, 1979).

Some variations do exist in the developmental processes of friendship experienced by men and women. Apparently young women feel stronger needs for **mutuality**—for equality in their relationships—than do young men; and the needs for intimacy of many middle-aged men become stronger at a time when those of middle-aged women aren't particularly strong. These patterns may be changing, however, as both men and women learn to interact in more open and intimate ways rather than to play out social stereotypes (Fiske & Weiss, 1977). A weakening of the stereotypes may bring friendship and intimacy (liking and loving) into a closer relationship, too. This would be an improvement over the current situation, in which women often both like and love their romantic partners while men most often love, but do not like, theirs (Rubin, 1975).

Kenneth Keniston (1977b) identifies a developmental process of interpersonal relationships that depends less on social conditions and life events—and more on psychological growth—than the research cited on friendship patterns suggests is the case. He describes four increasingly sophisticated phases of interpersonal relations: identicality, parity, complementarity, and mutuality. In the phase of identicality, closeness to another person is dependent on complete similarity and complete agreement, a typically adolescent pattern of relating. In the second, more realistic phase, parity, we can be close to others who are only fairly similar to us. When our relationship potential develops to the point that we can warmly relate to others who are quite different and, further, we value the differences, we have reached the phase of complementarity. And, finally, when another person can be recognized as truly separate from us, rather than a reflection of ourselves and our expectations, **mutuality** becomes possible.

Keniston draws parallels to the pattern of interpersonal relation-

ships that he's outlined in both sexual relationships (as individuals move from sexual interaction toward true intimacy) and in relationships with elders (as individuals move from being apprentices toward becoming peers with their mentors and parents). Keniston's parallel frameworks of growth are not tied to any chronology. He feels that, especially with the moratorium of "youth," in his definition of the period as a time to focus on interpersonal growth, the possibility of relating to others on a mutual and compassionate level is available at an early age (Keniston, 1977b).

To deal with interpersonal development in Keniston's terms is to move across the thin line between social and psychological processes, if such a line can be said to exist. In the next chapter we'll move to the psychological perspective, for a final survey of adult development.

Summary

Changes in the social environment cause changes in the traditional social patterns of adulthood. The patterns for the developmental processes of family and work life, usually maintained by social norms and social roles, break down with social change and often leave people socially uncomfortable and personally confused.

The social pattern that is central in most adult lives is the process of the unfolding of family experiences. The family has been undergoing some changes in form and timing over this century, but we still tend to perceive the family process in its mythical or traditional form, as the continuous creation of generations of nuclear families.

The family process, in both myth and tradition, consists of a sequence of substages in the lives of nuclear families: mariage, child rearing and launching, and postparenting. These stages require several role changes on the part of parents—changes that may be sources of family conflict.

Current trends that are modifying the patterns of family life include a shift in timing, a decrease in size, a variation in family forms, and a growing social acceptance of remaining child free and of staying single.

Like family patterns, work patterns have their myths and traditions, and the developmental process of work life is also undergoing changes. Most discussions of work development reflect a male version of the work pattern, as family care has been traditionally considered the work of women. A typical myth of work experience describes the phases of preparation and training, job experimentation, job commitment, and progress in a career that peaks, levels off, and fades out, ending in retirement. Some men do live out this pattern; some don't. Women seldom follow this pattern.

Trends in work development include variations in timing and form, particularly on the part of women, who may enter and leave the work force, taking time out for parenting. Timing is also changing because men and women require longer periods of preparation and training. Another trend is an emerging pattern of second careers, as technological and social changes affect the job market.

Another social pattern, which is directly related to both family and work cycles, is the process of education. In recent years the time for education has moved from early adult life only; people are educating themselves throughout the life course. There is more flexibility in the educational process now, for individualized choice in timing of training and retraining. The role of education as a source of personal enrichment also is becoming perceived more clearly.

There seems to be a pattern in friendship that may be related to the developmental processes of family and work. Needs for friendship and love relationships seem to be most intense in early adulthood, becoming less important at the end of young adulthood but emerging strongly again in later life. Men and women seem to differ in the timing and intensity of their friendship needs. There may exist a trend in the friendship cycle toward more openness and intimacy for both sexes and toward friendship over more of adult life. Keniston has suggested that relationships follow this trend when the partners have developed from having needs primarily for sameness to having acceptance of and respect for differences.

Terms and Concepts to Define

adult education _____

_____

blended family _____

_____

cohabitating couple _____

_____

communal family _____

_____

deferring a role _____

_____

developmental role changes _____

_____

empty-nest family _____

_____

extended family _____

_____

group marriage _____

_____

modified extended family _____

_____

mutuality _____

_____

nuclear family _____

_____

second careers _____

_____

single-parent family _____

_____

Experiences

To involve yourself with the concepts in this chapter, try these experiences described in the Appendix.

Alone
24. The Good Life
42. Goal Setting I: Long-Term Goals
43. Goal Setting II: Short-Term Goals
44. Goal Setting III: Lifetime Goals

With Others
38. Family Forms
39. Friendship
21. Social Roles

Going beyond the Text

1. Scan newspapers and magazines for materials that reflect new family and work patterns in contemporary life.
2. Identify your own changing pattern of relationships, from adolescence on, using Keniston's process theory. Does Keniston's theory fit? Do you have any complementary relationships? Do you have any that are truly mutual? What would you need to do to reach the level of mutuality in a relationship?

Suggested Readings

Gross, R. The lifelong learner. *New York: Simon & Schuster, 1975.*
Smelser, N., & Erikson, E. Themes of work and love in adulthood. *Cambridge, Mass.: Harvard University Press, 1980.*

13

Life Perceptions:
Psychological Changes over Time

When you have finished reading this chapter you should be able to:
Describe the forms of variability of the "psychological clock."
Discuss cognitive development during the adult years.
Summarize Kimmel's model of personality development.
Identify the life problems of early, middle, and late adulthood that require developmental changes in adaptive styles.

When we discuss psychological processes of change we are dealing with a form of development that is difficult to separate from biological and social development. One way to make the separation is to speak of the psychological aspects of experience in terms of perception, especially self-perception.

Perception is the most basic level on which we know our world. The act of perceiving is a two-step process that consists of selecting sensations to attend to and then interpreting these sensations on the basis of learned meanings. Both biological factors (accuracy and speed of sensory activity) and social factors (learning and expectations) are involved in perception, but in addition to these are psychological factors that shape our experience: cognitive styles (ways of thinking about the input) and personality styles, including adaptations (ways of reacting and behaving in response to the input of perceptions). These inner perceptual processes and their outer behavioral forms are the stuff of psychological change. We can discuss these changes in developmental terms, even while recognizing that it is impossible to separate them from changes in the body that experiences them or changes in the social settings in which the person is living and growing.

Adult Psychology

The history of the psychology of adult development is not very long. Although some work had been done on cognitive and behavioral changes by gerontologists earlier, it was not until 1966, in a paper Bernice Neugarten presented to the American Psychological Association, that the foundation for a true psychology of adult life was specified. Neugarten said it would be necessary to have an "overarching theory of human behavior." Such a theory would have to integrate biological and social changes as well as describe orderly and sequential psychological changes that were not traceable to physical decline or social change (Neugarten, 1968a).

Since Neugarten presented her paper, the work of both Gould and Levinson (which we have reviewed) as well as the work of Douglas Kimmel (which will be discussed in this chapter) have met the demand for "overarching theory." But an experimentally supported description of orderly and sequential changes in personality and other areas of psychological performance is still lacking. We do, however, have enough material—much of it supplied by Neugarten herself—to trace the probability that we do, psychologically, grow through time, or at least through experience. This chapter presents some of the evidence for these changes.

The developmental paths available for discussion are those that researchers have investigated. For example, cognitive changes that correlate to some degree with biological maturation, aging, and senescence have been identified. Personality changes that may be due to cumulative experience but may also relate to social developments have been recorded. And adaptive changes to evolving environmental demands have also been pointed out. So the specific topics of this chapter are some of the "psychological-clock" changes in cognition, personality, and adaptation.

The Psychological Clock

The timing of psychological changes is most often a question of an individualized **psychological clock**. Like biological- and social-clock timing, psychological-clock time is subject to personal and social variations. Psychological development may be the most variable process of the three. Most of the reasons for its variability are based in people's self-perceptions, although the environment may supply the sense of aging or the expectations for behavior. It is quite possible to feel psychologically "old" at the age of 20 (Sarason, 1977); the perception of having reached middle age may occur at any point in a 20-year span (Neugarten, 1968b). Yet a psychological sense of youth may be maintained as long as we're alive (Kanin, 1978). In other words, psychological age may have little correlation with chronology.

Psychological-clock time is not only individually variable and relatively unrestrained by chronology, it is also often internally variable within any adult. Robert Kastenbaum and his associates have developed a research framework called **The Ages of Me;** they apply it in surveys that gather personal and interpersonal definitions of aging. Their data indicates that a person may hold several perceptions of his or her own age; a person seldom specifies only one age in describing his or her appearance, physical condition, thoughts and interests, position in society, psychological sense of age, and age preference (Kastenbaum, Derbin, Sabatini, & Artt, 1972). Are your perceptions of your own age varied?

The age I appear to others to be is_____.
The age my body appears to me to be is_____.
The age that identifies the level of my thoughts and interests is_____.
The age for my social position is_____.
The age for my psychological self is_____.
The age I would prefer to be is_____.

Young adults estimating these ages may be fairly consistent, but, as time goes on, consistency becomes quite rare (Kastenbaum, 1979).

Psychological maturation and aging may be a matter of self-perception, for the most part, but there are some apparently biological factors that affect it—particularly in the area of cognitive processing.

Cognitive Development

The biological factors that affect cognition are mainly in the areas of sensory efficiency and speed of reaction. By the age of 20 the efficiency with which an individual reacts to physical stimuli has peaked. Reaction time—the length of time between a stimulus and a response to the stimulus—lengthens slightly between ages 20 and 25 and may increase as much as 17% between 20 and 40 (Bromley, 1974). This general slowing of reaction is often inaccurately generalized as being a slowdown of cognitive processes. Actually, a review of the literature suggests that the years between 20 and 40 are a time of peak performance in verbal learning, problem solving, short-term recall and creative thinking (Stevens-Long, 1979). These skills decline slowly if at all over the middle years because, as reaction time lengthens, other strategies are adopted to compensate for loss of quickness (Troll, 1975).

Intelligence testing is an example of a measure of cognitive processes that may indicate changes in quality of performance over the years of adult life but doesn't necessarily reflect a change in degree of intelligence. Although early cross-sectional studies seemed to show a general decline in intelligence (as measured by IQ tests) over time, their findings, you remember, were distorted by social changes in education, nutrition, and population. Longitudinal studies have indicated increases in IQ into the fifties (Troll, 1975). Recent research in intelligence has distinguished between two general types of intelligence, both of which IQ tests measure but typically have not measured separately. These two categories are called *fluid intelligence* and *crystallized intelligence.*

Fluid intelligence refers to kinds of intelligence that require quick thinking: recognition of relationships, for example, or rapid organization of data. Tests of memory span and timed problem solving tap fluid intelligence—which, because of its reliance on speed of reaction, does show some decline over time. **Crystallized intelligence,** on the other hand, is not a matter of quickness; it refers to a broad body of knowledge and a wide range of strategies. When time limits are eliminated from testing, crystallized intelligence is revealed to increase continuously over time. Because these two types of intelligence have been mixed in the results of IQ testing, the decrease in fluid intelligence and the increase in crystallized intelligence have averaged one another out, and the impression has been that little or no mental growth takes place in adulthood. But actually there may be a change in both intellectual quantity and quality (Horn, 1970).

Only with senescence is there any biological reason for significant decline in intellectual performance. In senescence, IQ drops significantly. Through administering the Wechsler Adult Intelligence Scale to an elderly population, Klaus Riegel has found that a significant drop in IQ often precedes death. In fact, this drop occurs in so many cases that it is an effective predictor. Riegel calls the phenomenon **terminal drop**. It is the point at which biological senescence catches up with cognition (1971).

Such cognitive behaviors as learning, problem solving, and creative thinking are affected only slightly, if at all, over the adult years by biological decline. And, given more time to think, more light to see by or whatever physical supports the individual tested needs, older adults can perform well indeed. Another factor that should be mentioned, however, is the effect of social beliefs and attitudes on cognitive processes. A belief system holding that to age is to grow forgetful, that "old dogs can't be taught new tricks," and that what's commonly termed *senility* is inevitable can create a self-fulfilling prophecy. As adults age they often believe that they can't learn; they often take refuge in forgetfulness. "If you don't use it, you lose it" may apply to cognitive as well as to physical functions. With adequate use, cognitive functions—especially those that relate to crystallized intelligence—may develop measurably over the years.

On a more theoretical level, the question of whether or not cognitive styles develop further in middle and late adulthood is an interesting open question. The most widely accepted model of growth in the ability to understand and in problem solving is the four-stage model described by Jean Piaget, which deals with childhood development of cognition. The Piagetian model consists of four stages: a simple sensory and motor reaction stage; "a pre-operational" stage, which precedes orderly and sequential thought; and then a "concrete operations" stage, in which thinking and problem solving about concrete objects and situations is possible. In the last stage, "formal operations" become possible. **Formal operations** include abstract thought and formal and creative reasoning. The first two stages—those of sensorimotor and preoperational processes—are identified with infancy and early childhood in Piaget's model. Concrete operations come later. Concrete operations are essential for adult functioning, and most people probably develop to this stage of cognitive processing as a direct function of maturation. Many people don't go beyond concrete thinking, but those who do develop formal operations may learn to think in abstract terms as early as the age of 11. Piaget believes that formal operations may develop in scope over the adult years, but he doesn't feel that any higher level of processing is achieved (1972).

Although Piaget believed that cognitive growth stops with the fourth stage he identified, a number of theorists are carrying the developmental model of cognitive process further. Lawrence Kohlberg, for instance, has created a sequential theory of moral reasoning that was originally based on stages of development that resemble Piaget's. To Kohlberg, as to Piaget, the higher cognitive processes seem to involve autonomous thinking that is free from the need for concrete details and specifics, which is relatively rare in the general population. In Kohlberg's later work, however, he emphasizes the importance not only of cognitive sophistication but of experience in shaping this autonomy. Perhaps the adult years of solving problems and experiencing difficult choices are necessary to bring us to the highest levels of social commitment and responsibility and of universal morality and compassion (Kohlberg, 1973). Like Erikson and Jung, Kohlberg describes an all-encompassing cosmic perspective that may emerge in middle life—the understanding of our essential unity with all things.

In addition to Kohlberg's extension of the cognitive model as a function of experience over time, a number of theorists have recently proposed that some adults may develop to a further, "dialectic" level in which they continue cognitive growth. This growth comes about by any or all of the following means: reconciliation of contradictions, seeking out problems and resolving them, and adapting to life's changes (Stevens-Long, 1979). If, as suggested in the proposed theories of further psychological growth, cognitive development can be extended through experience or openness to a wider range of conflicts and problems, the time-out for further personal growth that Keniston has identified in the twenties would allow for richer cognitive development as well as for broader personality development early in adult life.

Personality Development

Cognitive processing—the way we think—is an underlying part of personality—the way we act. Temperament, cognitive style, and environmentally learned emotional responses together with some other traits make up the predictable patterns that we call personality. Once formed in early childhood, does personality change?

A problem with many of the existing answers to the question of whether personality develops is that the answers have been given by theorists trained in the Freudian psychoanalytic tradition; Freud's answer, of course, is that personality development ends with adolescence. If researchers assume that personality remains stable, their research probably is designed to maintain that opinion (Levinson, 1980; Rubin, 1981).

Among those in structural schools of thought, only the neo-Freudians and ego psychologists allow room for the kind of growth orientation found in the work of Gould and Loevinger. However, the orientations of gerontology that are multidisciplinary, such as are found in the work of Neugarten, Levinson, Butler, and Kimmel, also allowed more bias-free research into personality changes. The results suggest that personality does develop or at least change in various ways through the years. Genetically inherited temperament may not modify much, but environmentally learned responses may, as the core, inner sense of oneself and the social demands of changing settings require new ways of being in the world.

On the theoretical level we have already reviewed a number of different points of view on personality change. The traditional psychoanalytic position is that there is no such change, except in the case of therapy or of an overwhelming life event. Even so, contemporary psychoanalytic theorists, including ego psychologists, have been apt to take positions similar to Erikson's: that the unfolding of the self depends on the individual's response to the social setting. Personality may develop over time or may fail to develop (Block & Haan, 1971; Erikson, 1968; Gould, 1978; Loevinger, 1976). Behaviorists and social-learning theorists also have taken the position that interaction with the environment over time can effect personality change, if learning takes place (Kimmel, 1974). Humanistic psychologists believe that human personality naturally develops over time, unless something blocks that natural psychological growth (Bühler & Massarik, 1968; Maslow, 1971; Rogers, 1968). In general, then, there's agreement that personality does change.

In reviewing the literature on personality change in adulthood, Zick Rubin has found that how much personality changes depends on how personality is defined, as well as on what aspects of behavior the researchers choose for their focus. Although temperament and some cognitive styles seem to remain fairly stable, self-esteem, sense of control over life, and value systems expand and are enriched over the years. Unless we get stuck, we will increase in mastery and integration—within the continuity and stability of our personal identities (Brim & Kagan, 1980; Rubin, 1981).

Jung, Bühler, Erikson, Gould, Levinson, and Loevinger all give us models of the potential for progressive integration of personality. Each of them sees personality change over time as potential but not necessarily inevitable. Not only does personality change not proceed automatically, it can be regressive; the change can be toward previously used psychological strategies as well as toward new, more adaptive ones (Fiske, 1978). To discuss personality change more fully, we need to have a clear model of how it works.

Douglas Kimmel (1974), a social gerontologist, has formulated a theoretical model of the development of the personality and the self that fits quite smoothly with the mixed contemporary views of personality. That is, Kimmel's model fits the views of personality unfolding in relationship to a social environment, being learned by an interacting organism, and constituting the core of a self-actualizing and growing human being. Although Kimmel's basic premise is the humanistic and existential belief that humans have an inborn striving to reach their highest potentials and greatest levels of competence, which creates the energy to grow psychologically, Kimmel also focuses on social interaction as a source of development over time.

How does personality develop? In Kimmel's view, the self and the environment interact constantly, as we attempt to self-actualize and to manage our social worlds. To cope, as either inner or outer conditions change, we adjust and readjust the fit of self to environment (see Figure 13-1).

Kimmel's model consists of three parts: a fairly stable inner world

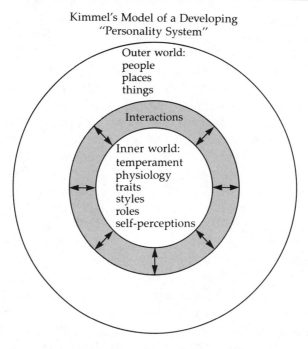

Kimmel's Model of a Developing
"Personality System"

Figure 13-1 Douglas Kimmel's model of development of the personality system combines temperament, physiology, roles, cognitive and behavioral styles, and self-perceptions in a conceptual "inner world" that is in constant interaction with the people, places, situations, and things of the "outer world." *(Source: Kimmel, 1974.)*

What's useful about Kimmel's model? _____

_____

Was the research method appropriate? _____

_____

What are the model's weaknesses? _____

_____

Does this model fit your life? How? _____

_____

_____

(of temperament, physiology, character traits, cognitive styles, behavioral styles, social roles, and self-perceptions), an often changing outer world (of social situations, other people, and social consequences of behavior) and the shifting interactions between inner and outer worlds (of physical responses, emotional responses, thoughts, and memories). The outer-world areas are constantly interacting with the inner-world areas, creating a **personality system.** Kimmel defines personality as an ongoing process of attempting to fit the self to the environment.

In this model, individual differences in personality are the effects of different inner worlds, outer worlds, or both. Cohort effects are the results of shared outer worlds. Personality change over time is the result of accumulated memories and strategies for interaction, changing physiology, changing roles, and changing self-perceptions. Development is the result of striving, interacting, and learning. Kimmel explains growth over time as being a natural function of adapting to the changes that time brings. Unlike biological and social processes, which can most often be illustrated by a curve that rises to a peak and then falls as the life course progresses, the psychological process of personality growth has the possibility of rising in an ever-upward-extending line.

When Kimmel was developing his model in the early 1970s, most of the work on adult life that we've reviewed in this text was not available. He had the Kansas City Studies to work from, and he had some material on the psychopathologies of aging. In spite of these limited resources he has described a model of psychological development that not only fits the research available then but that also holds up in light of later research. The work done in the seventies by Levinson, Gould, Vaillant, and Butler all support the following basic concepts: that psychological growth continues throughout adult life, and that the source of growth is interactions with the social environment.

Current research fits these concepts well. The Kansas City Studies showed that although such aspects of personality as styles of thinking, behaving, and responding emotionally were stable over time, adjustive interactions such as conformity to sexual stereotypes and degree of social involvement change over the years (Kimmel, 1974). A number of contemporary individual case studies in both Levinson's longitudinal work (Levinson et al., 1978) and Vaillant's (1977) also show these consistencies and changes. The conclusions reached by the two longitudinal studies are similar: in a sense, each of us is the same in late life as in early life, but over the life course our ways of adapting and of balancing our inner and outer lives may change dramatically. The issue of consistency or change in personality has more or less lost its meaning in recent years; the current issue isn't so much whether personality changes but which parts change and which are stable (Lazarus, 1976).

Bernice Neugarten's early contribution to the psychology of adult life (1968a) identified a number of parts of the personality in which changes are apt to occur over time. She called these parts of the self the **executive processes of personality;** they include mastery and control of the outer world and the awareness and cognitive processing that characterize the inner self. Self-awareness, self-understanding, and self-utilization became stronger over time in this early study of "successful" middle-aged adults between 45 and 55. As the central issues of their lives changed and their sense of competence grew stronger, these personality traits emerged consistently.

In Neugarten's study, differences in sex seemed to correlate with significant variations in personality change between men and women. It is in this study that sex-role reversals in men and women were first identified, to be supported by other, later studies. The shifts both in women's personalities toward independence and aggression in the later years and in men's personalities toward nurturance and sociability have been found to be a cross-cultural phenomenon (Gutmann, 1977), as well as an American one (Lowenthal, Thurnher, & Chiriboga, 1977). As outer-world variables such as status and autonomy change, and as older men lose social status with age and women grow more vulnerable to widowhood, inner-world shifts seem almost predictable.

Another inner-world shift, which Neugarten (1968b) has called **increased interiority** and Robert Butler (1975) calls "life review," also seems to develop in the middle and late years of life. This shift occurs as people become more self-aware, introspective, and reflective—as they rework the meanings of their lives in their minds. Butler, especially, has found that, in this process of adaptation to aging, dramatic personality changes occur. Even at the very end of life, as an adaptation to dying, personalities may change radically (Imara, 1975). In Kimmel's terms, the trend through time toward introspection may be seen as an internalized interaction between self-perceptions, another avenue for the adaptation he has described (Kimmel, 1974).

Adaptations over Time

Adaptations are changes in cognitive and behavioral patterns made as means of adjustment to situational changes. As typical ways of thinking and characteristic patterns of responding change, styles of adaptive behavior must change also. Often, if we are to adjust positively to changing situations, a new coping skill must be learned. It may be developed through experimentation, finding new role models, or seeking out new resources for mental health, such as therapy. New sources of self-esteem are often required, to replace physical qualities or social roles that drop away over the years. Learning to cope is one of life's ongoing lessons. We can adjust passively, changing our ways of thinking and behaving in order to limit the stresses presented by our changing situations. Or we can adjust actively, modifying the environment to bring it into harmony with our own needs (Lazarus, 1976). There are excellent self-help books available for all of the common rough spots in adult development: separation from family of origin, marital and vocational choices, sexual adjustments, parenting, divorce, mid-life changes, retirement, aging, death. And many communities supply supports for these transitions, as well as for the less common crises that may occur over the life course. Some of the typical community supports are hotlines, crisis counseling, and church and community counseling services, many of which offer help in coping with rape, suicide, marital assault, and other situations of immediate need. Given appropriate help at the appropriate time, most of us can deal with developmental changes adaptively.

In the work of most of the theorists reviewed, the assumption has been made that adaptations to life are increasingly positive. Yet negative adaptation or failure to adapt are also possibilities. We can become developmentally stuck.

In terms of Kimmel's model, our developmental process may become too centered on our inner worlds or too focused on our outer worlds, and then our interactions may become dysfunctional. Inner self-rejection or outer stresses may arrest development. It follows that psychotherapy should be concerned with helping the "stuck" person find ways to get the processes of personality working together again. This aspect of the model is consistent with most contemporary types of psychotherapy, including ego-centered, humanistic, client-centered, existential, and behavioral approaches. Their common ground is that the person has to do his/her own "unsticking" but can do that only with new inner understanding or new interactional coping skills, or with a new outer-world situation. Recent changes in psychiatric delivery systems also reflect this view: community outpatient centers and brief, crisis-intervention approaches to psychotherapy are designed around the concept that temporary and situational dysfunctions of personality process often only require some help in getting unstuck (Calhoun, Selby, & King, 1978).

Adaptive styles and failures of adaptation understandably vary over time, along with changing self-perceptions, roles, physical developments, and situational demands. And we all may find ourselves stuck at some points. However, ideally there should be an overall trend of increased understanding, balance, and autonomy (White, 1975). Life requires renewal. Gould has described the need for continuously eliminating illusions over the years, Levinson has described the necessity for continual re-creation of the life structure, and Vaillant has described the importance of modifying defenses in order to proceed with psychological growth. In early adulthood, successful adaptation involves achieving competence in the social world, which may require strategies of social conformity. In the middle years, other strategies are needed, for the task of bringing the needs of the inner personality into a dynamic balance with the realities of the outer world. And, in late life, successful adaptation may depend on the ability to expand the inner self. Whether psychological development is called *adapting,* or *growing,* or *self-actualizing,* it is a function of the personality system's flexibility in handling both inner and outer concerns (Kimmel, 1974).

A "life-problems" approach to adaptation may clarify the necessity for developmental changes over time (see Figure 13-2). Successful resolution of the life problems usually connected with early adulthood, which include decisions about autonomy, work, sex, aggression, intimacy, marriage, and parenting, all require some degree of outward conformity to the needs of others, rather than the needs of self, in the personality system. Adjustment in these years can be a struggle. Developing a clear sense of personal identity, dealing with sex and aggression appropriately, making meaningful commitments to the social setting—these adjustments aren't easy for everyone.

Life period	Adaptive process	Life problems
late adulthood	Personality system directed inward	adjusting to death adjustment to physical losses adjustment to social losses adjustment to role losses
transition to late life		transition to late life
middle adulthood	personality system balanced between inner and outer concerns	parental responsibilities sexual controls social maintenance aggression controls marriage maintenance work-role maintenance accepting vulnerability
transition to middle years		transition to middle years
early adulthood	personality system directed outward	parenting decisions marriage decisions establishing intimacy expression of sexuality expression of aggression work-role decisions accepting autonomy

Figure 13-2 Successful adaptation over the life course requires shifts in the personality system, as the problems of life make themselves felt.

Some young adults fit themselves to their outer worlds relatively painlessly; others suffer their ways through. In order to process these issues developmentally, big concessions and commitments have to be made on the outer-world side of the personality system (Kimmel, 1974; Lazarus, 1976; Levinson et al., 1978).

The life problems in the transition from early adulthood to the middle years brings an increase in the difficulties of adjustment. Responsibilities multiply. Situations that constitute the prime sources of life stress increasingly dominate life: marriage problems, family problems, and physical problems (Holmes & Rahe, 1967). Even acceptance of adult status can be a problem (Levinson, 1980). Development in this period calls for skills in coping with stress and in minimizing conflicts.

The same interactive strategies needed in the transition years after early adulthood are needed in the middle years. The adjustment problems themselves may not change much in middle adulthood, but they may increase in intensity. People who have difficulties with work or marriage in early adulthood have some hope of starting over. Yet, in the middle years, future possibilities shrink. People get set in their ways in this time of stability. To maintain sameness and illusions of security and to neglect growth can be tempting.

Transition to late life is another crisis in adaptation, especially for people who have been socialized to view growing older as a negative experience. The minimal condition for being able to continue growing psychologically from this point on is the belief that growing is possible.

Late-life problems are mostly losses—losses of people we love, of physical capabilities, and of familiar places and things. Successful adaptation requires a sufficiently strong sense of self in the individual that he/she can replace what's lost and continue to stay involved in living (Kart et al., 1978).

These developmental life problems are all just the result of living. Although categories of problems may be more common in some periods of life than in others, all of us don't experience the specific life problems in the same order. They can occur at any time in life, just when we least expect them. People we love can die at any age. Divorces and career setbacks can occur as total shocks, with no developmental markers to warn that they're coming: so can wars, disasters, and economic collapses. Whenever they happen, crises need to be met adaptively. Sometimes we can just go smoothly through life's changes. Sometimes we struggle for a while before we can fit ourselves back together comfortably. Inevitably there are times, and they can happen in any person's life, when we don't, can't, or won't adapt. We get stuck, and we need help.

Failures to Adapt

The failure to adapt is a failure to develop. Going through life as an eternal adolescent can be painful and lonely; and getting stuck in making the commitments that are most appropriately made in young adulthood can limit life narrowly over the years. Or, bogging down in the stability that is most typical of middle age can dwarf growth, at any time of life. These adaptive failures, however, are only slightly dysfunctional. There are far more disastrous maladaptations to living than failure to grow; for example, criminal behavior and mental illness also reflect dysfunctional social and personal adaptations to the demands of development.

Particularly in the early years of transition into adulthood, inappropriate expressions of sexuality or aggression may give rise to the kinds of behavior that are socially labeled *criminal*. Criminal behaviors peak in these early years. Of all U. S. crimes, 23.3% are committed by adolescents (U.S. Bureau of the Census, 1980). Late adolescence is also the most common time for those sets of maladaptive behaviors that are identified as mental illness and labeled *schizophrenia*. Social standards for mental health are based on expectations for adult behavior; people in the early years of adult life may not meet the standards for lack of skills to conform (Lazarus, 1976). Lack of ability to interact with the outer world productively sometimes defeats people before they start; suicides also are increasingly common in these years. In the past 20 years, the incidence of suicide has tripled for both sexes during the teens and twenties (Hyde & Forsythe, 1978).

Over the years, cognitive or behavioral change may be sufficient to allow the personality to come into balance. Criminal behavior decreases with age. Perhaps this is because violent people live short lives; but possibly it's because more appropriate ways of dealing with sex and aggression are learned. Mental illness does increase with age, however. People who are on the edge of mental illness may continue there for years; then at some point an adjustive crisis may push them over the line (Lazarus, 1976). **Mental illness** is a broad label for adjustive problems that are dysfunctional enough to require professional help. Mental and emotional maladjustments increase for both men and women in the middle years of life. The greatest number of outpatients in mental-health facilities are between the ages of 35 and 44; the numbers of patients increase with age after 25 until that peak is reached, and after it they steadily decline. Fewer people are being hospitalized now for mental illness, but in the number of hospitalizations that occur there is the same pattern of rise and fall in numbers of patients according to age that's been found with outpatients.

Depression and psychosomatic illness are two typical forms of maladaptive response that peak in the middle years (Torack, 1981). Suicide, as a solution to depression, peaks for women at this time also; for men it continues to increase in frequency as a solution over the life span. Although the elderly are only 11% of the population of the United States, they commit 25% of all the nation's suicides (USDHEW, 1978). The fact that so many older people have chosen to adapt to the problems of late life by ending it is not common knowledge (Hyde & Forsythe, 1978).

Along with the lack of knowledge in the general population about suicide in the late years, there is a common view of old age as the age of mental illness that is quite inaccurate. Although an estimated 15% of all people over 65 may have some problems in adjustment, only 5% have severe mental illnesses. Some of these illnesses are the result of brain diseases; others are the result of inappropriate drug use, of faulty nutrition, and of isolation, insecurity, and sensory loss (Butler & Lewis, 1977). It's hopeful to remember that the other 95% are coping, holding their lives in balance, and many are growing, still.

Of course, not all criminal behavior and mental illness and suicides are simply failures in psychological development, caused by the problems of life. There are social settings in which criminal

behavior is the only way to survive, in which what's been described as mental illness may be considered sanity, and in which suicide is socially acceptable. And there exist problems of body chemistry and neural function that constitute organic causes for both the social illnesses of criminals and the mental illnesses of disturbed and desperate people.

Still, enough of our problems of adaptation are developmental to make it useful to see them as natural side effects of living. In understanding our own developmental potentials for growth and nongrowth, we can be better prepared for dealing with the problems that life brings. We can be ready for the future. But can you be ready enough? In the next chapter you can explore that possibility.

Summary

It is difficult to separate psychological processes of development from biological and social processes, yet any description of psychological development must do that, while still recognizing both biological and social influences.

Three areas of development that are essentially psychological are cognitive development, personality changes, and adaptive changes. The timing of these changes constitutes the psychological clock and is extremely variable; individual differences and internal inconsistencies of self-perceived aging are common.

Although a gradual slowing of reaction time may affect physical performance over the adult years, there is very little slowing of cognitive processes as a result of aging. Intelligence (as measured by IQ) is actually fairly stable. Forms of intelligence that require quick thinking, called "fluid intelligence," may decrease. However, this is balanced by increase in the forms of intelligence that require broad knowledge and appropriate strategies, called "crystallized intelligence." With senescence—often, just preceding death—there may be a significant loss of cognitive function, called "terminal drop." Otherwise, biology affects cognition little over the adult years. Social belief systems with false built-in expectations of cognitive loss may be far more damaging than the effects of aging itself.

The possibility that higher-level cognitive development may occur in adult life and that it may be fostered by a wide range of experience is a current issue, but there has been no agreement on it.

Personality development, however, seems to be an issue with

many contemporary answers. Most theorists seem to agree that there are many aspects of the self that change. Bühler, Erikson, Fiske, Gould, Jung, Levinson, Loevinger, Maslow, Neugarten, and Rogers, to name only a few, all believe that personality can change.

Douglas Kimmel has created a theoretical model of the development of "personality systems" that synthesizes many current points of view on development. Kimmel describes the process of development as a result of a system of interaction between the self's inner world—which includes temperament and physiology as well as roles, styles, and self-perceptions—and the self's outer world—which consists of the situations, people, places, and things in the environment. Changes in personality are the products of striving, interacting, and learning, in Kimmel's model.

Some personality shifts over time that have been suggested by research are changes in self-awareness, self-understanding, self-utilization, sex-role conformity, and increased interiority and introspection.

Adaptive development involves changing cognitive and behavioral patterns to fit life's changing situations. Adaptive styles and failures to adapt both vary during the life span. Early adaptive strategies tend toward conformity; adaptation in the middle years strives toward balance; in the later years adaptation requires psychological growth. These trends are adjustive responses to the shifting life problems of biological and social development. Failure to adapt may be mildly dysfunctional or may result in criminal behavior or mental illness or self-destruction, although not all instances of these maladaptive behaviors are based in developmental failure. Social and biological causes also may be identified.

Terms and Concepts to Define

The Ages of Me _____

_____

crystallized intelligence _____

_____

executive processes of personality _____

_____

fluid intelligence _____

_____

formal operations _____

_____

increased interiority _____

_____

mental illness _____

_____

personality system _____

_____

psychological clock _____

_____

terminal drop _____

_____

Experiences

To involve yourself with the concepts in this chapter, try these experiences described in the Appendix.

Alone
22. Stable You/Changing You
45. Planning Strategies I: Taking Steps
46. Planning Strategies II: Realities

With Others
21. Social Roles
40. Suicide

Going beyond the Text

1. *Interview a sample of people in their middle years of life for self-reports on developmental changes in cognitive, interactive, and adaptive styles over the years of their lives.*
2. *Read and analyze an autobiography or biography for changes in personality over time.*

Suggested Readings

Calhoun, L. C., Selby, J. W., & King, H. E. Dealing with crisis: A guide to critical life problems. *Englewood Cliffs, N.J.: Prentice-Hall, 1976.*

PART FIVE

Looking Backward/ Looking Forward

By combining the stage and process theories, we can achieve an informed perception of adulthood as it often is lived. And, by projecting the potential of the current life-extension research, we can create an appropriate expectation of adult life as it may be in the future. In Part Five we look backward at the past and forward to the future.

14

Bottom Lines: Stages and Processes

When you have finished reading this chapter, you should be able to:

Identify the strengths and weaknesses of both the stage and process perspectives.

Discuss the practical applications of an integrated perception of adult development.

Explain why there can be no real bottom line to the subject of adult growth through time.

Now that we've surveyed development from both the chronological perspective and the process perspective, we're in a position to combine them for an integrated understanding of adulthood. Although there are no final formulas and because the bottom lines are forever changing, this combining of models can clarify our understanding of the drama of adult life now. First, however, we need a quick review of the contributions of each perspective, looking back to previous sections of the text.

Looking Backward

In the beginning, we traced the slow emergence of a science of adult development—the creation of theoretical models that fit the realities of living and then the design of research techniques to accurately

272

measure change. The pioneers, the ones to establish the first useful models, were Bühler, Jung, and Erikson. Then came the contemporary theorists: Gould and Levinson, Neugarten and Loevinger, among others. In recognizing the complexity of their subject, these contemporary developmental scientists have organized its diverse elements from varying perspectives.

Since the time of Erikson's publication on adult development, the field can be divided into the research mainly on the ordering, the sequence, and in many cases on the age links of adult changes or the research mainly on the specific processes and the continuous unfolding of developmental change. The first category includes the age/stage work of such researchers as Gould and Levinson; the second includes the continuity and process studies, such as those done by Neugarten and by Loevinger—to name a few of the many researchers.

Our first overview of adult life was from the chronological perspective, in order to get a sense of the sequence and the scope of development. We explored what seemed to be an ordered unfolding in time. For example we identified some typical conflicts, decisions, and transitions of the twenties. We recognized the characteristic settling in, restructuring, and reevaluation of the thirties. In the forties and fifties we found common crises, assessments, and anticipations. Predictable losses, reorientations, and readaptations of the retirement years and later life were explored. And the potential for continuing personal growth in late life in the face of senescence and death ended our survey. Much of the material in this section was drawn from the age/stage perspective, but the framework was filled out with work from the process viewpoint as well.

The perspective of continuity and process was our second go-round on the experiences of adult development. Freed from chronology, we examined some continuous biological, social, and psychological processes over time. We found that the biological processes of maturation, aging, and senescence are actually relatively free from age links—that they are a matter of function, not of time. We traced changes over time in the body's organs and systems and also traced the factors that modify the changes. The social processes, like the biological processes, also seem to be less time bound than the chronological framework had indicated—especially in the lives of contemporary cohorts. We identified changes in attitudes toward the social processes of family life, including marriage and parenting. The changes extend to the timing of these social processes as well as to the forms that families now take. In the social processes of work and career, we found comparable shifts in timing, forms, and expectations, as well as finding changes in the work orientations of both sexes. And both the family and the work changes affect other social processes in adulthood: particularly the patterns of education and perhaps the patterns of friendship. We also found that psychological processes are apt to correlate more with other developmental changes in an individual's life or with personal experience than with chronological age. Cognitive processes appear to be more closely tied to stimulation and experience than to age, although biological aging may affect cognition to some degree. Adaptive processes seem to be more clearly related to social and environmental stresses and to personality than to number of years lived. The process-perspective research supports the beliefs that adult life is a forever-unfinished process for all of us, and that most of us leave untapped at least some of our potential for productive growth and change.

This backward look adds credence to the essential blending of stage and process perspectives in our understanding of the human experience. It is, after all, a natural blending, which follows the actuality of our lives. Each perspective—stage and process—has its own strengths and weaknesses. Only an integration of the strengths of both can give us a whole perception of adult growth and change.

Putting It All Together

The stage perspective, as we pointed out earlier, gives us a grasp of the scope, the sequence, and the ordering of developmental tasks— the changing relationships of the self to its inner and outer worlds, over time (Gould, 1972; Levinson, 1980). These are the strengths of the stage perspective. One weakness is that attention to the broad framework and to age norms emphasizes sameness and blurs individual differences (Gould, 1972). Another weakness is that the studies that have indicated chronological stages of development deal with past cohorts, and they don't allow for cohort differences and the effects of social change (Fiske, 1980; Neugarten, 1980). This weakness becomes a real danger if the age/stage perspective is taken as a guideline for development—as a prescription, rather than a description (Rossi, 1980). If we recognize the strengths of stage theories in sketching out a model of a growing, changing, developmental structure of human life, this perspective can be of enormous value.

The process perspective fills out the model-of-life sketch with richer detail. Perhaps the greatest strength of the process perspective is that it frees the developmental experience from chronology (Neugarten, 1980). The process viewpoint's attention to the underlying motivations for growth is another strong point. A related weakness is that, with this perspective, one may assume growth exists even where there is none—where the potential for development has been stunted by personal or social factors (Fiske, 1980). Another weakness may be that attention to any individual process narrows the perception of the whole (Levinson, 1980). Still, in relaxing chronological expectations, the process point of view permits a thorough understanding of the effects of social change on individual lives and reflects the richness of individual differences.

Combining the strength of both stage and process perspectives gives us the potential for an integrated perception of the whole; this is the **holistic** vision that Neugarten was calling for in her request for an "overarching" integration of the biological, the social, and the behavioral aspects of human life in 1966, and that Levinson still calls for (1980). A number of the models that we have summarized in the course of this text do synthesize both stages and processes to some degree; Kimmel (1974), Loevinger (1976), Levinson and associates (1978), and Gould (1978) have each created an understanding of adult development that describes an unfolding process of growth through interaction with the environment within the framework of time. It is to be hoped that future work will extend this perspective.

An integrated life-span perspective is of practical as well as theoretical value. In the study of adult development, multidisciplinary efforts tend to produce coordination and cooperation rather than fragmented and redundant research. And this advantage extends to each of us who apply the research in our lives; with the combined energies of all the disciplines involved in the study of adult life, new and deeper knowledge of developmental changes can be attained.

Personal Applications

An integrated understanding that combines both a structured framework and a flexible sense of process has practical applications on many levels. An integrated perception of the complexities and potentials of adult living allows us to be more aware of our own development and potential; it makes us more aware and more understanding of the changes in the lives of other people. We can also step back and see the drama unfold with less attachments. Awareness gives us the opportunity to clarify our values, to give priority to the things in life that we value most. A **clarification of values** permits us to project the courses of our lives into the future realistically and so to set goals and to plan toward them consciously and effectively. Informed and deliberate personal choices enhance the future, they become not only possible but integral to our lives.

Predicting what time will bring—future projection—is tricky. Societal changes in the present affect the timing of future events and the patterns of development; societal changes in the future may affect the patterns of our development even further. As new developmental patterns appear, they in turn inevitably create new social changes, and so the trends follow and build on one another. Especially at the 20th-century rate of its escalation, change is the one thing we can be sure of; there can be no real bottom line to the subject of how we develop. Changes in social attitudes in the economy, in international relations, and in technology all will shape new scenarios for living. Life-extension technology, for example, may confront us with a future that requires all the creativity and understanding that we can muster. Looking backward at what already is known is never enough. We also have to look ahead—to what we may someday know.

Can you put together everything that you have learned so far in this text and identify what most intrigues or disturbs you? In your survey of the developmental framework of adult life and the processes on which the framework is based, what concerns you the most?

Summary

This brief chapter reviews the emergence of the stage and the process theories of adult development and the scope of their contributions. The chronological framework that characterizes the age/stage perspective is outlined over the life course; and the trends in the biological, social, and psychological aspects of life that are the concern of the process perspectives are summarized.

The strengths of the stage perspectives—the attention to order, sequence, and evolving framework associated with chronology—seem to outweigh the weaknesses—inattention to individual differences and cohort differences as well as the danger of the stages being interpreted as guidelines. Similarly, the strengths of the process models—their focus on specific processes and freedom from age constraints—are more important than the weaknesses—ignoring changes that are not developmental as well as the narrowness of the processes' scope. Integrating the strengths of the two kinds of perspectives creates a powerful synthesis, as we have seen in the work of Kimmel, Levinson, Loevinger, Erikson, and Gould.

The conceptual value of this integrated understanding is supplemented by its practical value, not only on the level of developmental research but on the personal level. A holistic vision of what life can be permits clarification of life values and life goals. A holistic vision allows for informed and deliberate personal choices, which enhance the way we live in every way—now and in the future.

Terms and Concepts to Define

clarification of values _____

_____

future projection _____

_____

holistic _____

_____

Experiences

To involve yourself with the concepts in this chapter, try these experiences described in the Appendix.

Alone

If you have not yet worked with the exercises in the "Being Prepared: Anticipation" section of the Appendix, now is the time to work your way through that set of experiences.

With Others

After completing the goal-setting and strategies exercises, group members may share their experiences by means of "47. Planning Strategies III" and "50. Exploring Alternatives III."

Going beyond the Text

Interview a person in late life and analyze the interview findings on the basis of successful completion of Erikson's, Gould's, and Levinson's stages as well as the freedom from stages and the variability in developmental processes on this individual. (Use the case study form that follows to record and evaluate your interview data.)

Case Study: Psychology of Adulthood and Aging

1. *Subject's Basic Data*

   A. Name _____ Age _____ Sex _____

   B. Occupation (include history if appropriate) _____

   Education (last year completed) _____

   C. Father's occupation _____ Mother's occupation _____

   D. Marital status (include history if appropriate) _____

2. *Subject's Self-Perception*

   A. Brief subjective self-description _____

   _____

   _____

   _____

   _____

   _____

   B. Self-described age grouping _____

   _____

   _____

   C. Attitudes toward life stages

   Late adolescence _____

   Early adulthood _____

   Middle adulthood _____

   Late adulthood _____

   D. Self-description of personal fit with social-age expectations _____

   _____

   _____

   _____

   _____

   _____

   _____

3. *Observations*

    A. Successful resolution of Erikson's eight stages of development (use Erikson's terminology):

_____

_____

_____

_____

_____

_____

_____

_____

_____

_____

_____

    B. Successful completion of Gould's tasks of adult life:

_____

_____

_____

_____

_____

_____

_____

_____

_____

_____

C. Correlations with Levinson's stages and transitions of adult life:

_____

_____

_____

_____

_____

_____

_____

_____

_____

_____

_____

_____

D. Relative freedom from stereotyped, socially-induced, age-related behavior patterns:

_____

_____

_____

_____

_____

_____

_____

_____

_____

_____

_____

15

Life Limits: Life-Extension Research

When you have finished this chapter you should be able to:
Summarize all of the cellular-damage and the wear-and-tear theories of physical aging.
Define "premature death."
Describe presently existing techniques for life extension.
List the characteristics of long-lived healthy people.

With change as the one condition we can count on in our social environment, looking ahead requires identifying the elements that may alter our future lives radically. Life-extension research certainly is one major potential source of innovation. In this chapter we return to the issue of potential changes in the human life span that have been briefly mentioned in previous pages.

Adult development may be quite different in the future as a result of two factors: shifts in biological processes made possible by life-extension technology and the social changes that they may produce. If, indeed, biological aging and senescence can be slowed or even reversed, adult life could become a long, long summer of maturity, ending only by disease, accident, or by choice. If, indeed, human life is extended significantly—by only 20 years, speculating conservatively—the effects on the individual life course will be profound. The effects on the economy, the work place, and the family in particular will be impressive. In the future, our lives may be carried far beyond the patterns and processes familiar to us now.

The Course of Life-Extension Research

In the first half of the century, life was extended through both disease control and disease prevention. At the turn of the century, five of the ten most frequent causes of death in North America were infectious diseases; they accounted for more than 35% of all deaths. Now infectious diseases are relatively under control; they cause less than 4% of all deaths (Leaf, 1975). The prevention of disease altogether accounts for most of the 20 years gained in average life span over this century. For the most part, this gain results from the elimination of childhood deaths from infection. But life extension has been achieved also through new methods of treating the chronic diseases of late life. Statistically, if in 1900 you lived to be 65, only 5 more years could be expected. Now, if you live to be 65, you can expect to make it to the age of 80 (U.S. Bureau of the Census, 1980).

By the second half of the century the most common causes of death had become cardiovascular failures—heart diseases and strokes—and cancer (Butler, 1978). Research on these killers has been accelerated. New methods of repairing and controlling malfunctions in the heart have been developed: transplants and implants, new valves, pacemakers, bypasses—a whole technology of the heart. New methods of preventing strokes have been developed; blood pressure is controlled through medication, diet, exercise, and biofeedback. New attacks on cancer also have been launched; radiation therapies, chemotherapies, and even psychotherapies continue the struggle against the second highest cause of death (Kart et al., 1978).

Add to the efforts countering disease an explosion of biochemical and electronic technologies; they are designed to detect dangerous malfunctions, to maintain malfunctioning body parts, and to preserve lives that are close to death from any cause. To this point, you have only a sampling of the spectrum of applied, medical life-extension work being done in the last quarter of this century. Next, include a network of basic research directed at any and all details of human life, at every level—from molecule to cell, organ, and system. Further add research on the causes and prevention of all the chronic diseases that humans suffer; prevention became a major focus during the 1960s and 1970s. This immensity of effort is made in the interest of life becoming healthier and longer.

The major gains in the life expectancy in this century have resulted from reduction in deaths from infections, chronic diseases, and accidents, which Alex Comfort (1978) calls **premature death**. He defines premature death as death due to any cause other than senescence. The human body has a potential "natural" span of about 85 years; each year after 85, senescence becomes more likely (Fries & Crapo, 1981). The various means to prevent disease, cope with malfunction, and repair accidental damage each have made premature death slightly less likely. But these simple solutions are only a part of the picture. Biologists have been aware for some time that "real" life extension—adding a significant number of years to the potential life span—will take more than the elimination of the causes of early death. To really extend life, scientists have to understand how the whole system works. They have to know what actually causes senescence. When they know how it works, they may be able to delay senescence. They might even reverse it.

Can we actually alter the seemingly inevitable biological changes of adult life? It could happen. If research continues at the present rate, it could conceivably happen in our lifetimes. A number of research biologists predict that they will understand senescence, to the point that they can slow it down, by the year 2000 (Comfort, 1978; Kurtzman & Gordon, 1977; Utke, 1978). If they know enough to slow it down, it's a short step to being able to reverse it—perhaps by the year 2025 (Kurtzman & Gordon, 1977).

Of course, breakthroughs in life extension might not come as soon as they're predicted. But there's some indication that actually the research is picking up speed (Utke, 1978). Drug companies are hotly competing to be the first with a control for biological decline, and as research jobs in the field multiply, so do the number of researchers. Cellular and molecular research in other areas—brain biochemistry, immunology, and cancer research, for example—produce findings that apply directly to the basic question of life extension: what makes human beings age?

Information is piling up that may ultimately provide answers to the question of why we age. The more we know about cell division, prenatal life, cellular growth, and cellular death, the more we know about the whole cell: the more we know about aging (Rosenfeld, 1976).

Life-Extension Theories

Contemporary research in senescence is focused on the microscopic levels of the body—on the cells and the molecules. It is on this level clues have been found that may eventually lead to the understanding and control of life itself.

Before we survey some of the current research approaches to life extension, a quick review of the functions of cells and how this relates to aging may be helpful.

Your body, almost all of it, is made up of millions of living, actively functioning cells. The cells, held together by connective tissues and supported by bones, carry on all the processes that you recognize as your life. They do everything. Depending on the organ in which it is located, each cell has a specialized function: nerve cells transmit information; lung cells transfer oxygen; pancreatic cells secrete insulin. But besides their specialized functions all cells have a general responsibility to manufacture proteins and enzymes. The proteins that they synthesize keep the cells alive and healthy. The proteins also maintain and repair the connective tissues and bones in the cell environment. In addition to the cells doing their specialized jobs and maintaining themselves, they are self-renewing. Skin cells, for example, can renew themselves fairly quickly. Other kinds of cells renew themselves more slowly but still do repair themselves eventually; some nerve-ending cells have this sort of capability. Some cells, such as those of the heart and the brain, can't replace themselves at all, but many body cells would be capable of renewing themselves forever if it were not for one problem. The problem is that the time a cell requires to renew itself increases over the years; eventually, the cell replaces itself too slowly to keep its functions going. The functions then falter and fail—that's senescence.

Aging begins, on the first level, in our cells. Eventually the inefficiency of the cells due to aging affects the functioning of whole organs. And when the inefficiency affects an organ, the organ system is affected as well. Then biological decline begins to be noticeable. But it all begins in our cells; substantial aging occurs when cells don't reproduce, don't renew themselves, and lose efficiency (Denny, 1975).

The first question that has to be asked about aging, then, is "What happens to the cell to make it inefficient or nonrenewing?" Nobody has a complete answer to the question, but many people are working on it. Researchers in a number of areas have been able to describe the changes that occur in cells over time. The problem is to separate changes that cause senescence from changes that are the effects. Identifying a change that comes with aging is one thing; proving that it's a cause of aging is more difficult. When you find several changes that correlate with age, how do you show which change causes which? Right now there are several promising solutions to the problem.

All the contemporary researchers in the field of gerontology are in agreement about the kinds of changes that occur in aging cells. Agreement also prevails that some mechanism acting as a biological clock is in some way responsible for the changes. The clock slows down cell functions and causes senescence. But how? The disagreements are about how the biological clock works and where the clock is located. These are issues that have led biologists, chemists, and biochemists in different research directions.

There are two general approaches to the "how" of aging. One approach is from the position that senescence is caused by wear and tear; not surprisingly, this is the **wear-and-tear theory.** From this point of view, aging is the result of an accumulation of mistakes and accidents over time. The process resembles wear and tear on a car, which "ages" it through use and abuse. If this approach turns out to be the best, the control of aging will be a matter of prevention, minimizing damage that occurs, and occasional repairs at the cellular level. A second approach, the **design-error theory,** conceives of senescence as built into the design of living things. From this point of view, aging is a design error that leads to malfunction gradually. The process can be compared to the deterioration of a car that's engineered so as to break down in three years. If aging is built into bodily design, controlling it requires finding out where the error is and then finding out how it can be corrected.

Wear-and-tear research begins at the molecular level of the cells. Within the broad wear-and-tear approach, one of the theories of aging is the **"free radical theory,"** first developed in the late 1960s by Denham Harman at the University of Nebraska. Free radicals are accidentally broken bits of molecules that are unstable until they join with other molecules. In the process of locating a completing molecule, free radicals damage other molecules, breaking off pieces that turn into free radicals and generally interfering with cell function. The cell's normal processes of oxidation routinely produce free radicals. As they accumulate over time, perhaps they cause senescence. Slowing down oxidation limits free-radical production; will slowing down oxidation limit senescence? Rodent studies suggest that this may be a possibility (Rosenfeld, 1976; Weg, 1976).

Closely connected to the free-radical research is another molecular study, on the wear-and-tear effects of "cross-linkages." **Cross-linkage theory** has been primarily the work of Johan Bjorksten. Cross-linkages, like "free radicals," are accidents: two large molecules get connected by mistake, and so become "cross-linked." At times cells may produce enzymes that apparently dissolve these linkages, but if they don't, the molecules stay linked. As these accidental linkages increase in the cells and in connective tissues, they get in the way of cellular function. And cross-linkages appear in greater numbers with age. Are they a cause of senescence or only a side effect? Can enzymes be administered to dissolve the links? Perhaps they can (Rosenfeld, 1976; Weg, 1976).

A third wear-and-tear effect that increases with age is a buildup in the cells of granules of waste materials called **lipofuscin.** Lipofuscin deposits may result from cross-linkages and free radicals. They aren't present in all cells, but the extent of lipofuscin buildup is clearly correlated with the passage of time. Does lipofuscin interfere with the cells' functioning? Does it slow them down and cause senescence? Of all the theories, this one is supported least by experimental evidence. Rather than a cause of aging, lipofuscin deposits are generally considered to be only an effect (Denny, 1975).

Wear-and-tear theories have been useful in identifying some of the clearly age-related changes in the cells. However, so far their usefulness is limited; they haven't established causal relationships.

The design-error approach to what causes aging has not yet produced any conclusive evidence that the biological clock is built in, but the feeling among biologists seems to be that this line of research is the most promising (Comfort, 1978).

One of the design-error theories is that the biological clock is built into the genetic coding of the cells. All the cells of a person's body carry the same genetic code, so they all age at about the same rate and in the same ways. A biologist at Stanford University in the 1960s, Leonard Hayflick, found that most normal human cells are capable of replacing themselves only about 50 times, plus or minus 10 divisions—this is called the **Hayflick limit.** Remember that as we age the cells reproduce more and more slowly. Hayflick believes he has demonstrated that the slowing mechanism in the biological clock is in the cell nucleus. He has transplanted young nuclei into old cells and old nuclei into young cells, and in either case it is the age of the nucleus that controls how many times the cell continues to double (Finch & Hayflick, 1977; Rosenfeld, 1976). Perhaps the genetic information in our DNA triggers "alarms" in our biological clocks.

Another possible cause of aging is that the cells all get instructions about aging from some common source in the body. This built-in timer may be in the brain. W. Donner Denckla, working at a research center funded by a drug firm, and Caleb Finch, at the University of Southern California, are convinced that the biological clock is in the hypothalamic region of the brain. The hypothalamus is suspected of sending messages about aging to the pituitary gland, causing the pituitary to send hormone messages to the cells, which in turn make the cells shut down their functions. The sequence is similar to that occurring when growth hormones stimulate growth or puberty (Finch & Hayflick, 1977). This is the **death-hormone theory.** Is aging indeed an endocrine function? Can such a "death hormone" be identified? Could it be blocked? If the answers are all yes, perhaps the biological clock can be reset, biochemically or nutritionally or even by using biofeedback (Comfort, 1978).

A final design-error theory, often identified with Ray Walford at the University of California at Los Angeles, is that aging is a result of decreases in immunity and increases in autoimmunity—the **autoimmune theory.** In this theory, the body progressively loses its protective immune responses, not only to invading bacteria but to its own internal dysfunctions, such as cells that have become cancerous. Biochemists Allen Goldstein and Abraham White have identified a naturally occurring hormone, which they've named thymosin, as a main source of the immune system's protection against disease and deterioration. The administration of artificially synthesized thymosin to replace the decreasing natural supply may be one of the first antidotes to aging to appear on the market (Rosenfeld, 1976).

If any of these lines of research is productive in accurately identifying, controlling, and even reversing the process of aging in the cells, it's very possible that you may someday live in a world where premature death has been eliminated, and where the aging process can be postponed indefinitely (Comfort, 1978). How do you feel about that possibility?

_____	disgusted
_____	depressed
_____	mildly negative
_____	neutral
_____	mildly positive
_____	pleased
_____	terrific!

Would you want to live for 300 or 400 years? Can you imagine a developmental study of adult life that covers 8 centuries instead of 8 decades? What would it be like?

_____

_____

_____

_____

_____

Life Limits Now

Aging may or may not be reversed in your lifetime. In fact, it probably won't be, but aging almost certainly will be modified. If you accept the possibility that this can happen, there are a number of strategies that you might consider as ways of coping with the incredible possibility. Building on what you now know about the biological, social, and psychological cycles, you'll need to recognize that, biologically, you should try to maintain your body in relatively good condition, rather than relegating exercise to moments when it's opportune; that, socially, you probably should anticipate a sequence of careers and interpersonal relationships, instead of one job and one social network; and that, psychologically, you ought to recognize your unending potential for psychological growth, instead of settling in at some level and considering that sufficient. Like the social mores of previous years, this is another set of "oughts" and "shoulds." But these are serious responsibilities to yourself, not to some social ideal. With a well-conditioned body, a varied framework, and an openness to psychological growth and change, you would be reasonably well prepared for whatever changes in life span the future brings. More importantly, you'll be prepared for changes of any sort in the present. And after all, the present is what you live in, always (Fries & Crapo, 1981).

There's a strong possibility that life extension technology may not become available in dramatic leaps but in small breakthroughs that accumulate almost unnoticeably over time. Life expectancies may be extended quietly, almost behind our backs. Joel Kurtzman and Phillip Gordon (1977), in a scenario for the future effects of life extension, have suggested that we can expect several areas of biochemical research to produce results in a predictable sequence. First, **bionic research**—the creation and implantation of artificial body parts—will be continued and perfected. Second, biochemical research will begin to pay off, with antioxidants developed to slow the formation of free radicals, with enzymes to dissolve cross-linkages, and with hormones to maintain the immune system. Third, genetic research will identify the biological clock and turn it off or even back. If Kurtzman and Gordon are right, these means of life extension will be operational within the next 50 years.

The first wave of life extension is already well under way. Bionic implants and biological transplants have become common everyday surgery. Electronic miniaturization has made it possible to replace worn-out body parts with devices that sometimes work better than the worn-out originals. The act of donating the organs of the body for transplantation after death to a stanger's body has become so common that in some states a form to permit it is part of the driver's license. The technology of freezing and preserving living organs now permits the creation of frozen-organ banks to supply the ever-increasing demand. **Bench surgery**—a sort of workbench surgical approach to replacing malfunctioning body parts—is a widespread present reality.

The second wave of life extension, biochemical research, is still in the animal-study stage. A number of techniques for successfully slowing the aging process at the cellular level have been developed in rodent studies. It's only a matter of time before these techniques can be made available for human beings. When the techniques are available for human use, they may slow down the rate of aging by from 10% to 20%—and it won't be long before they are available.

A number of biologists, including Denham Harman and Alex Comfort (1978), have demonstrated that the life expectancies of mice can be increased by slowing down the rate of oxidation in their cells. Antioxidants—vitamin E, among others—are simply fed to the mice along with their food. Harman has found that the antioxidants prevent free-radical damage in the cells of mice, even when the mice are exposed to radiation, which usually accelerates the formation of free radicals.

Another increase in life span, this time in rats, involves lowering their body temperatures. Barret Rosenberg and Gabor Kemeny, at Michigan State University, have lengthened rats' lives with a drug that drops their temperatures slightly below normal in their maturing years. Rosenberg and Kemeny also found that low body temperature in maturity can slow rats' decline significantly. And diet restriction, too, slows decline; by feeding a balanced diet that was severely limited in calories to rats from their early years, Clive McCay, at Cornell, almost doubled the rats' life spans. Their periods of decline occurred much later than those of rats from the same litters who were in a control group with no diet restriction.

Finally, Roy Walford has suppressed the autoimmune response in mice with drug therapy and extended their life spans considerably. In all, by slowing down oxidation in the cells of rodents, lowering the animals' body temperatures, restricting their diets, and giving them immunotherapy, they have been given long and healthy extended life spans (Rosenfeld, 1976; Weg, 1976). Alex Comfort has predicted (1978) that the findings from rodent studies could be extended to human life in inexpensive and safe forms within the next 15 years.

Antioxidants such as vitamins E and C and the element selenium are already available. Temperature-lowering drugs are still controversial; it's not yet known what their effects might be on other body systems. Substances that limit the body's absorption of calories from food are presently being developed, to restrict our diets even while we eat. Thymosin and other similar biochemicals are in experimental use with people who have abnormal immune functions; and there's a strong probability that inexpensive immunotherapy for those who function normally will soon be widely available, because of the commercial application of genetic recombination technology. In addition to these versions for humans of controls on aging that have been applied successfully on rodents, Comfort suggests that a hypothalamic biological clock could be reset with such biochemicals affecting the brain as tryptophan, L-dopa, and monoamino-oxydase (MAO) suppressors—drugs that are already in use for treating psychopathologies (Comfort, 1978).

The result of all these techniques would simply be that we would seem younger than our ages when we're old and that we'd be senescent for fewer years of our lengthened lives. People could be actively and dynamically alive "for life."

There are several locales in the world where the inhabitants claim to have lived extremely long lives while maintaining their health and energy. Of course, their claims may be exaggerated. Alexander Leaf (1975) and Sula Benet (1976) are two gerontologists who have studied these communities—Vilcabamba in Ecuador, Abkhasia in the Soviet state of Georgia, and the Hunza of Kashmir—to see what factors may contribute to their long lives.

Leaf and Benet have both found that these elderly yet vital people are very physically active all their lives, living in small mountain communities that require hard climbing and long walking distances for everyday tasks. They're also very sexually active. Far from the stresses and diseases and toxic substances of more "civilized" environments, these people live difficult but satisfying lives. Their diet is extremely low in calories with very little animal fat: natural grains, fresh fruits and vegetables, and yogurt. Aging isn't socially perceived to mandate a loss of status or attractiveness, so there is little sense of social loss over time. Although the brains of the older people do indicate the predictable decrease in number of cells, their physical health and positive attitudes seem to balance the loss (Benet, 1976; Leaf, 1975). High altitudes, cool climates, restricted diets, and lots of physical and endocrine activity: does this sound familiar? The people in these locales may have known all along what life-extension researchers have only recently discovered—that with positive sexual and social attitudes, physical fitness, and avoidance of stress, people can live long and healthy lives. Though the ages of these long-lived mountain dwellers could be exaggerated (Fries & Crapo, 1981; Neugarten, 1980), their health and vitality in the late years probably are not.

Similar predictors for old age have been identified in contemporary North American culture; if you don't smoke, if you stay socially involved, if you develop your interests, if you adapt positively to the changes of life, and if you keep a positive outlook on yourself and the world, your years are apt to be both many and lived in good health (Palmore & Jeffers, 1971). Together these factors can be considered basic guidelines for living a long life. Your maximum life limit now is about 85 good years, with luck. If you want to see what happens in the next century, integrating the steps of this list into your lifestyle is a sensible first step; the longer you're around, the better your chances to be here for each breakthrough that comes along. You may even manage to be around for the greatest breakthrough—when your biological clock can be reversed and you can think about living for another couple of centuries.

But do you really want to live so many years? Will everyone want to? What kinds of drastic changes would life extension make in our adult lives? The responses to these questions could fill another book; jot down the answers that seem to you the most critical. Stop and think, before you write, of the possible effects that life extension could have on society as a whole and how they could affect your life.

_____

_____

_____

_____

_____

Growing through Time

As you anticipate what your life may become, however long its span, my hope is that this book has helped you perceive more of the exciting potentials of adult development. The developmental theorists have described life's unfolding and creation; researchers with the stage perspective have chronicled common events and their predictable times; and the process-perspective theorists have freed developmental changes from any inevitable time table. You're now in a position to understand how your perceptions and expectations can control your future, how your choices and decisions can shape how your life changes, and how you can continue to develop who you are—all the way through time.

Summary

Life-extension research involves a two-branched attack on aging and death. The first branch, disease control, has moved from its successes with the infectious diseases early in the century to the current challenge of chronic diseases. The second branch, biochemical research, is reaching into the causes and effects of aging at the cellular level. This biochemical life-extension research has the goals of understanding, controlling, and eventually modifying the processes of senescence.

In general, biochemical researchers agree that aging is the result of a slowdown and a loss of efficiency in cellular functioning. They also agree that some internal mechanism exists that times and controls senescence. But the people who research aging are not in agreement on how the internal mechanism works or where it is located.

One point of view on the cause of aging—the wear-and-tear position—is that aging consists in cellular damage over time. Certainly the wear and tear on old cells is obvious. Various of the wear-and-tear theories rest on the cell's loss of normal functioning through accumulated damage at the molecular level (manifested by an abundance of free radicals), through molecular mistakes (cross-linkages), and through a buildup of cellular wastes (lipofuscin). However, it's hard to tell whether each of these breakdowns of cellular functions is a cause or an effect of senescence.

Scientists taking a slightly different point of view—the design-error position—argue that the cause of aging is a built-in program for bodily self-destruction. These researchers typically consider wear and tear more of an effect than a cause. Supporting the design-error approach are a theory that the biological clock controlling senescence is built into the hypothalamus of the brain and acts through the endocrine system and a theory that the clock is part of the body's immune system. Among the possible outcomes of biochemical research are elimination of premature death and extension of the life span by from 10% to 20%—or perhaps indefinitely. Such results could be accomplished within the next 50 years. To be prepared for these possibilities, it might be helpful to shift our physical, social, and psychological expectations about aging. We may have longer lives than we now anticipate.

Changes in life-span expectancy will probably develop in stages, moving from surgical repair and replacement techniques to biochemical manipulation of the body's systems to genetic controls. The first stage is well underway; researchers of the second stage anticipate major breakthroughs before the turn of the century; and the last stage may reach the point of general use not long after the third. Existing techniques for life extension may be applied to humans within the next few years, in readily available forms. Drugs to protect molecules from the effects of oxidation, to lower body temperatures, to limit diet, and to balance the body's immune system already are being developed and used extensively in studies of animals.

These life-extension techniques create bodily states that are very similar to those produced by the lifestyles characteristic of the healthy aged people found at several sites around the world. A high level of physical and sexual activity, a low level of calorie intake, an isolated and stress-free environment, and positive social attitudes toward older community members are common factors in long-lived populations.

Gerontologists studying long-lived individuals in North American culture agree that positive attitudes, physical activity, intellectual curiosity, and social involvement are all correlated with long and satisfying lives.

Terms and Concepts to Define

autoimmune theory _____

_____

bench surgery _____

_____

bionic research _____

_____

cross-linkage theory _____

_____

death-hormone theory _____

_____

design-error theory _____

_____

free-radical theory _____

_____

hayflick limit _____

_____

lipofuscin _____

_____

premature death _____

_____

wear-and-tear theory _____

_____

Experiences

To involve yourself with the concepts in this chapter, try these experiences described in the Appendix.

Alone
1. Experiencing Your Life Course
25. Life Extension II

With Others
23. Life Extension I

Going beyond the Text

1. *Scan the* Reader's Guide to Periodical Literature *and the* Social Science Index *for recent developments in life-extension research and for projected scenarios of mass longevity.*
2. *Survey a large sample of randomly selected people who are now in their twenties on the number of years they expect to live, barring major catastrophes, such as war. Determine how realistic their estimates are.*

Suggested Readings

Kurtzman, J., & Gordon, P. No more dying: The conquest of aging and extension of human life. *Atlanta: Dell, 1977.*

McQuade, W., & Aikman, A. The longevity factor. *New York: Simon & Schuster, 1979.*

Pelletier, K. Longevity: Fulfilling our biological potential. *New York: Delacorte, 1981.*

APPENDIX

Experiences

Being There: Awareness

The reading and remembering required of you in the chapters of this book are the usual route to learning, and indeed they are the first steps toward comprehension. But we can go farther. Getting involved—at the level of imagination and emotion and personal application—can be a big step toward the most fundamental kind of understanding.

This section contains a collection of exercises based on self questioning, empathy, and fantasy. The exercises will bring to your awareness some of your personal reactions to basic concepts in adult development, so you can understand them on a deeper level.

Some of the exercises can be done alone, some in twos or threes, and some in groups. Most of them are divided into two parts; the first part is an awareness experience, and the second part is an evaluation of the experience. Although you may not want to share the first part of an experience with other people, the second part may often be shared.

As you do these exercises, be receptive to your uncensored reactions. The more of your inner world that you allow to come out, the more clearly you can build on it. If an exercise makes you feel uncomfortable, you may want to skip it—but as you pass it by, you might ask yourself why you want to avoid it.

Mostly, these experiences are meant to be explored and enjoyed.

1. Experiencing Your Life Course

(alone)

Find a quiet place and a quiet hour and take the time to unfold the story of your life cycle—past and future. Part will be memory and part will be fantasy. Don't worry about forming sentences or about spelling, just sketch your life in words in any way that you feel comfortable doing it.

This exercise is for you, alone. If you don't want to share it, don't. The questions are just starters—add anything that comes to mind.

Begin with your birth. What do you know about it? What have you been told it was like?

_____

_____

_____

_____

_____

What are you like as a baby? What is your first word? What's your earliest memory? What are you afraid of? Have you had any serious illness? How do you fit into your family?

_____

_____

_____

_____

_____

What are you like as a 6-year-old? What do you most enjoy doing? least enjoy doing? What do you fear? How do you feel about school? church? How is your family life? Who is the most important person in your life?

_____

_____

_____

_____

_____

What are you like at 14 years? What is your body like? What do you most enjoy doing? least enjoy doing? What do you fear? How do you feel about your family? school? church? Who is most important in your life? What is the most exciting thing that happens to you this year?

_____

_____

_____

_____

_____

What are you like at 22? What is your body like? What do you most enjoy doing? least enjoy doing? What do you fear? What is your dream? How do you feel about school? work? family? religion? Who is most important in your life? What is the most exciting thing that happens this year? Where do you live, and with whom?

_____

_____

_____

_____

_____

What are you like at 33? What is your body like? What do you most enjoy doing? least enjoy doing? What do you fear? What is your dream? How do you feel about school? work? family? religion? Who is most important in your life? What is the most exciting thing that happens this year? Where do you live, and with whom?

_____

_____

_____

_____

_____

What are you like at 44? What is your body like? What do you most enjoy doing? least enjoy doing? What do you fear? What is your dream? How do you feel about school? work? family? religion? Who is most important in your life? What is the most exciting thing that happens this year? Where do you live, and with whom?

_____

_____

_____

_____

_____

What are you like at 55? What is your body like? What do you most enjoy doing? least enjoy doing? What do you fear? What is your dream? How do you feel about school? work? family? religion? Who is most important in your life? What is the most exciting thing that happens this year? Where do you live, and with whom?

_____

_____

_____

_____

_____

What are you like at 66? What is your body like? What do you most enjoy doing? least enjoy doing? What do you fear? What is your dream? How do you feel about school? work? family? religion? Who is most important in your life? What is the most exciting thing that happens this year? Where do you live, and with whom?

_____

_____

_____

_____

_____

What are you like at 77? What is your body like? What do you most enjoy doing? least enjoy doing? What do you fear? What is your dream? How do you feel about school? work? family? religion?

Who is most important in your life? What is the most exciting thing that happens this year? Where do you live, and with whom?

_____

_____

_____

_____

_____

How old do you want to be when you die? How will you die?

_____

_____

_____

_____

_____

(I'm aware that I can always change my mind about this.)

2. Uniqueness

(in twos)

Part I

Choose a partner. Sit facing each other. Look at each other without talking for a few minutes, paying attention to everything about the other person that reminds you of someone else you know. Let that drop, without commenting on it. Now pay attention to everything about the other person that is unique. (If it helps to write a list, do that.) Take turns telling each other what you notice that is different and special.

Part II

Now, with the same partner, take some time to think about the events in your life that are like those in most other lives. Let that drop. Now take some time to recall the events in your life that you feel have happened only to you. How has your life been different from most people's? Take turns sharing what you've experienced that is different—the mix of things that makes your life unique.

3. "Adults"

(group) What's an adult? Sitting in a circle, the members of the group take turns finishing each of the following sentences—one sentence in each round. Do it quickly; just free associate. Nobody can pass.

Part I

Adults always . . .
Adults never . . .
Adults think . . .
Adults look . . .
Adults wear . . .
Adults play . . .
When I feel like an adult I . . .
When I don't feel like an adult I . . .
The unbelievable thing about adults is . . .
The worst thing about adults is . . .
The best thing about adults is . . .

Part II

I define an adult as a person who _____

_____

_____

Did the members of the group agree on their definitions? Can you accept that?

_____

_____

4. Autobiography

(in twos) Charlotte Bühler's idea that biography and goals are closely related can be explored in this exercise.

Part I

You and your partner take turns telling each other the stories of your lives, with as much detail as you can supply in a 10- to 15-minute autobiography. The listener should take notes and listen closely for clues about the other person's life goals. When you've heard each other's biography, see whether you can identify the other person's central goals in life.

Part II

If you're in a group setting, share what happened with the rest of the group. Or just answer these questions for yourself.

Was telling your life story easy? difficult?
Was listening to your partner's story interesting? frustrating?
Could you identify each other's life goals accurately? If so, how? If not, why?

_____

_____

_____

_____

_____

5. Individuation

(alone or in a group)

Erik Erikson describes the self as unfolding; like a plant unfolds from its seed over time, we become more and more what we potentially are.

Get physically comfortable in a quiet place, at a quiet time. You're going to create a fantasy experience of the unfolding of your deepest inner self, so relax and empty your mind.

Part I

Picture your self as a tiny, unformed beginning, a long time ago, before you were born. What is it like, that little unshaped self? What are it's strongest emotions? needs? What's its main idea?

Now picture that self beginning to sprout and unfold. How is it changing? What about it is getting bigger? What new parts are beginning to develop?

Let it grow bigger yet. See if you can clearly imagine this larger self of yours, with all its parts. What is it like? What are its strongest emotions? its needs? its main goals in life?

Now picture your self unfolding, growing bigger and more complex than it is now. Let it grow. Where does it get bigger? stronger?

How does it grow more complex? What drops away? What gets added?

Let your self unfold as far as it wants to.

Part II

What was it like for you to observe your self as it grew? Could you let yourself really explore that fantasy? If you didn't want to let yourself do that, can you figure out why you didn't want to?

_____

_____

_____

_____

_____

6. Childhood Consciousness

(in twos)

Roger Gould describes the childhood consciousness that we carry with us as anger over not having our parents' total attention, over their leaving us sometimes, and over our not being all-powerful. Choose a partner; in this exercise you can experience being both parent and child.

Part I

You and your partner can get a feeling of this inner rage by role playing. Take turns being a child who demands attention, constant togetherness, and power to do everything and being a parent who wants to pay attention to something or someone else, to go away for a while, and to control the child by restricting his or her activity.

Part II

How did it feel to be the demanding child and the child's parent? Do you recognize any traces of those feelings in your present interactions with your parents or mate or friends?

_____

_____

_____

How much childhood consciousness do you have left? What can you do to get past it?

_____

_____

_____

_____

_____

_____

7. Transitions

(group)

Daniel Levinson describes the tensions that people experience as they move from one life stage to the next. How do you feel about transitions?

Divide the group into three or four small subgroups (depending on the size of the large group). Each subgroup will represent an age cohort: for example, the youngest, those who are less young, are older, and oldest. Do this exercise standing or sitting—whichever is most acceptable to the group.

Part I

The goal of this exercise is to give each person the opportunity to experience the tensions he or she feels about transitions.

Members of each subgroup should spend five minutes discussing the good things and the bad things about belonging to their assigned age cohort, getting a sense of being part of that time of life and noting the major changes that occur at that time. At the end of the five-minute period, one member of the group must volunteer to move on, to the next-older group. (The volunteers should try to be aware of how they feel about the move.)

Members who leave the oldest group are considered dead. But they immediately assume a new identity and begin again in the youngest group. For two minutes, the subgroups explain the pros and cons of their age cohort to the new member—and then another member of the group must volunteer to move on.

Everybody goes through each of the subgroups at least one time.

Part II

How did it feel to have to go through transitions? What did it make you aware of?

_____

_____

_____

_____

_____

8. Lifestyles

(alone)

Your lifestyle is made up of a complicated set of personal choices. It may or may not change over time. This exercise can put you in touch with your present lifestyle and how it differs from your past choices for living. It's also a chance to be aware of the changes in lifestyle that you'd like to make.

Part I

Ten years ago, I:

spent most of my time _____

worked _____

wore _____

spent most of my money for _____

depended most on _____

exercised by _____

ate a lot of _____

drank a lot of _____

smoked _____

believed in _____

read _____

relaxed by _____

interacted with my family _____

felt sex was _____

felt politics was _____

felt religion was _____

interacted with my friends _____

was most interested in _____

relied for transportation on _____

lived _____

had a dream of _____

questioned _____

interacted in the community by _____

Now, I:

spend my time _____

work _____

wear _____

spend most of my money for _____

depend on _____

exercise by _____

eat _____

drink _____

smoke _____

believe in _____

read _____

relax by _____

interact with my family _____

feel sex is _____

feel politics is _____

feel religion is _____

interact with my friends _____

am most interested in _____

rely for transportation on _____

live _____

dream of _____

question _____

interact in the community by _____

Part II

How could you realistically change your lifestyle to get more satisfaction from your life?

I could:

spend more of my time _____

work _____

wear _____

spend more/less money on _____

depend more/less on _____

exercise _____

eat more/less _____

drink more/less _____

smoke more/less _____

reexamine my beliefs about _____

read _____

relax by _____

interact with my family _____

reevaluate sex _____

reevaluate politics _____

reevaluate religion _____

interact with my friends _____

develop interests in _____

rely for transportation on _____

live _____

dream of _____

question _____

interact in the community by _____

9. Social Norms

(group)

Social expectations subtly shape our behavior as adult people. As a group, you can create a list of social norms for adults, then see whether all the norms are accepted by all the individuals in the group.

Part I

Someone should act as recorder, to write down all the norms the group suggests. The rest of the group completes three to five rounds (depending on the size of the group) of finishing the sentence "Mature adults should _____ to be socially acceptable." List as many norms as group members can think of, without questioning any of the suggestions.

Part II

The recorder reads one norm at a time and asks whether everyone is in complete agreement that this norm exists and then whether everyone accepts it in their own lives. Does this exercise increase your awareness of the norms you live with?

_____

_____

_____

10. Being 22

(in twos)

No matter what age you are, it's often helpful to be able to empathize with people at various points in their life spans. This is the first of several exercises concerning specific ages that can help you do that.

Part I

You and your partner take turns telling each other what it's like to be 22 years old, in the present. One partner can emphasize the good things and the other the bad things about being 22 now, or you can both think of pros and cons. Try to really empathize with people of this age and with the hopes and fears and pleasures and anxieties that go along with it.

Part II

How does it feel to be 22? What are the best and worst aspects of it?

_____

_____

_____

_____

_____

_____

11. Intimacy/Isolation

(group)

Erik Erikson sees the early years of adult life as a time for either creating intimate relationships or experiencing social isolation. To get in touch with the experience of that time, you can play a paper game.

Part I

Cut a small square of paper for each group member. An even number of squares should be marked with a *p*, for *partner*—half of them with an uppercase *P* and half with a lowercase *p*. Mark the rest of the squares (and there should be only a few of these) with an *i*, for *isolation*. Shuffle the squares, turn the blank side up, and let everybody pick one.

If you pick one marked *P*, actively choose a partner. Small *p*'s have to wait passively to be chosen; *i*'s cannot form partnerships. When you have a partner, sit down with him or her and talk about anything, signaling the relationship between you by holding your partner's hand or by the two of you turning your backs to the rest of the group. If your square is marked *i*, you can get up and move around, but you can't talk to anyone.

A round should continue for 5 minutes. When you've completed a round, take your original seats and reshuffle the squares. Pick another one, and play another round.

Part II

Did you get the same situation of intimacy or isolation in both rounds? How did it feel? If you experienced both intimacy and isolation, how were your feelings different?

_____

_____

_____

_____

_____

12. Perpetual Children

(in threes)

George Vaillant found that some men in the sample of his most influential study (1977) never took full responsibility in their lives—he called them "perpetual boys." They stayed in their parents' care for their entire adult lives. You may know a perpetual boy—or a perpetual girl, for that matter. Can you identify with this unwillingness to get involved in the cycles of normal life?

Part I

Three people role play in this exercise. One person will be the "perpetual child" (hanging on to dependency), one person the continuous parent (encouraging dependence), and one person will be the "voice of society," advocating social norms, the social clock, and other societal influences.

The "voice of society" will try every angle he or she can think of to persuade the perpetual child to become autonomous. The child will resist in any appropriate way. The parent will respond in any way that feels right.

Part II

What happened? How did it feel to be the child? the parent? the "voice of society"?

_____

_____

_____

What kinds of interactions went on between parent and child? between parent and "society"?

_____

_____

_____

_____

13. Being 33

(group)

This is a group exercise in empathy with people age 33. Members of the group should split into two subgroups, which sit facing each other. One subgroup focuses on the rewards of being 33; the other subgroup focuses on the difficulties. The positive and negative roles should be assigned arbitrarily.

Part I

One person from the group that's favorable to being 33 will announce: "One good thing about being 33 is . . . " and finish the sentence. A member of the negative group will reply with: "One bad thing about being 33 is . . .," and another person from the first group will reply to that.

Exchanges should be as fast as possible; they can be serious or funny—it doesn't really matter.

Part II

Did the feelings that your group had to express fit your own attitudes? Did any of the messages hit home with you, especially?

_____

_____

_____

_____

14. Evil and Death

(alone)

Roger Gould speaks of the difficulty in facing up to death and evil as real factors in our lives. Although freely dropping our own inner rage, hate, jealousy, and competitiveness is a last step to inner peace, in his view, Gould also feels that facing up to these feelings must precede dropping them, as the final step in achieving adult consciousness. This exercise can be a private, personal way to begin the process.

Complete the sentences for yourself; this is not to share, unless you feel the need to.

Sometimes, inside, I'm angry at ＿＿＿＿＿＿＿＿＿＿＿

because ＿＿＿＿＿＿＿＿＿＿＿＿＿＿＿

Sometimes, inside, I'm angry at ＿＿＿＿＿＿＿＿＿＿＿

because ＿＿＿＿＿＿＿＿＿＿＿＿＿＿＿

Sometimes, inside, I'm angry at ＿＿＿＿＿＿＿＿＿＿＿

because ＿＿＿＿＿＿＿＿＿＿＿＿＿＿＿

Sometimes, inside, I'm angry at ＿＿＿＿＿＿＿＿＿＿＿

because ＿＿＿＿＿＿＿＿＿＿＿＿＿＿＿

Sometimes, inside, I'm angry at ＿＿＿＿＿＿＿＿＿＿＿

because ＿＿＿＿＿＿＿＿＿＿＿＿＿＿＿

This anger is part of me, but someday I will let it drop away.

Sometimes, inside, I hate ＿＿＿＿＿＿＿＿＿＿＿＿

because ＿＿＿＿＿＿＿＿＿＿＿＿＿＿＿

Sometimes, inside, I hate ＿＿＿＿＿＿＿＿＿＿＿＿

because ＿＿＿＿＿＿＿＿＿＿＿＿＿＿＿

Sometimes, inside, I hate ＿＿＿＿＿＿＿＿＿＿＿＿

because ＿＿＿＿＿＿＿＿＿＿＿＿＿＿＿

Sometimes, inside, I hate ＿＿＿＿＿＿＿＿＿＿＿＿

because ＿＿＿＿＿＿＿＿＿＿＿＿＿＿＿

Sometimes, inside, I hate ＿＿＿＿＿＿＿＿＿＿＿＿

because ＿＿＿＿＿＿＿＿＿＿＿＿＿＿＿

This hatred is part of me, but someday I'll let it drop away.

Sometimes, inside, I'm jealous of ＿＿＿＿＿＿＿＿＿＿

because ＿＿＿＿＿＿＿＿＿＿＿＿＿＿＿

Sometimes, inside, I'm jealous of _____

    because _____

Sometimes, inside, I'm jealous of _____

    because _____

Sometimes, inside, I'm jealous of _____

    because _____

Sometimes, inside, I'm jealous of _____

    because _____

This jealousy is part of me, but someday I'll let it drop away.

Sometimes I want to get ahead of _____

    because _____

Sometimes I want to get ahead of _____

    because _____

Sometimes I want to get ahead of _____

    because _____

Sometimes I want to get ahead of _____

    because _____

Sometimes I want to get ahead of _____

    because _____

This competitiveness is part of me, but someday I can let it drop away.

(Facing up to our inner negative feelings is a first step toward achieving adult consciousness; dropping them freely is a last step to inner peace.)

15. Being 44

(group)

Bernice Neugarten invented the expression "age-irrelevant society." It's a concept that could change our point of view particularly of the years that in the past have been identified with mid-life crisis and middlescence, since one of the major factors in mid-life crisis is the awareness that people in this period are treated differently from the way younger people are treated. This exercise is an experience in bringing age irrelevance to the middle years of adult life.

Part I

Separately or in small groups, members of the group make lists of realistic ways that maturing people can be free of age stereotypes and norms. The lists can include things to do, ways to act, mental attitudes—all the lifestyle choices you can list.

As each list is finished, it is written on a blackboard. When all the lists are up, somebody can cross out any duplicates, leaving one nonrepetitive list.

Part II

Are all the items on the list realistic? Are all of the items acceptable to you? Is it good to be age irrelevant? Why is or isn't it good?

_____

_____

_____

_____

16. Retiring

(alone or in twos)

Part I

To get a clear sense of your feelings about retirement, map them on this set of scales. Put an X at the point on each scale that reflects

young	old
creative	destructive
closeness	separation
aliveness	deadness
calm	stressful
growing	static
positive	negative

your attitude toward retirement and connect the points. Is the line more toward the left, or toward the right? Is it straight, or does it zig-zag? The more it is oriented toward the left and the more consistent it is, the more enthusiastically you anticipate retirement.

Part II

Can you share your answers and have a dialogue about them? How do you feel about the idea of retirement? Could it be a productive time in your life? Is it threatening? In what way?

_____

_____

_____

_____

17. Getting There

(alone)

Carl Jung, Charlotte Bühler, Erik Erikson, Robert Peck, and Abraham Maslow all describe a positive and whole state of being that we can potentially reach in life. Jung calls it "individuation"; Bühler calls it "fulfillment"; Erikson and Peck call it "integrity"; Maslow calls it "self-actualization." Generally speaking, each of these terms means becoming your own person, valuing your self and your life, seeing life clearly, and seeing it whole. What would it take for you to reach that level of development?

Part I

To be completely individuated, my most developed self, I would have to:

_____

_____

_____

To feel that my life was completely fulfilled, I would have to:

_____

_____

_____

To completely accept my life for what it has been, I would have to:

_____

_____

_____

To purely value life and living, beyond my own self-existence, I would have to:

_____

_____

_____

Part II

Are your answers based on conditions that you feel you will reach? If so, could you push your possibilities farther? If not, could you lower your sights a little, to have the conditions possible?

_____

_____

_____

18. Ego Transcendence

(alone or in a group)

Robert Peck describes the final developmental stage as "ego transcendence"—growing beyond your own small self into an awareness of the whole of human history and the masses of humankind. Abraham Maslow, too, describes "self-transcendence" as a furthest level of growth. You're going to create a fantasy experience of what that might be like. Relax. Empty your mind.

Part I

See if you can clearly imagine your self as it is now. Picture all its needs, its desires, its hopes, its fears. Take some time to fully develop your awareness of this self. What are its strongest emotions? its goals?

Try to create an image of how that self could be if all its needs and desires were met or became unimportant; if all its hopes were fulfilled or were dropped as unnecessary; if all its fears became less and less meaningful.

Next fill that self full of acceptance—of all people and all events and all living things and all material things. Fill it with confidence that the universe is the way it should be, and with a sense of humor that recognizes absurdity as OK.

Now let that self look openly at you, your life history, your mind, and your body; let it recognize that you are fully human. Accept that everything you are and have been is part of the flow of life in the universe. Relax and accept that.

Part II

What was this experience like for you? Did you let yourself go with it? Did you fight it? Did you feel silly? uncomfortable? Is there any time in life when this experience might be of more value to you?

_____

_____

_____

_____

19. Ageism

(group)

Robert Butler invented the term *ageism* for our negative stereotypes and our prejudices about age. Ageism includes both the hostility of younger people toward older people and the self-hatred of older people, for being aged. To get in touch with the ageism that we're all socially conditioned to feel, try being old.

Part I

Everybody in this group will suddenly become 86. Zap. We're all 86 years old. Feel it? The members of the group will take turns complaining about how awful it is to be old. Really try to identify with the "bad" things about being old. Go around the group two or three or more times (depending on the number of people) until you get a strong sense of all the negative values that our society places on age. It might help to get started by completing a sentence, such as: "It's terrible to be so old, because . . ."

Part II

How real are these prejudices? Where do they come from? Do you want to carry them with you? How could they influence your life?

_____

_____

_____

_____

20. Biological Aging

(alone)

For this exercise you'll need to be alone somewhere with a big mirror—preferably one that's full-length. You're going to take a quick trip through your biological life cycle. You'll probably be able to work only with the superficial level of appearance, but it's a start toward empathizing with older people and the older person in you.

Part I

Stand in front of your mirror, dressed or undressed—whichever is comfortable. Take some time to see yourself as you are, physically, right now. When you have a clear sense of your bodily condition now, you can start taking your body through its biological cycle.

Look at yourself as you are right now:

How does this face look? skin texture? expression? What's nicest about this face now?

_____

_____

How does this body look? size? posture? muscles? fat? What's nicest about this body now?

_____

_____

What's healthiest about this body now? What's strongest about it?

_____

_____

Now picture yourself at 22:

How does this face look? skin texture? expression? What's nicest about this face now?

_____

_____

How does this body look? size? posture? muscles? fat? What's nicest about this body now?

_____

_____

What's healthiest about this body now? What's strongest about it?

_____

_____

Now picture yourself at 33:

How does this face look? skin texture? expression? What's nicest about this face now?

_____

_____

How does this body look? size? posture? muscles? fat? What's nicest about this body now?

_____

_____

What's healthiest about this body now? What's strongest about it?

_____

_____

Now, at 44:

How does this face look? skin texture? expression? What's nicest about this face now?

_____

_____

How does this body look? size? posture? muscles? fat? What's nicest about this body now?

_____

_____

What's healthiest about this body now? What's strongest about it?

_____

_____

Now, at 55:

How does this face look? skin texture? expression? What's nicest about this face now?

_____

_____

How does this body look? size? posture? muscles? fat? What's nicest about this body now?

_____

_____

What's healthiest about this body now? What's strongest about it?

_____

_____

Now, at 66:

How does this face look? skin texture? expression? What's nicest about this face now?

_____

_____

How does this body look? size? posture? muscles? fat? What's nicest about this body now?

_____

_____

What's healthiest about this body now? What's strongest about it?

_____

_____

Now, at 77:

How does this face look? skin texture? expression? What's nicest about this face now?

_____

_____

How does this body look? size? posture? muscles? fat? What's nicest about this body now?

_____

_____

What's healthiest about this body now? What's strongest about it?

_____

_____

Now, at 88:

How does this face look? skin texture? expression? What's nicest about this face now?

_____

_____

How does this body look? size? posture? muscles? fat? What's nicest about this body now?

_____

_____

What's healthiest about this body now? What's strongest about it?

_____

_____

Part II

What happened during this experience? Could you get involved in doing it? If not, why not? What was the best thing about it? What was the worst thing?

_____

_____

_____

_____

_____

_____

What do you fear about aging? What do you look forward to in old age?

_____

_____

_____

_____

_____

_____

21. Social Roles

(in twos)

The social cycle of your life involves a complex collection of social roles. You begin with a baby role and from then on it's a nonstop process of role collecting, until eventually you get to play "dying person." See how many you can identify.

Part I

With a partner, take turns asking each other "Have you ever played the role of _____?" You can include family, educational, work, sexual, legal, economic, and any other roles. Keep a running list of each other's roles. When you can't think of any more roles to ask your partner about, make another column and list all the social roles that you have played that your partner didn't think of. Share your lists and see whether that makes you aware of more roles.

Part II

How many roles did you identify all together? Have you ever thought of yourself as having such a big collection of social roles? What effect do they have on your life? How do you feel about that?

_____

_____

_____

_____

_____

22. Stable You/Changing You

(alone)

Daniel Levinson and Douglas Kimmel describe adult personality development as a process that involves a stable, inner aspect as well as a changing, outer aspect that adapts to the outer world's demands. This is an exercise in differentiating these aspects.

Part I

You may be able to identify many parts of your personality and whether they change, if you stop and think about it. Check the appropriate blank.

	Stable	Changing
My sense of how I feel about myself	_____	_____
My sense of how I appear to other people	_____	_____
The way I think about problems	_____	_____
The way I think about people	_____	_____
My usual mood, in general	_____	_____
My level of emotional reaction	_____	_____
My level of physical energy, in general	_____	_____
My level of emotional energy, in general	_____	_____
My physical health, in general	_____	_____
My physical strength, in general	_____	_____
My physical endurance, in general	_____	_____
My tendency to act without thinking	_____	_____
My tendency to think before acting	_____	_____
My ways of interacting with intimates	_____	_____

	Stable	Changing
My ways of interacting with friends	———	———
My ways of interacting with people, in general	———	———
My ways of reacting to hostility	———	———
My ways of reacting to authority	———	———
My ways of reacting to danger	———	———
My ways of relating to responsibility	———	———
My ways of relating to new ideas	———	———
My ways of relating to change	———	———
My skills in expressing myself	———	———
My skills in communicating intimately	———	———
My skills in social conversation	———	———
My skills in logical thinking	———	———
My skills in problem solving	———	———
My skills in generalizing	———	———
My skills in empathizing	———	———
My sense of what is fair	———	———
My sense of what is beautiful	———	———
My sense of what is honest	———	———
My sense of what is right	———	———
My sense of what is wrong	———	———

(Fill in anything that's been left out.)

_____   ———   ———

_____   ———   ———

_____   ———   ———

_____   ———   ———

Part II

List the things about you that have been stable over time.

_____

_____

_____

_____

_____

Would you like any of those aspects of yourself to change? How could you accomplish those changes?

_____

_____

_____

_____

List the things that have changed over time.

_____

_____

_____

Do you wish any of them hadn't changed? Can you do anything to change them back?

_____

_____

_____

_____

23. Life Extension I

(group)

If life-extension technology keeps developing at the present rate, you might be faced with living a much longer life than you've been anticipating. Take some time to get in touch with the feeling of living 150 years or more.

Part I

Divide your group in half and make two circles—an inner circle of people who are going to talk about their long lives and what it's like to live so long plus an outer circle of people who are going to listen and take notes on the verbal and nonverbal messages that the inner circle communicates.

Each outer-circle member picks one inner-circle member to watch and listen to and begins taking notes on that person's messages. The inner-circle group members talk to each other, covering how they feel about their long lives, what it's like, what they do, what they plan to do, and so forth. The discussion should cover as much of life as the members can get in touch with—it should last for 15 minutes or more. If pauses occur, let them; somebody will probably think of something else to add.

Part II

Members in the outer circle share their notes. How did your person feel about his/her long life? Did the nonverbal and the verbal messages match? How do you feel about that person's point of view? Do you agree? disagree? What was it like, listening but not getting involved in the discussion?

24. The Good Life

(alone)

What is "the good life" to you? This is an opportunity to assess the importance of some basic aspects of your ideal lifestyle.

Part I

Put an X in the appropriate place on the lifestyle scales.

For me, the good life is when:

I'm involved closely with my parents, siblings, relatives.	⌊_⌊_⌊_⌊_⌋	I'm not involved closely with my parents, siblings, relatives.
Marriage is central in life.	⌊_⌊_⌊_⌊_⌋	Marriage isn't necessary.
Parenting is central in life.	⌊_⌊_⌊_⌊_⌋	Parenting isn't necessary.
I have close and intimate friends.	⌊_⌊_⌊_⌊_⌋	I have surface relationships with friends.
I have social contact with many people.	⌊_⌊_⌊_⌊_⌋	I have little social contact.
My work life involves me with people.	⌊_⌊_⌊_⌊_⌋	My work life doesn't involve me with people.
My job demands involvement and responsibility.	⌊_⌊_⌊_⌊_⌋	My job is structured and undemanding.
My work setting is comfortable and attractive.	⌊_⌊_⌊_⌊_⌋	My work place is challenging and rough.
I can have a variety of work experiences.	⌊_⌊_⌊_⌊_⌋	I have an unchanging work situation.

Work is important in my life.	⊢—⊥—⊥—⊥—⊣	Work is incidental in my life.
I can live in many different places.	⊢—⊥—⊥—⊥—⊣	I can settle in one location.
My home reflects my taste and my social class.	⊢—⊥—⊥—⊥—⊣	My home is not a matter of aesthetics or status.
I have the chance to travel widely.	⊢—⊥—⊥—⊥—⊣	I stay in one familiar place.
I have more money than I need.	⊢—⊥—⊥—⊥—⊣	I have enough money to survive.
I have complete financial security.	⊢—⊥—⊥—⊥—⊣	Easy come, easy go.
I have many material possessions.	⊢—⊥—⊥—⊥—⊣	I don't have unnecessary material possessions.
I have luxuries and expensive possessions.	⊢—⊥—⊥—⊥—⊣	I have essentials and cheap, expendable things.
Most of my choices in life are made for me by my social world.	⊢—⊥—⊥—⊥—⊣	I make my own, conscious lifestyle choices.
I am aware and in touch with my inner feelings, thoughts, self.	⊢—⊥—⊥—⊥—⊣	My inner world is insulated and hidden.
I am stimulated and excited.	⊢—⊥—⊥—⊥—⊣	I am at peace and relaxed.
My life is full of stress but challenging.	⊢—⊥—⊥—⊥—⊣	My life is free from stress and challenge.
My body is physically fit and active.	⊢—⊥—⊥—⊥—⊣	My body is sedentary and rested.
My health is maximal.	⊢—⊥—⊥—⊥—⊣	My health is at maintenance level.
I have a lot of available energy.	⊢—⊥—⊥—⊥—⊣	I have low energy drives.
I am highly sexually active.	⊢—⊥—⊥—⊥—⊣	I'm minimally sexually active.
I am free to act on impulse.	⊢—⊥—⊥—⊥—⊣	I have my impulses under complete control.
I am dominant in my interpersonal relations.	⊢—⊥—⊥—⊥—⊣	I am passive in my interpersonal relations.
I can play a variety of social roles.	⊢—⊥—⊥—⊥—⊣	I have few social roles to play.
My social roles are in control of my behavior.	⊢—⊥—⊥—⊥—⊣	I am totally free of social-role controls.
My social roles are a source of status.	⊢—⊥—⊥—⊥—⊣	My status has little connection with roles.
I am free to express myself fully.	⊢—⊥—⊥—⊥—⊣	I can control myself completely.

| My time is free and unstructured. | ⌊___⌊___⌊___⌊___⌋ | My time is organized and structured. |
| My potential to grow and change is being tapped. | ⌊___⌊___⌊___⌊___⌋ | My ability to stabilize and limit my experience is being tapped. |

Part II

Can you think of more areas in your lifestyle that you could assess? Does evaluating your lifestyle suggest any changes that you would like to make in your life now? in your future goals?

_____

_____

_____

_____

_____

Being Clear: Alternatives

Besides absorbing information about ideas and getting in touch with your feelings and fantasies about them, there's another way to understand ideas a little more completely: you can evaluate their usefulness in your own value system.

To relate an idea to your own values you have to go through at least four processes. The first process is to think about the idea in relationship to other ideas that could substitute in their usefulness to you. In other words, you have to become clearly aware of alternatives.

Each of the alternatives may have very different consequences. A second process, then, is to determine what the consequences may be of every alternative. Once you're clear about the alternatives and their consequences, a third process is to decide which alternatives are most attractive to you. That is, you have to weigh each of the alternatives in terms of your values.

Once you've weighed the alternatives individually, you can set up a personal scale of exactly how valuable each alternative is to you. The fourth process, then, is to decide how the alternatives fit your priorities.

This section contains a collection of exercises based on exploring alternatives, examining consequences, weighing the alternatives on their own merits, and deciding how the alternatives fit your priorities. They're designed to give you a chance to clarify your values about some of the basic concepts in this book. There are some exercises to do alone, some to do alone or in groups, and some to do in twos or threes. In general, the more you share and compare values with others, the clearer your values can become.

As you do these exercises, you may find that sometimes your values are unclear, or that they're in conflict with each other. Sometimes you'll be very clear about them. In any case, integrating the ideas into your own set of priorities will help you understand them in a personal way.

25. Life Extension II

(alone or in a group)

The possibility of extending human life is a possibility for social change with far-reaching consequences. You can explore some of the consequences by thinking about the areas listed below as well as any other areas that occur to you.

Part I

If you're doing this exercise alone, use the lines below. If you're doing it with a group, maybe a blackboard would be better.

Extended longevity, if it involves a large percentage of the population, might have some of the following effects

on personal life satisfaction: _____

_____

_____

on the family: _____

_____

_____

on work: _____

_____

_____

on the economy: _____

_____

_____

on the government: _____

_____

_____

on population size: _____

_____

_____

_____

on the energy supply: _____

_____

_____

on the food supply: _____

_____

_____

on religion: _____

_____

_____

on friendship networks: _____

_____

_____

on medical services: _____

_____

_____

on social services: _____

_____

_____

on legal services: _____

_____

_____

on other institutions and facets of society: _____

_____

_____

_____

_____

_____

Part II

Did you find far-reaching effects? Do you think they can be handled positively in our society? What was the least positive effect? The most positive?

_____

_____

_____

_____

_____

26. Cohort Values

(group or alone)   Because cohorts are born into history at different times, they experience different sets of historical events, or experience them in different ways than do other cohorts. Each cohort tends to learn a slightly different set of values. Can you generalize about a cohort's values to some degree?

The chart that follows lists a number of social changes, scratching the surface of the set of events that may influence a cohort's values. Examine the three cohorts illustrated, one at a time, and then rank the order of the values you would expect them to hold, explaining why.

Part I

Fill in the appropriate number from *1* for the highest to *12* for the lowest according to the values you would expect each cohort to hold. In each case, explain why you think the number you assigned reflects the cohort's value most closely.

Cohort born in 1900

_____ exciting experiences—because _____

_____ material possessions—because _____

_____ family closeness—because _____

_____ personal freedom—because _____

_____ hard work—because _____

Born 1900

Born 1930

Born 1960

	1900	1910	1920	1930	1940	1950	1960	1970	1980	1990	2000
Family	Extended family		Nuclear family	Increasing divorce rate	Modified nuclear family	Birth control technology		Experimental family styles			
Location	Move from farms to cities					Move from cities to suburbs					
Economy	Rising industrialism			Great Depression	Economic boom		Easy credit	Inflated economy			
Work	Most labor unskilled		Few jobs open		Many more jobs open		Most labor skilled		Few jobs open		
Military action		World War I (won)			World War II (won)	Korean War (ambiguous result)	Vietnam War (troops withdrawn)				
Technology	Electricity, Telephone	Automobile	Radio	Air travel	Television	Atomic bomb	Computer age, Space technology, Satellite communications				
Resources	Exploitation of natural resources					Destruction and shortage of natural resources					

_____ self-expression—because _____

_____ peace—because _____

_____ patriotism—because _____

_____ financial security—because _____

_____ equal opportunity—because _____

_____ protection of the environment—because _____

_____ technical industrial progress—because _____

Cohort born in 1930

_____ exciting experiences—because _____

_____ material possessions—because _____

_____ family closeness—because _____

_____ personal freedom—because _____

_____ hard work—because _____

_____ self-expression—because _____

_____ peace—because _____

_____ patriotism—because _____

_____ financial security—because _____

_____ equal opportunity—because _____

_____ protection of the environment—because _____

_____ technical industrial progress—because _____

Cohort born in 1960

_____ exciting experiences—because _____

_____ material possessions—because _____

_____ family closeness—because _____

_____ personal freedom—because _____

_____ hard work—because _____

_____ self-expression—because _____

_____ peace—because _____

_____ patriotism—because _____

_____ financial security—because _____

_____ equal opportunity—because _____

_____ protection of the environment—because _____

_____ technical industrial progress—because _____

Part II

Were each cohort's value priorities substantially similar or at variance to the other cohorts'? If they differed more than they were the same, did you find reasons for the differences?

_____

_____

_____

_____

_____

27. Values over Time

(alone)

This exercise is a sort of values autobiography. It will give you the opportunity to establish a personal list of values and to think about how that list may change during your adult life span.

Part I

For each period in your life, make up a list of at least ten people, places, things, beliefs, or activities that you feel were, are, or will be most valuable, and briefly explain why.

Late teens to late twenties

1. _____ because _____

2. _____ because _____

3. _____ because _____

4. _____ because _____

5. _____ because _____

6. _____ because _____

7. _____ because _____

8. _____ because _____

9. _____ because _____

10. _____ because _____

_____ because _____

_____ because _____

_____ because _____

Early thirties to late thirties

1. _____ because _____

2. _____ because _____

3. _____ because _____

4. _____ because _____

5. _____ because _____

6. _____ because _____

7. _____ because _____

8. _____ because _____

9. _____ because _____

10. _____ because _____

_____ because _____

_____ because _____

_____ because _____

Early forties to mid-fifties

1. _____ because _____

2. _____ because _____

3. _____ because _____

4. _____ because _____

5. _____ because _____

6. _____ because _____

7. _____ because _____

8. _____ because _____

9. _____ because _____

10. _____ because _____

_____ because _____

_____ because _____

_____ because _____

Mid-fifties to mid-sixties

1. _____ because _____

2. _____ because _____

3. _____ because _____

4. _____ because _____

5. _____ because _____

6. _____ because _____

7. _____ because _____

8. _____ because _____

9. _____ because _____

10. _____ because _____

_____ because _____

_____ because _____

_____ because _____

Mid-sixties to mid-seventies

1. _____ because _____

2. _____ because _____

3. _____ because _____

4. _____ because _____

5. _____ because _____

6. _____ because _____

7. _____ because _____

8. _____ because _____

9. _____   because _____
10. _____   because _____
   _____   because _____
   _____   because _____
   _____   because _____

The mid-seventies and later

1. _____   because _____
2. _____   because _____
3. _____   because _____
4. _____   because _____
5. _____   because _____
6. _____   because _____
7. _____   because _____
8. _____   because _____
9. _____   because _____
10. _____   because _____
   _____   because _____
   _____   because _____
   _____   because _____

Part II

Which values stayed with you all through life? Which ones became more important? Which ones became less important? Which ones did you drop?

_____

_____

_____

_____

_____

28. Seasons

(group)

Daniel Levinson describes the ages of life as seasons, like the seasons of the year—each having its own special beauties and each contributing something special to the whole of life.

Divide your group into four subgroups: spring, summer, fall, and winter. The groups get in touch with the values of their assigned season of life by focusing on it and exploring the image as deeply as possible. (Each group should try to get in touch with both the positive and the negative aspects of the seasons.)

Part I

Take 15 minutes or more to focus on your group's assigned season of life. (Spring extends to the late twenties; summer, to the thirties; fall, to the fifties and sixties; winter, to the seventies and eighties.) Try relating everything about your season of the year to everything about that time of life. Carry the image as far as you can.

Part II

Share your findings with the whole group. Did the image work for you? What were the positive aspects of the season? the negative aspects?

29. Mature Defenses

(alone)

Although Freud considered defense mechanisms to be maladaptive, George Vaillant has made some value judgments about some "defense mechanisms" that he feels are mature and constructive. All of these can be useful adaptations. This exercise is aimed at becoming more conscious of how you use these mature defenses.

Part I

List two recent situations in which you used each of the mature defenses named.

altruism: reaching out, giving to someone else, or helping someone else

_____

_____

humor: seeing the funny side of a difficult situation

_____

_____

suppression: deciding not to deal with an issue until you're ready

_____

_____

sublimation: putting your negative energy into positive and satisfying behavior

_____

_____

anticipation: realistic planning for a specific outcome

_____

_____

Part II

Did you find that you're putting these positive defenses to use in your life? Can you see that there are situations in which they could be helpful?

_____

_____

_____

_____

_____

30. Adult Family

(in twos)

Quentin and Emily Schenk describe the ideal situation for young adults and their parents as being an "adult family"—a family in which both children and parents avoid role playing and relate to one another as equal adults. What is your idea of the ideal family situation in your life?

Part I

With a partner, take turns sharing how your family could create better parent/child relationships. Try to be very specific. Keep a list. Use your agreements and disagreements with your partner as a way to create a fuller picture of your ideal adult family.

Part II

What is most important to you in family life? How could parent/child conflicts be minimized in your family? How could sibling relationships be better?

_____

_____

_____

_____

_____

_____

31. Intimacy

(in twos)

Erikson identifies the first years of adult life as a time when each person has to learn to establish intimacy with another person. To establish intimacy requires openness and honesty—the ability to share inner worlds, yours and theirs. One path to intimacy begins with learning about the other person's memories and feelings and preferences.

Part I

Pick a person you would like to know better and spend a half hour or more moving toward intimacy, using the following questions. Try to answer the questions briefly, so that you can move through the whole set.

Partner 1: What's the best movie you've seen recently? Why?
Partner 2: What's your favorite television program? Why?
Partner 1: What do you like to do best on Sunday afternoons? Why?
Partner 2: What kind of music do you like to listen to most? Why?
Partner 1: What's your favorite color?
Partner 2: What kind of clothes do you feel best in?

Partner 1: What's the most embarrassing thing that's ever happened to you?

Partner 2: What's the best thing that's happened to you in your whole life?

Partner 1: What are you most afraid of? Why?

Partner 2: What do you hate the most? Why?

Partner 1: How old are you? How do you feel about being this age?

Partner 2: How old are you? How do you feel about being this age?

Partner 1: What is your best friend like?

Partner 2: What is your father like?

Partner 1: What makes you feel really happy?

Partner 2: What do you want to know more about?

Partner 1: What do you like most about yourself?

Partner 2: What's the best thing that you've ever done?

Partner 1: What do you think people dislike about you?

Partner 2: What is the most unpleasant thing about you?

Partner 1: What's your favorite smell?

Partner 2: What's your favorite flower?

Partner 1: Can you play a musical instrument? Which one?

Partner 2: Can you make things by hand? What?

Partner 1: What's the earliest thing you remember from childhood?

Partner 2: How old do you want to be when you die?

Partner 1: What would you do with a million dollars?

Partner 2: What countries would you like to tour?

Partner 1: Do you speak any language besides English?

Partner 2: What games or sports are you best at?

Partner 1: If you were a dog, what kind of dog would you be?

Partner 2: If you were a bird, what kind would you be?

Partner 1: What's your favorite season?

Partner 2: What's your favorite holiday?

Partner 1: When do you feel most lonely? Why?

Partner 2: What depresses you most? Why?

Partner 1: What do you want to be doing in ten years?

Partner 2: What do you wish you had done ten years ago?

Partner 1: What world problem worries you most? Why?

Partner 2: What environmental problem is the most serious? Why?

Partner 1: When do you feel most comfortable?

Partner 2: When are you happiest?

Partner 1: Which of my answers was closest to the way you would have answered?

Partner 2: Which of my answers was closest to the way you would
have answered?

Partner 1: Which of my answers told you most about me?

Partner 2: Which of my answers told you most about me?

Part II

Did this exercise help you get a feeling of what intimacy with your
partner might be like? If not, what was missing?

_____

_____

_____

32. Thirties Roots

(group)

In the thirties, many people settle into family living. Gail Sheehy
calls this time of life "rooting and extending." As a group, you can
generate a list of the values of marriage, parenting, the PTA, community involvement, homemaking—all the basic ground for the
roots of the thirties. You can also contribute some of the drawbacks.

Part I

Go around the group several times (depending on the size of the
group) until you have established a list of the values that are most
important to people in their thirties.

1. _____	2. _____
3. _____	4. _____
5. _____	6. _____
7. _____	8. _____
9. _____	10. _____
11. _____	12. _____
13. _____	14. _____
15. _____	16. _____
17. _____	18. _____
19. _____	20. _____

21. _____   22. _____

23. _____   24. _____

25. _____   26. _____

27. _____   28. _____

29. _____   30. _____

31. _____   32. _____

33. _____   34. _____

35. _____   36. _____

37. _____   38. _____

39. _____   40. _____

Part II

When you have the list, open it up for discussion of the consequences—social and personal, positive and negative—of these values.

33. Polarities

(alone)

Carl Jung identified a list of inner polarities that we need to recognize and integrate in order to become individuated adults. This exercise is an opportunity to recognize some of your own polarities.

Part I

The youthful things about me (such as being fresh, enthusiastic, energetic, innocent, new) are:	The old things about me (such as being dull, bored, jaded, sophisticated, worn out) are:
1. _____	1. _____
2. _____	2. _____
3. _____	3. _____
4. _____	4. _____
5. _____	5. _____
6. _____	6. _____

The destructive things about me (such as denying, destroying, no-saying, rejecting, and being aggressive, negative) are:

1. _____
2. _____
3. _____
4. _____
5. _____
6. _____

The creative things about me (such as accepting, problem solving, constructive, imaginative, and being positive, curious) are:

1. _____
2. _____
3. _____
4. _____
5. _____
6. _____

The masculine things about me (such as being strong, active, dominant, hard, rational) are:

1. _____
2. _____
3. _____
4. _____
5. _____
6. _____

The feminine things about me (such as being nurturant, passive, submissive, soft, emotional) are:

1. _____
2. _____
3. _____
4. _____
5. _____
6. _____

My attachment needs (for dependency, protection, acceptance) are:

1. _____
2. _____
3. _____
4. _____
5. _____
6. _____

My separation needs (for independence, self-sufficiency, being alone) are:

1. _____
2. _____
3. _____
4. _____
5. _____
6. _____

Part II

In this exercise, did you find aspects of yourself that you don't usually notice? If so, were you comfortable recognizing these other sides of yourself?

_____

_____

_____

34. Middle Age

(in twos)

Bernice and Morton Hunt have described two perceptions of middle age: those of the "old middle age" of the past and the "new middle age" of the present. Many attitudes from the old-middle-age concept are still strong in our social world.

This role-playing exercise is designed to help you be more fully aware of the negative attitudes of the old middle age and also the positive attitudes of the new middle age.

Part I

One partner will play a 60-year-old who's suffering from the old middle age. Playing this role involves changing posture and facial expression accordingly and altering thoughts as though "thinking sick" and "thinking old" and being inactive.

The other partner will play a 60-year-old who is living the new middle age. Face and body should be congruent with "thinking fit," "thinking healthy," and being active.

The partners talk to one another for about 15 minutes, describing their lifestyles: what they eat, drink, and do for entertainment; how they spend their days; what they're looking forward to.

Part II

How did it feel to be 60? Was it fun? uncomfortable? Did your partner irritate you? What does that tell you?

_____

_____

_____

_____

35. Losses

(alone)

One characteristic of late adult life is that it involves a number of inevitable losses. Some potential losses may be more important to you than others.

Part I

Using the list that follows, rate the typical losses, with *1* indicating the one most difficult for you and *27* indicating the least difficult.

Social losses	*Physical losses*	*Psychological losses*
___ work roles	___ speed	___ belonging
___ friendship roles	___ flexibility	___ confidence
___ marriage roles	___ endurance	___ emotional satisfaction
___ time structure	___ sensory functions	___ social intimacy
___ variety of interactions	___ physical activity	___ autonomy
___ domestic routines	___ health	___ self-expression
___ social structure	___ attractiveness	___ security
___ group identity	___ self-sufficiency	___ power
___ couple status	___ competence	___ self-awareness

Part II

Which loss would make you most unhappy? How could you compensate for it? Which losses would matter the least?

_____

_____

_____

_____

_____

36. *Disengagement versus Activity*

(group) Some people are more comfortable withdrawing from the social world as they grow older; some people thrive on active involvement in their late years. You can use your group to generate pros and cons for disengagement and for remaining active.

Part I

Split the group into three subgroups. Identify one subgroup as people who want to use their last years as a phase of disengaging from involvement with life; one subgroup will be people who insist on involving themselves in life at every level until they die; and one subgroup will attempt to combine disengagement and involvement.

The "disengagers" collect as many specific reasons as they can think of for eliminating from the last years of life physical, social, personal, sexual, sensual, intellectual, emotional, and other activity. The "involvers" collect as many specific reasons as they can think of for continuing to experience all of these aspects of life as fully as possible in their last years. The "combiners" sort out some areas of activity and some areas of disengaging.

Part II

Each subgroup will select a person to state its position. (Summarizers may want to list arguments on a blackboard instead of stating them verbally.) Then each member of the group votes—each person choosing disengagement, activity, or a combination of the two for the style he or she expects to prefer at the end of his or her life.

37. *Body Systems*

(alone) All of your body systems are interconnected and interrelated. Can you consider them separately and decide which is most valuable to you and why?

Part I

Rank the eight bodily systems 1 through 8, with the system filled in at 1 the one you consider most valuable. Then, on the accompanying lines, explain why you ranked each system the way you did.

	Value	Explanation
nervous system	_____	_____
cardiovascular system	_____	_____
respiratory system	_____	_____
skeletomuscular system	_____	_____
digestive system	_____	_____
excretory system	_____	_____
endocrine system	_____	_____
immune system	_____	_____

Part II

Was ranking the systems' importance to you difficult? Are any of your answers questionable? Why? Can you survive if any one of these systems stops functioning? How?

_____

_____

_____

_____

_____

38. Family Forms

(group)
The American family has taken a number of forms in recent years that may become more and more common in the future. This exercise for a group is to point up some of the positive and negative aspects of these family forms.

Part I

The group members sit in a circle. Each person answers each of the following sentences, going around the circle on each sentence.

1. A child in a communal family has an advantage because . . .
2. Parents who bring together their children from other marriages have problems because . . .

3. Couples who decide to have no children miss . . .
4. One good thing about a group marriage is . . .
5. In a changing society, the nuclear family is valuable because . . .
6. Children brought up in a single-parent family may have problems because . . .
7. Maintaining close ties with extended-family members is helpful because . . .
8. Institutional families, such as group homes, are socially valuable because . . .
9. The nuclear family can be considered the best form because it . . .
10. A blended family gives children from other marriages a positive experience by . . .
11. Growing up in an extended family is healthy for a child because . . .
12. When you're brought up by a single parent, you have an advantage because . . .
13. The big problem with an institutional family is that it . . .
14. Group marriages are socially destructive because . . .
15. The best thing about being child free is . . .
16. The advantage to society of communal families is . . .
17. Single parents have a rough life sometimes because . . .
18. Marriage, divorce, and remarriage can be a valuable experience because . . .
19. Children in a group marriage have problems because . . .
20. If too many people are child free, society will . . .
21. Society needs to support single parents by . . .
22. Communal life could be difficult for parents because . . .
23. The nuclear family creates psychological problems because . . .
24. One good thing about being a single parent is . . .
25. A series of marriages and divorces isn't good for a person, because . . .
26. Parenting in a group marriage would be confusing because . . .
27. Too much contact with extended-family members causes problems such as . . .
28. When many people choose to be child free, society gains because . . .
29. The existence of alternative family forms is . . .
30. The family form that I think would be most comfortable for me is . . .

Part II

Did you find that your openness to variations in family forms increased during this exercise? decreased? Were positive values raised that hadn't occurred to you? Were negative points raised that you had never considered?

----

39. Friendship

(in twos)

The friendship cycle is an important social cycle in life. This experience is directed at getting you in touch with your own values concerning friendship.

Part I

Partners will take turns interviewing each other on experiences of friendship. Ask such questions as:

Who is your best friend? Why?
How do you choose your friends?
What does it take for an acquaintance to become a friend?
What do you like to do with your friends?
What do you expect from a friend?
What does having a friend add to your life?
How could you make your friendships more valuable?

Part II

In asking questions did you learn anything about your own values about friendship? Did you become more aware of your own friendship patterns?

----

40. Suicide

(group)

One of the most serious blocks to adjusting to life is the refusal to adjust. All through the life span, suicides mark situations in which people have chosen not to adjust.

This exercise is a loose discussion of the reasons for self-destruction, the arguments for and against it, and the methods of dealing with it.

Part I

Using the following statements as guidelines, members of the group share experiences and opinions about suicide.

I've known/heard about a person who attempted/committed suicide because:
   of depression about the present/the future.
   someone the person admired committed suicide.
   of a crime that he or she had committed.
   of an unhappy love affair.
   of the desire to punish the survivors.
   the person was trying to save someone else.
   of heavy involvement with drugs or alcohol.
   of a desire for attention.
I believe that suicide:
   can't ever be justified.
   is a sin.
   is almost always a mistake.
   can be justified in some circumstances.
   is stupid.
In dealing with a threatened suicide:
   it's important to be there for the person, because . . .
   it's better to listen and ask questions than it is to give advice or
      preach because . . .
   it's helpful to encourage the person to clarify the problem be-
      cause . . .
   it's important to refer the person to a trusted professional (such as
      a priest, doctor, counselor, or psychologist) because . . .
We all ought to be familiar with suicide-prevention hot lines in our community because . . .

Part II

Do you know more about suicide now than you did before? Are you clearer on your own feelings about it?

_____

_____

_____

_____

_____

Being Prepared: Anticipation

Being aware of your feelings about elements of life may be helpful in your future; and being clear about some of your values may be useful. In this third section, the theme is anticipating the directions that your life might take in the future.

What follows is a collection of exercises to help you set goals, plan strategies, and explore alternatives. In the process of working your way through it you can learn:

to identify your goals
to plan systematically
to open up some alternatives
to accept changes more flexibly

The plans you make may or may not work out. In fact, they seldom do. Right? Plans aren't the important thing; the planning process is what counts. Having a strategy for planning available to you, one that's realistic and flexible, gives you the opportunity to shape your life more consciously. (You're shaping it unconsciously, anyway.)

Go ahead. Do it! I hope your life unfolds in just the very best way.

41. The Life Game

(alone, in twos, or in a group) Just to emphasize that any systematic planning you do in life is always open to forces that you can't control, this game is an experience in taking life as it comes and then dealing with it on your own terms. It's a combination of fate, luck, the will of God, random chance, and personal choice—like real life.

You can play the game alone or with other people. (Sometimes having people around to suggest some options you haven't thought of is useful.) To play this game, each player (or group) needs one die.

Part I

To play the game, each player rolls the die three times for each period of adult life.

On the first roll, the number that comes up determines the biological events on the period's life chart.

On the second roll, your number indicates what happens in your social world—family, work, and friendships.

On the third roll, your number is your psychological condition.

When you've rolled three times, you'll have one period's life situation to deal with. On the lines accompanying the chart, you can outline your solutions to any problems that have cropped up, the adaptations that you may have to make, and the new directions you can move in.

For any of the periods, if you roll a 6 on the first roll your life is finished. (But you can choose to live another time around, if you want to.)

Now you're in your late teens to late twenties.

	Biological factors	*Social factors*	*Psychological factors*
1	Super physical condition and health	Intimate relationship Career training	High emotional well-being High life satisfaction High growth
2	Good condition and health	Limited relationship Promising career	Good emotional well-being Good life satisfaction Moderate growth
3	Average condition and health	Satisfying marriage Promising career Children	Average emotional stability Average life satisfaction Little growth
4	Temporary disability	Unsatisfying marriage Promising career	Shaky emotional stability Little life satisfaction No growth
5	Serious disability	Divorced Limited career Children	High emotional stress Little life satisfaction No growth
6	Death	Isolated Little career direction	Emotional crisis No life satisfaction No growth

How will you solve your new problems? _____

_____

_____

How can you adapt most positively? _____

_____

_____

What new directions will you move in? _____

_____

_____

Now you're in your early to late thirties.

Biological factors	*Social factors*	*Psychological factors*
1 Super physical condition and health	Satisfying marriage Promising career Children	High emotional well-being High life-satisfaction level High growth
2 Good condition and health	Satisfying marriage Promising career	Good emotional well-being Good life satisfaction Moderate growth
3 Average condition and health	Unsatisfying marriage Promising career Children	Average emotional stability Average life satisfaction Little growth
4 Temporary disability	Divorced Promising career Children	Shaky emotional stability Little life satisfaction No growth
5 Serious disability	Unsatisfying marriage Limited career Children	High emotional stress Little life satisfaction No growth
6 Death	Isolated Limited career	Emotional crisis No life satisfaction No growth

How will you solve your new problems? _____

_____

How can you adapt most positively? _____

_____

What new directions will you move in? _____

_____

Now you're in your early forties to mid-fifties.

Biological factors	*Social factors*	*Psychological factors*
1 Super physical condition and health	Satisfying marriage Promising career Launched children	High emotional well-being High life satisfaction High growth
2 Good condition and health	Satisfying marriage Promising career	Good emotional well-being Good life satisfaction Moderate growth
3 Average condition and health	Unsatisfying marriage Promising career Children at home	Average emotional stability Average life satisfaction Little growth
4 Temporary disability	Unsatisfying marriage Limited career Children at home	Shaky emotional stability Little life satisfaction No growth

5	Serious disability	Divorced	High emotional stress
		Limited career	Little life satisfaction
		Launched children	No growth
6	Death	Isolated	Emotional crisis
		Limited career	No life satisfaction
			No growth

How will you solve your new problems? _____

_____

How can you adapt most positively? _____

_____

What new directions will you move in? _____

_____

Now you're in your mid-fifties to mid-sixties.

		Biological factors	*Social factors*	*Psychological factors*
1	Super physical condition and health	Satisfying marriage Satisfying career	High emotional well-being High life satisfaction High growth
2	Good condition and health	Satisfying marriage Early retirement	Good emotional well-being Good life satisfaction Moderate growth
3	Average condition and health	Unsatisfying marriage Early retirement	Average emotional stability Average life satisfaction Little growth
4	Temporary disability	Divorced Limited career	Shaky emotional stability Little life satisfaction No growth
5	Serious disability	Widowed Retired	High emotional stress Little life satisfaction No growth
6	Death	Isolated Limited career	Emotional crisis No life satisfaction No growth

How will you solve your new problems? _____

_____

How can you adapt most positively? _____

_____

What new directions will you move in? _____

_____

Now you're in your mid-sixties to mid-seventies.

Biological factors	Social factors	Psychological factors
1 Super physical condition and health	Satisfying marriage Satisfying career	High emotional well-being High life satisfaction High growth
2 Good condition and health	Unsatisfying marriage Retired	Good emotional well-being Good life satisfaction Moderate growth
3 Average condition and health	Divorced Limited career	Average emotional stability Average life satisfaction Little growth
4 Temporary disability	Divorced Retired	Shaky emotional stability Little life satisfaction No growth
5 Serious disability	Widowed Retired	High emotional stress Little life satisfaction No growth
6 Death	Isolated Retired	Emotional crisis No life satisfaction No growth

How will you solve your new problems? _____

_____

How can you adapt most positively? _____

_____

What new directions will you move in? _____

_____

Now you're in your mid-seventies and later.

Biological factors	Social factors	Psychological factors
1 Super physical condition and health	Satisfying marriage Retired	High emotional well-being High life satisfaction High growth
2 Good condition and health	Satisfying relationships Retired	Good emotional well-being Good life satisfaction Moderate growth
3 Average condition and health	Self-sufficient Retired	Average emotional stability Average life satisfaction Little growth
4 Temporary disability	Dependent Retired	Shaky emotional stability Little life satisfaction No growth

5 Serious disability	Institutionalized Retired	High emotional stress Little life satisfaction No growth
6 Death	Isolated Retired	Emotional crisis No life satisfaction No growth

How will you solve your new problems? _____

_____

How can you adapt most positively? _____

_____

What new directions will you move in? _____

_____

Part II

Can you win this game? How? Could you find positive ways of dealing with most of life's changes?

_____

_____

_____

_____

_____

42. Goal Setting I: Long-Term Goals

(group)

One way to get through life is to follow the pattern that emerges, as in the "Life Game"—waiting to see what happens and then trying to deal with it constructively.

A less random way of relating to the events of your life is to give them a framework in which to happen, by establishing some long-term goals for your life span. Once you have some life goals, you can begin to perceive the things that happen from a new perspective: how does the new experience relate to what I want from my life?

This exercise is a search for broad, general goals for your life. What do you want to become? What do you want to contribute to society? What do you want to achieve?

Part I

The group will act as a forum established to create a universal set of goals for all human beings.

Divide the group into three subcommittees: a committee for personal-development goals, a committee for social-participation goals, and a committee for physical, intellectual, creative, and financial achievement goals.

Each committee takes 15 or 20 minutes to generate a list of possible long-term life goals in each area.

When the lists are complete, they should be shared with the whole group (a blackboard would be useful).

After an open discussion during which goals are added or deleted, each member (secretly) selects two goals from each list.

Part II

What goals did you choose? Why? Do you have any private life goals that you didn't share with the group? What are they?

_____

_____

_____

_____

_____

_____

_____

_____

_____

_____

_____

43. Goal Setting II: Short-Term Goals

(alone)

Long-term goals tend to be broad and general; short-term goals have to be much more specific, if you want to keep track of a number of them and to know exactly when they are achieved.

This exercise is a step toward outlining some specific short-term goals that fit within your long-term goals but that could bring you earlier payoffs.

Part I

Long-Term Goals: (These may be from the previous exercise.)

My personal-development goals (for becoming the kind of person I want to be) are:

_____

_____

_____

My social-participation goals (toward what I want to contribute) are:

_____

_____

_____

My achievement goals (the physical, intellectual, creative, and financial tasks I want to accomplish) are:

_____

_____

_____

Short-Term Goals: (These are specific, small, short-range goals that contribute to the longer-term goals you have just stated.)

Personal development

(When) Within the next ten years

(What) I want to_____

(How) I can do this by_____

(When) Within the next five years

(What) I want to_____

(How) I can do this by_____

(When) Within the next year

(What) I want to_____

(How) I can do this by_____

Social participation

(When) Within the next ten years

(What) I want to_____

(How) I can do this by_____

(When) Within the next five years

(What) I want to_____

(How) I can do this by_____

(When) Within the next year

(What) I want to_____

(How) I can do this by_____

Achievement

(When) Within the next ten years

(What) I want to_____

(How) I can do this by_____

(When) Within the next five years

(What) I want to_____

(How) I can do this by_____

(When) Within the next year

(What) I want to_____

(How) I can do this by_____

Part II

Which goals will you accomplish most easily? Which goals will you know for sure that you've accomplished? If any of them are vague, can you make them more specific?

_____

_____

_____

_____

_____

44. Goal Setting III: Lifetime Goals

(alone)

Now that you have some clear-cut ideas on how to go about setting goals, you can rough out a set of goals for your lifetime. Obviously, your goals always have to be open to modification, but they're a beginning toward consciously shaping your life.

Part I

For each time period named, complete the sentences by first identifying a goal you'd like to have for that period and then explaining how you would work to accomplish the goal.

Late teens to late twenties

1. In this period, I want to_____

   I can do this by_____

2. In this period, I want to_____

   I can do this by_____

3. In this period, I want to_____

   I can do this by_____

4. In this period, I want to_____

   I can do this by_____

5. In this period, I want to_____

   I can do this by_____

Early thirties to late thirties

1. In this period, I want to_____

   I can do this by_____

2. In this period, I want to_____

   I can do this by_____

3. In this period, I want to_____

   I can do this by_____

4. In this period, I want to_____

   I can do this by_____

5. In this period, I want to_____

   I can do this by_____

Early forties to mid-fifties

1. In this period, I want to _____

   I can do this by _____

2. In this period, I want to _____

   I can do this by _____

3. In this period, I want to _____

   I can do this by _____

4. In this period, I want to _____

   I can do this by _____

5. In this period, I want to _____

   I can do this by _____

Mid-fifties to mid-sixties

1. In this period, I want to _____

   I can do this by _____

2. In this period, I want to _____

   I can do this by _____

3. In this period, I want to _____

   I can do this by _____

4. In this period, I want to _____

   I can do this by _____

5. In this period, I want to _____

   I can do this by _____

Mid-sixties to mid-seventies

1. In this period, I want to _____

   I can do this by _____

2. In this period, I want to _____

   I can do this by _____

3. In this period, I want to _____

   I can do this by _____

4. In this period, I want to_____

   I can do this by_____

5. In this period, I want to_____

   I can do this by_____

Mid-seventies and later

1. In this period, I want to_____

   I can do this by_____

2. In this period, I want to_____

   I can do this by_____

3. In this period, I want to_____

   I can do this by_____

4. In this period, I want to_____

   I can do this by_____

5. In this period, I want to_____

   I can do this by_____

Part II

Could you identify a rough set of life goals? Did they contradict each other in any way? How do you feel about doing this?

_____

_____

_____

_____

_____

45. Planning Strategies I: Taking Steps

(alone or in twos) Knowing where you want to go comes first; deciding the route that will take you there is the next step.

This is an exercise in breaking down short-term goals into specific, small steps—each step a stage of progress. You can do the exercise alone, but it can be helpful to do it with a partner, who might see some steps that you've missed.

Part I

At each of the three schematics that follow, write your goal on the bottom line. For each goal, state exactly what you want to accomplish, how, and when. Then, decide on the small steps that you'll need to take to reach the goal. Check each step to see whether it can be broken down into smaller steps. You may not need all of the steps.

Steps	*Smaller steps*
1. _____	1½. _____
2. _____	2½. _____
3. _____	3½. _____
4. _____	4½. _____
5. _____	5½. _____
6. _____	6½. _____
7. _____	7½. _____
8. _____	8½. _____
9. _____	9½. _____
10. _____	10½. _____

Goal: _____

Steps	*Smaller steps*
1. _____	1½. _____
2. _____	2½. _____
3. _____	3½. _____
4. _____	4½. _____
5. _____	5½. _____
6. _____	6½. _____
7. _____	7½. _____
8. _____	8½. _____
9. _____	9½. _____
10. _____	10½. _____

Goal: _____

Steps	*Smaller steps*
1. _____	1½. _____
2. _____	2½. _____
3. _____	3½. _____
4. _____	4½. _____
5. _____	5½. _____
6. _____	6½. _____
7. _____	7½. _____
8. _____	8½. _____
9. _____	9½. _____
10. _____	10½. _____

Goal: _____

Part II

Are your goals sufficiently specific? What's helpful about thinking in terms of steps?

_____

_____

_____

_____

_____

_____

46. Planning Strategies II: Realities

(alone)

Once you have an idea of some of the directions that you'd like your life to go in and the steps that will take you there, the next process is to test how real those goals are for you.

In this exercise, you'll work through a set of testing strategies that explore the realistic problems and challenges that might block you from reaching some goals, the ways that you can deal with these problems and challenges, and the resources that you can turn to for help.

Part I

Fill in the chart as completely as you can.

Short-term goal:_____

(What, how, and when)

Steps	Possible problems and challenges	Possible solutions to problems	Resources that can help
1.			
2.			
3.			
4.			
5.			
6.			

Steps	Possible problems and challenges	Possible solutions to problems	Resources that can help
7.			
8.			
9.			
10.			

Want to try doing a chart for one more goal?

Short-term goal:_____

(What, how, and when)

Steps	Possible problems and challenges	Possible solutions to problems	Resources that can help
1.			

Steps	Possible problems and challenges	Possible solutions to problems	Resources that can help
2.			
3.			
4.			
5.			
6.			
7.			
8.			

Steps	Possible problems and challenges	Possible solutions to problems	Resources that can help
9.			
10.			

Part II

Did you find that most of the problems/challenges could be overcome? Why is it important to identify the possible blocks to a goal?

47. Planning Strategies III: Resources

(group)   To get a more complete idea of the scope of resources that are available to help you reach your goals, you can use a group to generate ideas about possible resources.

Part I

Each member of the group will try to complete each of the following sentences; the group will go around once for each sentence. It's OK to have the same answer repeated more than once, but new ideas are better.

If you need special credentials to accomplish your goal, you can . . .
If you need to learn some new skills to accomplish your goal, you can . . .
If you need some new information to accomplish your goal, you can . . .
If you need a role model in order to accomplish your goal, you can . . .
If you need some more money to accomplish your goal, you can . . .
If you need additional space or another location to accomplish your goal, you can . . .
If you need special materials to accomplish your goal, you can . . .

If you need other people to help you to accomplish your goal, you can . . .

If you need people to share your goal with you, you can . . .

If you need emotional support to accomplish your goal, you can . . .

If you need an organization to help you, you can . . .

If you need a social institution (government, church, school, or other) to help you, you can . . .

Part II

The group has explored resources of skills, materials, and people. Can you think of any other kinds of resources?

_____

_____

_____

_____

_____

48. Exploring Alternatives I: Widening Your Goals

(alone)   If you have been working your way through this section systematically, you have identified some long-term life goals, some short-term goals, some steps that you need to take to accomplish your goals, some blocks that can get in your way, and some resources for dealing with the blocks. You're prepared to begin shaping your future actively.

Despite preparedness for planning the future, however, if you played the "Life Game" at the beginning of this section—and even if you didn't—you're probably aware that many of the events of your life aren't under your control. How does this affect your planning processes? To be able to adapt your plans to the unexpected, you need to develop another planning skill—flexibility.

This exercise gives you a chance to widen your goals for the period of your life by considering some alternatives.

Part I

Identify some short-term goals you want to achieve in each of the time periods listed. For each goal you name, decide on an alternative goal you might have if you can't accomplish your original goal.

Then decide on a second alternative goal you can aim for if your first alternative doesn't work.

Late teens to late twenties

Short-term goal	*First alternative goal*	*Second alternative goal*
1. _____	_____	_____
2. _____	_____	_____
3. _____	_____	_____
4. _____	_____	_____
5. _____	_____	_____

Early thirties to late thirties

Short-term goal	*First alternative goal*	*Second alternative goal*
1. _____	_____	_____
2. _____	_____	_____
3. _____	_____	_____
4. _____	_____	_____
5. _____	_____	_____

Early forties to mid-fifties

Short-term goal	*First alternative goal*	*Second alternative goal*
1. _____	_____	_____
2. _____	_____	_____
3. _____	_____	_____
4. _____	_____	_____
5. _____	_____	_____

Mid-fifties to mid-sixties

Short-term goal	*First alternative goal*	*Second alternative goal*
1. _____	_____	_____
2. _____	_____	_____
3. _____	_____	_____
4. _____	_____	_____
5. _____	_____	_____

Mid-seventies and later

	Short-term goal	*First alternative goal*	*Second alternative goal*
1.	_____	_____	_____
2.	_____	_____	_____
3.	_____	_____	_____
4.	_____	_____	_____
5.	_____	_____	_____

Part II

Could you find satisfactory alternatives? Could alternative goals lead your life in new directions?

_____

_____

_____

_____

_____

49. Exploring Alternatives II: Future Fantasies

(alone)

Here's another way to determine possible alternatives for your future. This exercise consists of imagining three alternative futures for yourself: one really imaginative one and two other possible patterns for your future. Use the information available from this text to shape your alternatives as much as possible.

Part I

If your wildest dreams come true, how will you be living and working 5 years from now, 10 years from now, and 20 years from now?

	5 Years	10 Years	20 Years
Occupation			

	5 Years	10 Years	20 Years
Personal life (married? family?)			
Financial level			
Leisure			
Other details (location, lifestyle, and others)			

If a more conservative plan works out, what will you be doing?

	5 Years	10 Years	20 Years
Occupation			
Personal life (married? family?)			

	5 Years	10 Years	20 Years
Financial level			
Leisure			
Other details (location, lifestyle, and others)			

Can you think of an another possible future for yourself, working from the same base as for the previous scenario?

	5 Years	10 Years	20 Years
Occupation			
Personal life (married? family?)			
Financial level			

	5 Years	10 Years	20 Years
Leisure			
Other details (location, lifestyle, and others)			

Part II

Could you find satisfactory alternatives? Did alternative goals lead your life in new directions?

_____

_____

_____

_____

_____

_____

_____

_____

_____

50. *Exploring Alternatives III: Unfolding*

(group)

In reality, the events of life can present you with endless alternative opportunities. Goals may conflict and have to be reexamined; social changes may cancel old goals and introduce new ones; personal changes may open up whole new futures. To get a sense of some of the complexities that your unfolding life could bring, try the following exercise.

Part I

1. Everybody in the group starts with the same decision: to marry or not to marry. Half of the group will be assigned to marriage, the other half to not marrying.
2. After being assigned to their groups, members individually decide on two alternative goals that their marital status has generated. These alternatives should be written on the branched lines extending from "to marry" and "not to marry."
3. Each member then chooses one of the new alternative goals and thinks of two further alternative goals that this choice has generated. These alternatives should be written on the branched lines extending from the line where the previous choice is written.
4. Each member then chooses one of the new alternative goals and thinks of two further alternative goals that this choice has generated, to be written on the next set of branched lines.

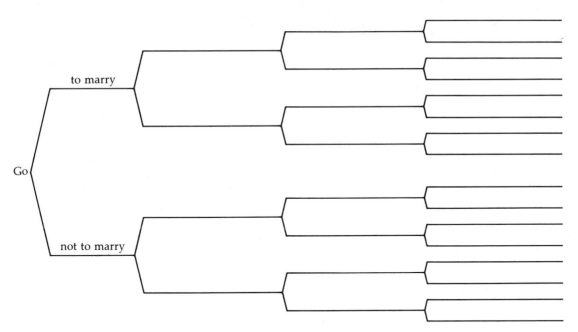

Part II

Do you get the sense of how alternative goals can stem from your life choices?

Share your goals. Were the final goals set by the "married" people at all similar? How about the final goals set by the "not-married" people? Did the two groups have a lot in common? little in common?

_____

_____

_____

_____

_____

References

Appleton, W. S. *Fathers and daughters.* New York: Doubleday, 1981.

Arkin, A. M., & Battin, D. A technical device for the psychotherapy of pathological bereavement. In B. Shilenberg (Ed.), *Bereavement: Its psychosocial aspects.* New York: Columbia University Press, 1975.

Atchley, R. C. *The sociology of retirement.* New York: Schenkman, 1976.

Atchley, R. C. *The social forces in later life* (2nd ed.). Belmont, Calif.: Wadsworth, 1977.

Baltes, P. B., & Goulet, L. R. Status and issues of a lifespan developmental psychology. In L. R. Goulet & P. B. Baltes (Eds.), *Lifespan developmental psychology: Research and theory.* New York: Academic Press, 1970.

Baltes, R., & Schaie, K. W. (Eds.). *Lifespan developmental psychology.* New York: Academic Press, 1973.

Batten, M. *Study guide to accompany development of the adult.* New York: Harper & Row, 1977.

Bem, S. L., & Bem, D. J. *Training the woman to know her place: The social antecedents of women in the world of work.* Harrisburg, Pa.: Pennsylvania Department of Education, 1973.

Benet, S. *How to live to be 100: The lifestyle of the people of the Caucasus.* New York: Dial Press, 1976.

Bengtson, V. L., & Haber, D. A. Sociological approaches to aging. In D. Woodruff & J. Birren (Eds.), *Aging: Scientific perspectives and social issues.* New York: Van Nostrand, 1975.

Bengtson, V. L., Kasschau, P. L., & Ragan, P. K. The impact of social structure on aging individuals. In J. E. Birren & K. W. Schaie (Eds.), *Handbook of the psychology of aging.* New York: Van Nostrand Reinhold, 1977.

Bengtson, V. L., & Manuel, R. C. The sociology of aging. In R. H. Davis (Ed.),

Aging: Prospects and issues (3rd ed.). Los Angeles: University of Southern California Press, 1976.

Bensman, J., & Lilienfield, R. Friendship and alienation. *Psychology Today,* October 1979, p. 4.

Birren, J. *The psychology of aging,* Englewood Cliffs, N. J.: Prentice-Hall, 1964.

Birren, J. A gerontologist's overview. In L. F. Jarvik (Ed.), *Aging into the 21st century.* New York: Gardner Press, 1978.

Birren, J. E., & Schaie, K. W. (Eds.). *Handbook of the psychology of aging.* New York: Van Nostrand Reinhold, 1977.

Bischof, L. *Adult psychology.* New York: Harper & Row, 1976.

Blau, Z. S. *Aging in a changing society.* New York: Watts, 1981.

Block, J., & Haan, W. *Lives through time.* Berkeley, Calif.: Rodcroft Books, 1971.

Block, M., Davidson, J., & Grambs, J. *Women over forty: Visions and realities.* New York: Springer, 1981.

Brill, P., & Hayes, J. B. *Taming your turmoil: Managing the transitions of adult life.* Englewood Cliffs, N. J.: Prentice-Hall, 1981.

Brim, O., & Kagan, J. (Eds.). *Constancy and change in human development.* Cambridge, Mass.: Harvard University Press, 1980.

Bromley, D. B. *The psychology of human aging* (2nd ed.). Baltimore, Md.: Penguin, 1974.

Broverman, I., Broverman, D., Clarkson, F., Rosenkrantz, P., & Vogel, S. Sex-role stereotypes and clinical judgments of mental health. *Journal of Consulting Psychology,* 1972, 34, 1–7.

Bruner, J. *Process of cognitive growth: Infancy.* Worcester, Mass.: Clark University Press, 1968.

Bühler, C. Meaningfulness of the biographical approach. In L. Allman & D. Jaffe (Eds.), *Readings in adult psychology: Contemporary perspectives, 1977–1978.* New York: Harper & Row, 1977.

Bühler, C., & Massarik, F. (Eds.). *The course of human life: A study of goals in the humanistic perspective.* New York: Springer, 1968.

Butcher, L. *Retirement without fear.* Princeton, N. J.: Dow Jones Books, 1978.

Butler, R. The facade of chronological age: An interpretive summary. In B. Neugarten (Ed.), *Middle age and aging.* Chicago: University of Chicago Press, 1968.

Butler, R. Humanistic perspectives in gerontology. In S. Spicker (Ed.), *Aging and the elderly.* Atlantic Highlands, N. J.: Humanities Press, 1978.

Butler, R., & Lewis, M. *Aging and mental health: Positive psychosocial approaches* (2nd ed.). St. Louis, Mo.: Mosby, 1977.

Butler, R. N. *Why survive?: Being old in America.* New York: Harper & Row, 1975.

Calhoun, L. G., Selby, J. W., & King, H. E. *Dealing with crisis: A guide to critical life problems.* Englewood Cliffs, N. J.: Prentice-Hall, 1976.

Cameron, P. Age parameters of young adult, middle-aged, old and aged. *Journal of Gerontology,* 1969, 24, 201–202.

Carter, E. A., & Orfanidis, M. M. *The family life cycle.* New York: Halsted, 1980.

Chess, S., Thomas, A., & Birch, H. *Annual progress in child psychiatry and child development.* New York: Brunner/Mazel, 1968.

Clore, G. L. *Interpersonal attraction: An overview.* Morristown, N. J.: General Learning Press, 1975.

Cohen, J. Z. *Hitting our stride: Good news about women in their middle years.* New York: Delacorte, 1980.

Comfort, A. *A good age.* New York: Crown, 1976.

Comfort, A. A biologist laments and exhorts. In L. F. Jarvik (Ed.), *Aging into the 21st century.* New York: Gardner Press, 1978.

Cowgill, D. O., & Holmes, L. D. (Eds.). *Aging and modernization.* New York: Appleton, 1972.

Cumming, E., & Henry, W. H. *Growing old.* New York: Basic Books, 1961.

Cutler, N., & Harootyan, R. Demography of the aged. In D. Woodruff & J. Birren (Eds.), *Aging.* New York: Van Nostrand, 1975.

Dangott, L., & Kalish, R. *A time to enjoy: The pleasures of aging.* Englewood Cliffs, N. J.: Prentice-Hall, 1979.

Davitz, J., & Davitz, L. *Making it from 40 to 50.* New York: Random House, 1976.

DeBeauvoir, S. *The coming of age.* New York: Warner, 1972.

Denny, P. Cellular biology of aging. In D. Woodruff & J. Birren (Eds.), *Aging: Scientific perspectives and social issues.* New York: Van Nostrand, 1975.

Derenski, A., & Lansburg, S. B. *The age taboo: Older women–younger men relationships.* Boston: Little, Brown, 1981.

deVries, H. A. Psychology of exercise and aging. In D. Woodruff & J. Birren (Eds.), *Understanding aging.* New York: Appleton, 1975.

Dibner, A. S. The psychology of normal aging. In D. Woodruff & J. Birren (Eds.), *Aging: Scientific perspectives and social issues.* New York: Van Nostrand, 1975.

Dressler, D., & Willis, W. *Sociology: The study of human interaction* (3rd ed.). New York: Knopf, 1976.

Eisdorfer, C., & Lawton, P. M. *The psychology of adult development and aging.* Washington, D. C.: American Psychological Association, 1973.

Erikson, E. *Childhood and society* (2nd ed.). New York: Norton, 1963.

Erikson, E. *Identity: Youth and crisis.* New York: Norton, 1968.

Erikson, E., & Erikson, J. Reflections on aging. In S. F. Spicker (Ed.), *Aging and the elderly.* Atlantic Highlands, N. J.: Humanities Press, 1978.

Finch, C. E., & Hayflick, L. H. *Handbook of the biology of aging.* New York: Van Nostrand Reinhold, 1977.

Fiske, M. The reality of psychological change. In L. F. Jarvik (Ed.), *Aging into the 21st century.* New York: Gardner Press, 1978.

Fiske, M. Changing hierarchies of commitment in adulthood. In N. Smelser & E. Erikson (Eds.), *Themes of work and love in adulthood.* Cambridge, Mass.: Harvard University Press, 1980.

Fiske, M., & Weiss, L. Intimacy and crisis in adulthood. In N. Schlossberg & A. Entine (Eds.), *Counseling adults.* Monterey, Calif.: Brooks/Cole, 1977.

Foner, A., & Schwab, K. *Aging and retirement.* Monterey, Calif.: Brooks/Cole, 1981.

Fortinberry, A. Father's increasing empty nest blues. *Psychology Today,* October 1979, p. 36.

Fozard, J. L., Nuttal, R. L., & Waugh, N. C. Age-related changes in mental performance. *Aging in Human Development,* 1972, 3, 19–43.

Fracchia, C. A. *Living together alone: The new American monasticism.* San Francisco: Harper & Row, 1979.

Frankel-Brunswik, E. Adjustments and reorientation in the course of the life span. In B. L. Neugarten (Ed.), *Middle age and aging.* Chicago: University of Chicago Press, 1968.

Freedman, J. L. *Happy people: What happiness is, who has it, and why.* New York: Harcourt Brace Jovanovich, 1978.

Freud, S. *The Standard Edition of the Complete Psychological Works* (J. Strachey, Ed.). London: Hogarth, 1953.

Fries, J. F., & Crapo, L. M. *Vitality and aging.* San Francisco: W. H. Freeman, 1981.

Galinsky, E. *Between generations: The six stages of parenthood.* New York: Times Books, 1980.

Gartner, A., & Riessman, F. Is there a new work ethic? In H. J. Peters & J. C. Hansen (Eds.), *Vocational guidance and career development.* New York: Macmillan, 1977.

Giele, J. Adulthood as transcendence of age and sex. In N. Smelser & E. Erikson (Eds.), *Themes of work and love in adulthood.* Cambridge, Mass.: Harvard University Press, 1980.

Gillies, J. *A guide to caring for and coping with aged parents.* Nashville, Tenn.: Thomas Nelson, 1981.

Gould, R. The phases of adult life: A study in developmental psychology. *American Journal of Psychiatry,* 1972, *129*(5), 33–45.

Gould, R. Adult life styles: Growth toward self-tolerance. *Psychology Today,* February 1975, pp. 74–78.

Gould, R. *Transformations: Growth and change in adult life.* New York: Simon & Schuster, 1978.

Gould, R. Transformations during early and middle adult years. In N. Smelser & E. Erikson (Eds.), *Themes of work and love in adulthood.* Cambridge, Mass.: Harvard University Press, 1980.

Gross, M. L. *The psychological society.* New York: Random House, 1978.

Gruman, G. J. Cultural origins of present day ageism: The modernization of the life cycle. In S. F. Spicker (Ed.), *Aging and the elderly.* Atlantic Highlands, N. J.: Humanities Press, 1978.

Gubrium, J. F. Being single in old age. *International Journal of Aging and Human Development,* 1975, *6,* 29–41.

Gutmann, D. L. The cross-cultural perspective: Notes toward a comparative psychology of aging. In J. E. Birren & K. W. Schaie (Eds.), *Handbook of the psychology of aging.* New York: Van Nostrand Reinhold, 1977.

Hansen, L. S. Counseling and career (self) development of women. In H. Peters & J. C. Hansen (Eds.), *Vocational guidance and career development* (3rd ed.), New York: Macmillan, 1977.

Havighurst, R. Social roles, work, leisure, and education. *The psychology of adult development and aging.* Washington, D. C.: American Psychological Association, 1973.

Havighurst, R. J. *Developmental tasks and education* (3rd ed.). New York: David McKay, 1972.

Havighurst, R. J., Neugarten, B. L., & Tobin, S. S. Disengagement and patterns of aging. In B. Neugarten (Ed.), *Middle age and aging.* Chicago: University of Chicago Press, 1968.

Hennig, M., & Jardim, A. *Women and management.* New York: Doubleday, 1977.

Holmes, T. H., & Rahe, R. H. The social readjustment rating scale. *Journal of Psychosomatic Research,* 1967, *11,* 213–218.

Horn, J. L. Organization of data on lifespan development of human abilities. In L. R. Goulet & P. B. Baltes (Eds.), *Lifespan developmental psychology: Research and theory.* New York: Academic Press, 1970.

Hunt, B., & Hunt, M. *Prime time: A guide to the pleasures and potentialities of mid-life today.* New York: Stein & Day, 1974.

Hunt, M. *Sexual behavior in the 1970's.* New York: Dell, 1974.

Hyde, M. O., & Forsythe, E. H. *Suicide: The hidden epidemic.* New York: Watts, 1978.

Imara, M. Dying as the last stage of growth. In E. Kübler-Ross (Ed.), *Death: The final stage of growth.* Englewood Cliffs, N. J.: Prentice-Hall, 1975.

Irwin, R. *The $100,000 decision: The older American's guide to selling a home and choosing retirement housing.* New York: McGraw-Hill, 1981.

Jacques, E. *Work, creativity, and social justice.* New York: International Universities Press, 1970.

Jung, C. *Man and his symbols.* New York: Doubleday, 1964.

Jung, C. The stages of life. In J. Campbell (Ed.), *The portable Jung.* New York: Viking Press, 1971.

Kalish, R. Death and dying in a social context. In R. Binstock & E. Shemas (Eds.), *Handbook of aging and social sciences.* New York: Van Nostrand Reinhold, 1976.

Kalish, R. A. *Late adulthood: Perspectives on human development.* Monterey, Calif.: Brooks/Cole, 1975.

Kanin, G. *It takes a long time to become young.* New York: Berkeley, 1978.

Kart, C. S., Metress, E. S., & Metress, J. F. *Aging and health: Biologic and social perspectives.* Menlo Park, Calif.: Addison–Wesley, 1978.

Kastenbaum, R. *Growing old: The years of fulfillment.* New York: Harper & Row, 1979.

Kastenbaum, R., & Candy, S. E. The 4% fallacy: A methodological and empirical critique of extended care facility population statistics. *Aging and Human Development,* 1973, *4,* 15–22.

Kastenbaum, R., Derbin, V., Sabatini, P., & Artt, S. The ages of me: Toward personal and interpersonal definitions of functional aging. *Aging and Human Development,* 1972, *3*(2), 197–211.

Katchadourian, H. A. Medical perspectives on adulthood. *Daedalus,* Spring 1976.

Keniston, K. *All our children: The American family under pressure.* New York: Harcourt Brace Jovanovich, 1977. (a)

Keniston, K. Youth: A new stage of life. In L. Allman & D. Jaffe (Eds.), *Readings in adult psychology.* New York: Harper & Row, 1977. (b)

Kimmel, D. *Adulthood and aging: An interdisciplinary developmental view.* New York: Wiley, 1974.

Kline, C. The socialization process of women. *The Gerontologist,* December 1975, pp. 486–492.

Knopf, O. *Successful aging.* New York: Viking, 1975.

Kohlberg, L. Continuities in childhood and adult moral development revisited.

In P. B. Baltes & K. W. Schaie (Eds.), *Lifespan developmental psychology: Personality and socialization.* New York: Academic Press, 1973.

Kroll, A. M., Dinklage, L. B., Morely, E. D., & Wilson, E. A. *Career development: Growth and crisis.* New York: Wiley, 1970.

Kübler-Ross, E. *On Death and Dying.* New York: Macmillan, 1969.

Kübler-Ross, E. *Questions and answers on death and dying.* New York: Macmillan, 1974.

Kübler-Ross, E. *Death: The final stage of growth.* Englewood Cliffs, N. J.: Prentice-Hall, 1975.

Kübler-Ross, E. *To live until we say goodbye.* Englewood Cliffs, N. J.: Prentice-Hall, 1978.

Kurtzman, J., & Gordon, P. *No more dying.* Atlanta: Dell, 1977.

Laing, R. D. *The politics of the family and other essays II.* New York: Pantheon, 1969.

Lazarus, R. S. *Patterns of adjustment.* New York: McGraw-Hill, 1976.

Leaf, A. *Youth in old age.* New York: McGraw-Hill, 1975.

Levine, S. *Who dies?: An investigation of conscious living and conscious dying.* New York: Anchor Books, 1982.

Levinson, D. Conception of the adult life course. In N. Smelser & E. Erikson (Eds.), *Themes of work and love in adulthood.* Cambridge, Mass.: Harvard University Press, 1980.

Levinson, D., Darrow, C., Klein, E., Levinson, M., & McKee, B. *The seasons of a man's life.* New York: Knopf, 1978.

Lidz, T. *The person: His development throughout the life cycle.* New York: Basic Books, 1976.

Loevinger, J. *Ego development: Conceptions and theories.* San Francisco: Jossey-Bass, 1976.

Lopata, H. *Family fact book.* Chicago: Marquis Academic Media, 1978.

Lott, B. *Becoming a woman: The socialization of gender.* Springfield, Ill.: Charles C Thomas, 1981.

Lowenthal, M. F. Some potentialities of a life-cycle approach to the study of retirement. In F. M. Carp (Ed.), *Retirement.* New York: Behavioral Publications, 1972.

Lowenthal, M., Thurnher, M., & Chiriboga, D. *Four stages of life: A comparative study of men and women facing transitions.* San Francisco: Jossey-Bass, 1977.

Luce, G. G. *Your second life.* New York: Delacorte, 1980.

Ludel, J. *Introduction to sensory processes.* San Francisco: W. H. Freeman, 1978.

Lygre, D. *Life manipulation: From test-tube babies to aging.* New York: Walker, 1979.

Marshall, G. N. *Facing death and grief: A sensible perspective for the modern person.* Buffalo, N. Y.: Prometheus Books, 1981.

Maslow, A. H. *Motivation and personality* (2nd ed.). New York: Harper & Row, 1971.

Masters, W. H., & Johnson, V. *Human sexual response.* Boston: Little, Brown, 1970.

Masters, W. H., & Johnson, V. *The pleasure bond: A new look qt sexuality and commitment.* Bostn: Little, Brown, 1974.

Maynard, J. *Growing up old in the sixties.* New York: Doubleday, 1973.

McClusky, H. Y. Designs for learning. In L. F. Jarvik (Ed.), *Aging into the 21st century.* New York: Gardner Press, 1978.

McFarland, D. The aged in the 21st century: A demographer's view. In L. F. Jarvik (Ed.), *Aging into the 21st century.* New York: Gardner Press, 1978.

McGill, M. E. *The 40 to 60 year old male.* New York: Simon & Schuster, 1980.

McLeish, J. A. B. *The Ulyssean adult: Creativity in the middle and later years.* New York: McGraw-Hill, 1976.

Merriam, S. Middle age: A review of the literature and its implication for educational intervention. *Adult Education,* 1978, *29*(1), 39–54.

Michaels, J. *Prime of your life.* New York: Facts on File, 1981.

Minuchin, S. *Families and family therapy.* Cambridge, Mass.: Harvard University Press, 1974.

Montague, A. *Growing young.* New York: McGraw-Hill, 1981.

Moody, R. A. *Life after life.* New York: Bantam, 1975.

Mussen, P. H., Conger, J., Kagan, J., & Geiwitz, J. *Psychological development: A life-span approach.* New York: Harper & Row, 1979.

Neugarten, B. Adult personality: Toward a psychology of the life cycle. In B. Neugarten (Ed.), *Middle age and aging.* Chicago: University of Chicago Press, 1968. (a)

Neugarten, B. The awareness of middle age. In B. Neugarten (Ed.), *Middle age and aging.* University of Chicago Press, 1968. (b)

Neugarten, B. Personality and the aging process. *The Gerontologist,* Spring 1972, 9–15.

Neugarten, B. Adaptation and the life cycle. In N. Schlossberg & A. Entine (Eds.), *Counseling adults.* Monterey, Calif.: Brooks/Cole, 1977.

Neugarten, B. (Interviewed by E. Hall.) Acting one's age: New rules for old. *Psychology Today,* April 1980, pp. 66–80.

Neugarten, B. L. The future and the young-old. In L. F. Jarvik (Ed.), *Aging into the 21st century.* New York: Gardner Press, 1978.

Neugarten, B., Moore, J., & Lowe, J. Age norms, age constraints, and age socialization. In B. Neugarten (Ed.), *Middle age and aging.* Chicago: University of Chicago Press, 1968.

Newman, P. R., & Newman, B. M. *Living, the process of adjustment.* Homewood, Ill.: Dorsey Press, 1981.

Palmore, E., & Jeffers, F. C. (Eds.). *Predictions of life span: Recent findings.* Lexington, Mass.: Heath, 1971.

Parlee, M. B. The friendship bond. *Psychology Today,* October 1979.

Pattison, E. M. *The experience of dying.* Englewood Cliffs, N. J.: Prentice-Hall, 1977.

Peck, R. Psychological development in the second half of life. In W. Sze (Ed.), *Human life cycle.* New York: Aronson, 1975.

Pellegrino, V. *The other side of thirty.* New York: Rawson Wade, 1981.

Pelletier, K. *Longevity: Fulfilling our biological potential.* New York: Delacorte, 1981.

Peters, H. J., & Hansen, J. C. (Eds.). *Vocational guidance and career development.* New York: Macmillan, 1977.

Piaget, J. Intellectual evolution from adolescence into adulthood. *Human Development*, 1972, *15*, 1–12.

Puner, M. *Getting the most out of your fifties.* New York: Crown, 1977.

Ram Dass. Dying: An opportunity for awakening. *Grist for the mill.* Santa Cruz, Calif.: Unity Press, 1977.

Ramsay, R., & Noorbergen, R. *Living with loss: A dramatic new breakthrough in grief therapy.* New York: Morrow, 1981.

Raskin, A., & Jarvik, L. F. (Eds.). *Psychiatric symptoms and cognitive loss in the elderly.* New York: Wiley, 1979.

Reichard, S., Livson, F., & Petersen, P. Adjustment to retirement. In B. Neugarten (Ed.), *Middle age and aging.* Chicago: University of Chicago Press, 1968.

Riegel, K. F. The predictors of death and longevity in longitudinal research. In E. Palmore & F. Jeffers (Eds.), *Predictions of life span.* Lexington, Mass.: Heath, 1981.

Rogers, C. *On becoming a person.* Boston: Houghton Mifflin, 1968.

Romer, N. *The sex-role cycle: Socialization from infancy to old age.* New York: McGraw-Hill, 1981.

Rosenfeld, A. *Prolongevity.* New York: Knopf, 1976.

Rosow, I. *Socialization to old age.* Berkeley, Calif.: University of California Press, 1974.

Rossi, A. S. Lifespan theories and women's lives. *Signs*, Autumn 1980, pp. 4–32.

Rubin, L. *Women of a certain age: The midlife search for self.* New York: Harper & Row, 1979.

Rubin, Z. *Doing unto others.* Englewood Cliffs, N. J.: Prentice-Hall, 1975.

Rubin, Z. Does personality really change after 20? *Psychology Today*, May 1981, pp. 18–27.

Sabom, M. B. *Recollections of death: A medical investigation.* New York: Harper & Row, 1981.

Sarason, S. B. *Work, aging, and social change.* New York: Free Press, 1977.

Sarason, S., Sarason, E., & Cowden, G. Aging and the nature of work. *American Psychologist*, May 1975, 584–592.

Saunders, C. *The management of terminal illness.* London: Hospital Medicine Publications, Ltd., 1967.

Schenk, Q., & Schenk, E. *Pulling up roots.* Englewood Cliffs, N. J.: Prentice-Hall, 1978.

Sheehy, G. *Passages.* New York: Dutton, 1976.

Sheehy, G. Introducing the postponing generation. *Esquire*, October 1979, pp. 25–30.

Sheehy, G. *Pathfinders.* New York: Morrow, 1981.

Sheppard, H. L. The emerging pattern of second careers. *Vocational Guidance Quarterly*, December 1971, 89–95.

Sheppard, H., & Rix, S. *The graying of working America.* New York: Free Press, 1977.

Smelser, N., & Erikson, E. (Eds.). *Themes of work and love in adulthood.* Cambridge, Mass.: Harvard University Press, 1980.

Sontag, S. The double standard of aging. *Saturday Review*, September 23, 1972.

Speck, R., & Attneave, C. *Family networks.* New York: Pantheon, 1973.

Spencer, M., & Dovi, C. (Eds.). *Understanding aging: A multidisciplinary approach.* New York: Appleton-Century-Crofts, 1975.

Spicker, S. F., Woodward, K. M., & Van Tassel, D. D. *Aging and the elderly: Humanistic perspectives in gerontology.* Atlantic Highlands, N. J.: Humanities Press, 1978.

Sroufe, A. Attachment and the roots of competence. *Human Nature,* October 1978.

Stevens-Long, J. *Adult life: Developmental processes.* Palo Alto, Calif.: Mayfield, 1979.

Timiras, P. S. *Developmental physiology and aging.* New York: Macmillan, 1972.

Tobin, S., & Lieberman, M. *Last home for the aged.* San Francisco: Jossey-Bass, 1976.

Toffler, A. *Future shock.* New York: Random House, 1970.

Toffler, A. *The third wave.* New York: Morrow, 1980.

Torack, R. M. *Your brain is younger than you think: A guide to mental aging.* Chicago: Nelson-Hall, 1981.

Troll, L. *Early and middle adulthood.* Monterey, Calif.: Brooks/Cole, 1975.

Troll, L., Miller, S., & Atchley, R. *Families in later life.* Belmont, Calif.: Wadsworth, 1979.

U. S. Bureau of the Census. *Statistical Abstract of the United States, 1979,* Washington, D. C.: Government Printing Office, 1980.

U. S. Department of Health, Education & Welfare. *Changes: Research on aging and the aged.* Publication No. (NIH) 78–85. Bethesda, Md.: National Institute of Health, 1978.

Utke, A. R. *Bio-babel: Can we survive the new biology?* Atlanta: John Knox Press, 1978.

Vaillant, G. *Adaptation to life.* Boston: Little, Brown, 1977.

Van Dusen, R., & Sheldon, E. B. The changing status of American women: A life-cycle perspective. In H. J. Peters & J. C. Hansen (Eds.), *Vocational guidance and career development* (3rd ed.). New York: Macmillan, 1977.

Varga, L. Occupational floundering. *Personnel and Guidance Journal,* 1973, *52,* 225–231.

Volkan, V. D. The linking objects of pathological mourners. *Archives of General Psychiatry,* 1972, *27,* 215 ff.

Wantz, M. S., & Gay, J. E. *The aging process: A health perspective.* Cambridge, Mass.: Winthrop, 1981.

Weg, R. The changing physiology of aging. In R. H. Davis (Ed.), *Aging: Prospects and issues* (3rd ed.). Los Angeles: University of Southern California Press, 1976.

Weisman, A. *On dying and denying.* New York: Behavioral Publications, 1972.

White, R. *Lives in progress* (3rd ed.). New York: Holt, Rinehart & Winston, 1975.

Woodruff, D. S. A physiological perspective of the psychology of aging. In D. Woodruff & J. Birren (Eds.), *Aging: Scientific perspectives and social issues.* New York: Van Nostrand, 1975.

Yankelovich, D. *New rules: Searching for self-fulfillment in a world turned upside down.* New York: Random House, 1981.

Name Index

Subject Index